ISBN - 979-8-9995918-4-5

THE SMART INVESTOR'S GUIDE TO COMMERCIAL REAL ESTATE:

How to Analyze, Value, and Invest in Commercial Real Estate with Confidence

NED GANDEVANI, PHD, MBA

For my daughters, **Ariana, Analisa, and Malisa**,
Your kindness, brilliance, and laughter fill my world with a beauty that words can barely hold.

This work, and every effort of my life, is dedicated to you, with a love that grows deeper with every passing day.

Always,
Dad

PROLOGUE

Commercial real estate today is far more than just location and physical assets. It has evolved into a complex, data-driven, and globally connected asset class that requires both analytical discipline and strategic foresight. Investors operate in a landscape shaped by demographic changes, rapid technological advances, shifting consumer patterns, regulatory complexities, and flows of global capital. In this environment, the ability to identify true value, measure risk accurately, and execute disciplined investment strategies has become essential.

This book aims to close the gap between theory and action. It's crafted for institutional and private investors, analysts, and portfolio strategists who want to make confident, well-informed decisions. Combining structured frameworks, real-world data, and illustrative case studies, it lays out how to evaluate markets, understand risks at both property and portfolio levels, design capital structures, and align incentives within sophisticated investment vehicles.

The journey begins with the fundamentals of commercial real estate as an asset class and builds toward advanced topics like adaptive reuse, mixed-use developments, and cross-border capital strategies. Along the way, readers will see examples of smart investments, from industrial logistics hubs to life sciences campuses, as well as cautionary lessons where governance failures, mistimed moves, or behavioral biases led to losses.

By the book's conclusion, the reader will be equipped not just to understand how commercial real estate functions but to turn insight into effective action. The goal is to provide a framework for disciplined, repeatable, and future-ready CRE investing that delivers consistent results across cycles, sectors, and geographies.

CONTENTS

PREFACE

Why This Book

Commercial real estate used to feel like a mysterious, exclusive club, full of insiders with the know-how, fragmented data, and high barriers to entry. But that's changing fast. Capital is pouring into CRE on a scale we've never seen before. Markets are opening up. Tools that were once Wall Street's secret weapon are now at your fingertips, whether you're an individual investor, part of a family office, or an emerging manager. The line between local expertise and global opportunities is blurring quicker than ever.

Still, most resources fall into two traps: they either dumb down CRE to simplistic rules or drown you in technical jargon without giving you practical ways to apply it. I wrote this book to fill that gap. It's a modern, rigorous, clear guide built for the investor you are today. Here, I bring together institutional insights, analytical tools, and real-world smarts into one playbook designed to help you invest smarter, operate more strategically, and make decisions with real confidence.

Why Now?

We're right in the middle of the biggest shakeup commercial real estate has seen in decades.

- **Technology is rewriting the rules.** AI, PropTech, automation, and data science are transforming everything, from leasing to asset management.
- **Global capital flows are running hot and fast.** Sovereign funds, pension plans, private investors, and cross-border players are reshaping price discovery and liquidity worldwide.

- **Demographics and behaviors are shifting.** Hybrid work, e-commerce, life sciences, logistics, and adaptive reuse are creating new winners while shaking up the old guard.
- **Market cycles are speeding up.** Interest rates, inflation, geopolitical risks, and supply-demand imbalances mean you face more volatility and quicker moves than before.
- In this environment, the winners will be the investors who embrace a wider perspective, who are analytical, strategic, data-savvy, globally aware, and disciplined in execution. This book is here to help you become one of them.

What Is The Smart Investor's Guide to Commercial Real Estate?

Think of this book as your comprehensive roadmap to mastering CRE investing like a pro. I blend four key ingredients:

1. A deep understanding of CRE as an asset class, its structure, cycles, players, and what drives performance.
2. Analytical mastery, market research, financial modeling, valuation, capital structures, and risk management.
3. Strategic portfolio thinking, diversification, resilience, ESG leadership, and creating long-term value.
4. Forward-looking insight, technology trends, global capital, changing demand, and emerging sectors.

This isn't your traditional textbook or surface-level how-to. I take a holistic, integrated approach to show how real investors pull all these pieces together, and how you can too.

The book's structure mirrors the journey you're on:

- Part I lays the foundation.

- ☐ Part II shows you where to look.
- ☐ Part III teaches how to underwrite.
- ☐ Part IV dives into building and protecting your portfolio.
- ☐ Part V helps you prepare for what's next.
- ☐ Part VI reveals how experts put it all into practice.

By the end, you won't just understand deals, you'll master the bigger systems and frameworks that separate top investors from the rest.

How Should You Use This Book?

This book adapts to where you are in your investing journey, whether you're just starting out, sharpening your edge, or running major institutional portfolios. Here's how to get the most out of it:

1. **Read it cover-to-cover like a full course.**

   If you want a complete, clear system from fundamentals to case studies, this is your path. You'll move through foundational concepts, market analysis, financial modeling, portfolio strategy, future trends, and real-world examples, like a private masterclass in CRE investing.

2. **Use it as a go-to reference.**

   Each part stands alone, so you can dive in where you need help:

   - ☐ Pricing a deal? Head to Part III.
   - ☐ Evaluating a market? Check Part II.
   - ☐ Diversifying your portfolio? Flip to Part IV.
   - ☐ Understanding global flows? Part V's got you.
   - ☐ Learning from case studies? Part VI will guide you.

3. **Come back again and again.**

   CRE investing evolves with you. What feels complex today becomes second nature with time. As your deals grow, your portfolio deepens, and markets shift, this book grows with you, offering tools, tactics, and insights for every stage.

Closing Thoughts

The modern CRE investor can't rely on rules of thumb anymore. You need clarity in complexity, discipline in uncertainty, and a forward-thinking approach that holds up across cycles, markets, and asset types.

Whether you're picking up your first property, building a diversified portfolio, launching a fund, exploring cross-border deals, or just craving a deeper understanding of commercial real estate, this book is here to equip you with the tools, insights, and confidence to invest smarter and thrive for years to come.

PART I

The Investor's Landscape

OVERVIEW

Let's start by laying down the strategic groundwork you need to understand commercial real estate (CRE) as a complex, data-driven, and globally connected investment arena. We'll break down the economic forces, market structures, and investor behaviors that move capital into property markets, and ultimately shape your investment returns. Blending analytical tools, institutional insights, and real-life examples, this section gives you a clear picture of the structural and cyclical dynamics that drive CRE performance.

Across four chapters, we'll clarify what commercial real estate really is, map out how its markets are organized, uncover why different investors have varying objectives, and explore how market cycles affect valuations and decision-making. This foundation will prepare you for the advanced financial modeling, valuation techniques, and risk management strategies we cover later.

Our journey begins with the basics: how CRE generates income and appreciates in value, how it stacks up against stocks, bonds, and other asset classes, and how investors break down risk and shape their strategies. From there, we expand to look at the dance between institutional and private capital in a financial ecosystem growing ever more sophisticated.

We then dive into the diverse goals you'll see across the investor spectrum, from public REITs to family offices, and how those goals influence underwriting, leverage, holding periods, and expected returns. Finally, we tackle CRE's market cycles head-on, giving you practical frameworks to spot turning points and align your investment moves with the larger economic story.

Overview of Chapters

Chapter 1 – Understanding Commercial Real Estate as an Asset Class

We start by breaking down what really drives CRE returns, steady income streams and long-term appreciation. You'll see where CRE fits in the broader investment landscape and how it stacks up against stocks, bonds, and alternatives across different market cycles. We make sense of the various CRE strategies by risk level, core, core-plus, value-add, opportunistic, and explore how different property types react as the economy shifts. Plus, we take a close look at how office and industrial sectors performed side by side from 2000 to 2025.

Chapter 2 – The Structure of the Commercial Real Estate Market

Here, we unpack the financial, institutional, and operational framework that keeps CRE running. You'll get a front-row seat to the ecosystem of capital providers, investment vehicles, regulations, and operating platforms. We'll guide you through the entire deal cycle, from sourcing and underwriting to raising capital and closing, while comparing heavyweight institutional players with private market investors. Expect profiles of giants like Blackstone, Brookfield, KKR, and Carlyle, alongside the growing role of family offices and ultra-high-net-worth individuals.

Chapter 3 – Divergent Investor Objectives and Strategic Implications

Not all CRE investors play the same game. This chapter highlights why public REITs, private equity funds, pension plans, insurance companies, and family offices have distinct timelines, risk tolerances, and return targets. Those differences ripple through everything, from underwriting and leverage to asset management and exit strategies. We wrap up by showing how the top global players use flexible capital structures and strategic positioning to stay ahead through every phase of the market cycle.

Chapter 4 – The CRE Market Cycle

CRE isn't static, it pulses through four well-known phases: Expansion, Hypersupply, Recession, and Recovery. We unpack how macroeconomic trends, capital markets, and sector-specific fundamentals interact to push markets through these stages. You'll learn how to apply cycle awareness practically, timing your acquisitions, dispositions, developments, and refinancing moves. Real-world examples highlight how sectors like multifamily and office respond differently as markets shift.

Key Takeaways from Part I

- ☐ Commercial real estate blends income with capital appreciation, adding valuable diversification alongside stocks and bonds.
- ☐ The CRE market functions as a layered ecosystem, you need to understand the players, capital flows, and investment structures to stay competitive.
- ☐ Investors come with varied objectives, shaping underwriting approaches, capital stacks, leverage, holding horizons, and performance goals.
- ☐ Understanding CRE's cyclical rhythm is essential for timing your moves, managing risk, and building resilient portfolios.
- ☐ Mastering these fundamentals sets you up to tackle the more advanced modeling, valuation, and portfolio strategies we dive into next.

CHAPTER 01

Understanding Commercial Real Estate as an Asset Class

Introduction

When you think of commercial real estate (CRE), it's easy to picture the towering buildings and sprawling complexes shaping our cities, and while that's true, CRE is way more than just physical space. It's actually a fundamental pillar in the world of both institutional and private investment portfolios all around the globe. By early 2024, the U.S. investable CRE market was estimated to be a massive $26.8 trillion. Of that, $11.7 trillion represented institutional-grade assets managed by pensions, insurers, and some of the biggest asset managers out there (MSCI Real Assets, 2024). But don't stop there, zoom out and the global figure towers beyond $50 trillion. And that number doesn't just reflect the traditional sectors we know, office, industrial, retail, and multifamily, but also an ever-expanding roster that includes alternatives like data centers and healthcare facilities, sectors growing fast and demanding attention (CBRE, 2025).

1.1 The Role of CRE in Diversified Portfolios

Now, here's why CRE should matter to you as an investor or professional working in finance: it's not just about owning buildings. For institutional investors, CRE is a powerful way to weave stable income streams, inflation protection, and genuine diversification into the fabric of their portfolios. You know how stocks can wildly swing based on earnings reports or market mood, and bonds dance to the tune of interest rate changes? CRE behaves differently, it's tied to real, physical usage, longer-term leases, and local market supply and demand dynamics, grounding its value in the real world (Cohen & Steers, 2024).

Studies back this up. Private U.S. real estate shows a low-to-moderate correlation to the S&P 500, between 0.20 and 0.40, and even has a slightly negative correlation to long-term bonds, ranging from -0.10 to -0.20 (NCREIF, 2025). Why care? Because those numbers mean CRE often moves on a different beat than stocks and bonds. It becomes especially valuable when financial markets get rough. Combine that with income locked in from contracts and potential for property appreciation, and you have a recipe for attractive risk-adjusted returns that sophisticated investors just can't ignore.

1.2 How CRE Generates Returns

Let's talk about how you actually make money in CRE, because that's what everyone wants to know. Returns come mainly from two places: income and appreciation. Picture a modern logistics warehouse leased to a third-party logistics provider (3PL) under a triple-net lease. What does that mean for the landlord? The tenant takes care of property taxes, insurance, and maintenance, leaving the landlord with a rock-solid, predictable net operating income (NOI) (TowerCorp, 2025). This kind of setup is exactly what core and core-plus investors look for, steady income without nasty surprises.

Now, appreciation is a bit more nuanced. It's about market forces and savvy management. Here's a classic example: imagine a property producing $100,000 in NOI, bought with a capitalization rate (cap rate) of 7%. That puts its valuation around $1.43 million. If interest rates fall or demand heats up, and the cap rate compresses to 6%, the property's value jumps to about $1.66 million, just like that, a 17%

increase without one extra dollar of income (FNRP USA, 2022). On top of market-driven upticks, active hands-on management, think renovating an aging apartment complex to fill vacancies and raise rents, can seriously boost your returns. Take a multifamily project in Atlanta as an example: after a major renovation and re-tenanting, it raked in a five-year internal rate of return of 15% (Marcus & Millichap, 2021).

1.3 CRE Strategy Segmentation: Balancing Risk and Return

You'll quickly find that not every commercial real estate investment plays by the same rules. Investors segment strategies to hit different risk and return targets, each with a distinct place in portfolio construction. As outlined in Table 1.1, CRE investments break down into four main categories, core, core-plus, value-add, and opportunistic, each offering a different blend of expected annual returns and asset types.

Core properties, for example, are the classic low-risk bets: stabilized, well-leased urban office buildings delivering steady returns and minimal surprises. Core-plus assets build on that base, providing stable income but with extra upside from modest improvements or operational enhancements, like renovated suburban multifamily properties. Value-add takes things further, targeting underperforming or outdated buildings where upgrades and repositioning can spur rent growth and reduce vacancies. At the far end of the spectrum are opportunistic strategies, think ground-up development or distressed assets. These deals come with higher risk but the potential for outsized returns if managed well (Preqin, 2025).

Table 1.1 summarizes these CRE investment strategies, their typical return expectations, and representative asset types (Century 21 Edge, 2024; Marcus & Millichap, 2021; Related Companies, 2020).

Understanding this segmentation is critical: it shapes how institutional investors balance growth, income, and liquidity in their portfolios.

Table 1.1 CRE Investment Strategy Segmentation and Typical Returns

Strategy	Expected Annual Return (%)	Example Asset Type
Core	4-7	Stabilized urban office
Core-Plus	6-9	Renovated suburban multifamily
Value-Add	8-12	Repositioned apartments
Opportunistic	12+	Development/distressed assets

Note. Adapted from Century 21 Edge, 2024; Marcus & Millichap, 2021; Related Companies, 2020.

1.4 Major Institutional Players

The commercial real estate market wouldn't move without some serious players steering the ship. Blackstone Group is one of those giants, executing a multi-strategy plan. Their recent $7.6 billion buy of PS Business Parks alongside a $20 billion Real Estate Partners X fund showcases their laser focus on global logistics and value-add plays (Blackstone, 2025b).

Not far behind, Ares Management made waves with the acquisition of GLP Capital Partners' international logistics assets for $44 billion. That move is all about expanding their reach into resilient, cash-flowing global logistics hubs, including Goodman Logistics Centres across Europe (Financial Times, 2024).

Then there's Brookfield Asset Management, managing over $1 trillion across multiple segments, multifamily through Greystar, life sciences, core logistics, highlighting their scale and versatile platform approach (Brookfield Asset Management, 2025b).

Public REITs like Prologis dominate the industrial scene, holding a staggering 1.2 billion square feet of distribution space and long-term tenant relationships with giants like Amazon and FedEx. Prologis's focus on high-barrier, last-mile distribution has powered its market cap beyond $100 billion (Prologis, 2025).

1.4.1 Sector Trends and Examples

The industrial and logistics sectors exploded in 2024. Duke Realty reported record leasing activity across its 141 million square feet of U.S. properties, fueled largely by the e-commerce boom (Duke Realty, 2024; Statista, 2025). Meanwhile, office real estate is feeling the strain. Tenants are shrinking their spaces amid hybrid work models, Boston Properties is a case in point, with notable downsizing (Boston Properties, 2024). Others like SL Green have shifted resources away from office, putting capital toward multifamily and industrial spaces instead (SL Green, 2024).

1.4.2 Sector Divergence: Office vs. Industrial

This contrast between office and industrial sectors is striking. Industrial rents climbed 6.8% year-over-year as of early 2025, hitting $8.35 per square foot. Quarterly returns in some regions even topped 20% (Sidra Capital, 2024; Scottmax, 2025). The NCREIF Industrial index confirms these assets are outperforming many broader market benchmarks. Meanwhile, office vacancy rates now often exceed 20%, and valuations in major cities have dropped by over 30% since 2020, major clients and institutions are rethinking where their money goes (Keiter CPA, 2024; JLL, 2025; Cohen & Steers, 2024).

1.5 CRE Performance Across Market Cycles

CRE's ability to weather market cycles is impressive. Post the 2008–09 financial crisis, property values dipped but steadily recovered, ultimately beating public equities during the rebound. The COVID-19 pandemic reshaped everything, industrial and logistics assets gained in prominence and performance, while office and retail suffered (JLL, 2025; NAREIT, 2025).

Looking across 2010-2024, the NCREIF Property Index delivered average annual returns of 9.3%, trailing the S&P 500's 11.2% but outperforming bonds, which averaged just 3.5%, all with comparatively less roller-coaster volatility (NCREIF, 2025; Bloomberg, 2024).

1.6 Market Size and Sector Composition

To grasp CRE's scale, think of the 2024 U.S. investable market at $26.8 trillion, with $11.7 trillion classified as institutional-grade (Clarion Partners, 2024). Traditional sectors, multifamily, industrial, office, retail, hospitality, hold about 70% of the pie, but alternatives like data centers, self-storage, and healthcare grow their pieces yearly.

Take a look at Table 1.2 to see exactly how institutional capital is spread across the different sectors.

Table 1.2 Sectoral Composition of Institutional U.S. CRE (2024)

Sector	Share (%)	Value ($ Trillion)
Multifamily	22.5	2.63
Retail	18.5	2.17
Office	12.3	1.44
Industrial	11.5	1.35
Hospitality	5.1	0.60
Alternatives	30.5	3.58

Note. Data adapted from Clarion Partners, 2024; Commercial Observer, 2024.

Think about Prologis holding more than 150 million square feet of U.S. "last-mile" logistics space by 2024. Or Blackstone's $14.5 billion acquisition of Logicor, both moves showing why scaling up in logistics matters so much (Blackstone, 2017).

1.6.1 U.S. CRE Market Growth and Institutional Share

Institutional involvement in CRE has steadily increased over the past decade. Table 1.3 shows how the U.S. market and the institutional share have expanded from 2010 to 2024:

Table 1.3 Growth of U.S. CRE Market and Institutional Share (2010–2024)

Year	Total CRE ($T)	Institutional-Quality CRE ($T)	% Institutional
2010	13.0	5.5	42%
2014	15.0	6.5	43%
2018	16.0	7.0	44%
2020	20.0	10.0	50%
2024	26.8	11.7	44%

Note. Sources: Clarion Partners, 2024; Blue Vault, 2018.

1.7 Major Institutional Players and Strategic Shifts

A handful of powerhouse firms dominate the commercial real estate landscape, steering massive amounts of capital and shaping industry trends. Blackstone, for instance, continues to make waves by managing roughly $320 billion in real estate assets and topping $1 trillion in total AUM. Their focus has sharpened on logistics, digital infrastructure, and large-scale platform acquisitions, constantly redefining the market's direction (Blackstone, 2025a, 2025b).

Brookfield Asset Management is another heavyweight, overseeing more than $1 trillion globally, with $272 billion allocated to property holdings spanning diverse sectors and regions (Brookfield AM,

2025a, 2025b). Ares Management has recently strengthened its foothold in logistics, acquiring GLP Capital Partners' international logistics platform in a landmark $44 billion deal, an ambitious move aimed at global scale (Financial Times, 2024; Ares Management, 2025). Prologis stands out among public REITs, boasting a market cap above $130 billion and leading the way in industrial and logistics real estate (Prologis, 2025).

To provide a clear comparison of these market movers, Table 1.4 presents the top global institutional real estate managers in 2025 and their respective holdings.

Understanding the positions and strategies of these major players is central to grasping how capital flows and strategic priorities set the tone for the broader CRE market.

Table 1.4 Top Global Institutional Real Estate Managers (2025)

Manager	Total AUM ($B)	Real Estate AUM ($B)	Key Focus/ Highlights	Source
Blackstone	~1,040	~320	Logistics, Digital Infrastructure, Acquisitions	Blackstone (2025a, 2025b)
Brookfield	~1,000	~272	Diversified Global Platforms, Operator Model	Brookfield AM (2025a, 2025b)
Ares	~450	~115	Logistics/Industrial, International Expansion	Ares; Financial Times (2024/25)
Prologis	~130 (mkt cap)	~130	Industrial/Logistics, 1.2B sq. ft. under management	Prologis (2025)

1.7.1 The Evolving CRE Landscape

Each economic cycle shuffles capital in new directions. Institutional investors are increasingly funneling money into growth areas like logistics and data infrastructure. The big players, Blackstone,

Brookfield, don't just follow these trends; they shape and accelerate them, even as old guard sectors like office face steady challenges (Blackstone, 2025a; Brookfield Asset Management, 2025b).

1.8 Summary and Key Investor Takeaways

In short, commercial real estate occupies an undeniable slot in institutional portfolios focused on stability, dependable cash flows, and upside potential (MSCI Real Assets, 2024). Industrial and logistics assets have emerged as the new engines powering growth, while alternative property types steadily chip away at legacy sectors. The giants like Blackstone, Brookfield, and Ares aren't just managing capital, they're steering market currents. For you as an investor or market watcher, know this: deep sector knowledge, disciplined allocation, and nimbleness to adapt remain your best bets for lasting success in CRE (Cohen & Steers, 2024; JLL, 2025).

1.9 Transition to Chapter 2: The Structure of the Commercial Real Estate (CRE) Market

Now that we've laid out the essential contours of CRE as an asset class, we'll shift gears in Chapter 2 to explore the capital ecosystem powering it, REITs, private equity funds, pension funds, family offices. Understanding their mandates, investment criteria, and deal structures will give you the foundation you need to navigate this complex, fast-evolving market.

References

Ares Management Corporation. (2025, March 3). *Ares Management Corporation completes acquisition of GCP International* [Press release]. https://ir.aresmgmt.com/news/ares-management-corporation-completes-acquisition-of-gcp-international

Blackstone. (2025a, January 30). *Blackstone reports fourth quarter and full year 2024 results* [Press release]. https://www.blackstone.com/wp-content/uploads/sites/2/2025/01/Blackstone4Q24EarningsPressRelease.pdf

Blackstone. (2025b, April 10). *Blackstone announces €9.8 billion final close of largest ever European real estate drawdown fund (BREP Europe VII)* [Press release]. https://www.blackstone.com/news/press/blackstone-announces-10-6-billion-final-close-largest-ever-european-real-estate-drawdown-fund

Blackstone. (2025c). *Blackstone Real Estate Partners X: Opportunistic logistics and value-add fund.*

Bloomberg. (2024, December 30). *Bloomberg U.S. aggregate bond index: 2024 performance summary.* https://www.bloomberg.com

Boston Properties. (2024). *Q4 earnings report: Office portfolio adjustments.*

Brookfield Asset Management. (2025a, February 12). *Brookfield Asset Management announces record 2024 results and 15% dividend increase* [Press release]. https://www.globenewswire.com/news-release/2025/02/12/3024869/0/en/Brookfield-Asset-Management-Announces-Record-2024-Results-and-15-Dividend-Increase.html

Brookfield Asset Management. (2025b, July 1). *The Brookfield Real Estate Advantage* [White paper]. https://www.brookfieldoaktree.com/sites/default/files/2025-07/the-brookfield-real-estate-advantage.pdf

Brookfield Asset Management. (2025c). *Greystar real estate platform overview.*

Brookfield Asset Management. (n.d.). *Real estate* [Company webpage]. https://www.brookfield.com/about-us/capabilities/real-estate

CBRE. (2025, April 12). *Global real estate outlook 2025: Alternatives and logistics lead growth* [Market report]. https://www.cbre.com/insights

CBRE Investment Management. (2025, April 2). *CBRE Investment Management 2025 global outlook: Sustainable growth in real assets* [Report]. https://www.cbreim.com

Clarion Partners. (2024, August 19). *The ongoing outperformance of U.S. industrial real estate.* https://www.clarionpartners.com/insights/ongoing-outperformance-of-us-industrial-real-estate

Cohen & Steers. (2024, November 15). *Listed real assets performance review 2023–2024* [White paper]. https://www.cohenandsteers.com

Cohen & Steers. (2025, January 25). *Drivers of commercial real estate returns in 2025.* https://www.cohenandsteers.com/insights/the-real-estate-reel-drivers-of-commercial-real-estate-returns-in-2025

Duke Realty. (2024). *Annual market report: Industrial leasing and occupancy.*

Financial Times. (2024, October 8). *Ares bolsters real estate business with US $5.2 billion takeover of GLP Capital Partners International.* https://www.ft.com/content/f3fe6c43-4f31-44ba-981e-21433a65efce

FNRP USA. (2022). *Cap rate compression: Value effects in commercial real estate.*

Garman, J., Kuney, K., & Zutshi, A. (2025, July 30). *Finding a firmer footing: The case for commercial real estate.* Goldman Sachs. https://am.gs.com/en-sg/advisors/insights/article/2025/finding-firmer-footing-case-for-commercial-real-estate

JLL. (2025, May 2). *U.S. industrial market update Q1 2025* [Market insight report]. https://www.jll.com/en-us/insights/market-dynamics/industrial-market-statistics-trends

Keiter CPA. (2024, September 30). *U.S. office sector vacancy and absorption report Q3 2024.* https://keitercpa.com

KKR & Co. Inc. (2025, March 15). *KKR real estate platform expands with $2.1 billion student housing acquisition* [Press release]. https://www.kkr.com/newsroom

MacKinnon, G. (2018). Yes, stocks, bonds, and real estate are exposed to different risk factors (PREA Research Insights). Pension Real Estate Association. https://docs.prea.org/pub/45CA1E42-A07F-E5EA-C448-19C346183AAF

Marcus & Millichap. (2021). *Multifamily value-add investment case study: Atlanta market.*

MetLife Investment Management. (2024, December 31). *MetLife Investment Management annual report 2024.* https://investments.metlife.com

MSCI Real Assets. (2024, October 18). *U.S. commercial real estate market size 2024* [Data brief]. https://www.msci.com/our-solutions/real-assets

National Association of Real Estate Investment Trusts. (2022). *Estimating the size of the commercial real estate market in the U.S.* https://www.reit.com/data-research/research/nareit-research

NAREIT. (2025, January 5). *REIT market data and sector performance review 2024.* https://www.reit.com

NCREIF. (2025, January 10). *NCREIF property index historical performance data* [Quarterly report]. https://www.ncreif.org

Nuveen Real Estate. (2025, May 20). *Nuveen Real Estate European logistics expansion continues with €1.4 billion acquisitions* [Press release]. https://www.nuveen.com/real-estate

Origin Investments. (2016, January 19). *Private real estate improves your portfolio of stocks & bonds.* https://origininvestments.com/why-private-real-estate-portfolio-stocks-bonds-diversification

PGIM Real Estate. (2025, April 15). *PGIM Real Estate global AUM surpasses US $210 billion* [Press release]. https://www.pgim.com/real-estate

Preqin. (2025, March 25). *Global real estate report 2025: Capital allocation and strategy trends.* https://www.preqin.com

Prologis. (2025, March 31). *Prologis Q1 2025 results* [Investor report]. https://www.prologis.com/investors

Prologis. (2025). *Annual report: Global logistics footprint and customer base.*

Scottmax. (2025, February 20). *U.S. industrial property market rent growth statistics 2025.* https://www.scottmax.com

Sidra Capital. (2024, November 8). *Global real estate outlook: Industrial sector performance analysis.* https://www.sidracapital.com

SL Green Realty. (2024). *Strategic portfolio rebalancing disclosure.*

Statista. (2025, January 12). *Global e-commerce sales from 2014 to 2025 (in trillion U.S. dollars).* https://www.statista.com/statistics/379046/worldwide-retail-e-commerce-sales

TowerCorp. (2025). *Triple net lease structures and income predictability in logistics real estate.*

U.S. Federal Reserve Bank of St. Louis. (2025). *Commercial real estate prices for United States* [Data set COMREPUSQ159N]. FRED. https://fred.stlouisfed.org/series/COMREPUSQ159N

CHAPTER 02

The Structure of the Commercial Real Estate (CRE) Market

Introduction

The global CRE market isn't just about buildings and land anymore. It's a massive, intertwined ecosystem where capital providers, investment vehicles, regulations, and operating platforms all play their parts. While "real estate" used to mean just property, today's CRE financial landscape is more like a high-level capital market with complex funds, trusts, and asset classes.

You've got REITs, private equity funds, pension plans, insurance companies, sovereign wealth funds, and increasingly, family offices, each bringing capital with their own unique risk appetites, timelines, and strategies. They're shaping how fast money flows, the types of deals that get done, and even how properties are managed day to day (CBRE, 2025; Clarion Partners, 2024).

In this chapter, we're going to map out the main players, the deal mechanics, the different goals driving investment, and how capital is deployed and recycled by the big players. We'll also break down detailed case studies of global titans like Blackstone, Brookfield, KKR, and Carlyle, and dive into family offices, the rising force redefining CRE with their long game.

2.1 Capital Providers in Global CRE

2.1.1 Real Estate Investment Trusts (REITs)

If you want to see CRE's most visible and liquid capital sources, look no further than REITs. They connect everyday retail investors and large institutions to diversified income-producing real estate portfolios (Blackstone Real Estate Income Trust, n.d.; Clarion Partners, 2024).

REITs are required by law to distribute most of their taxable income, around 90%, so they're built around steady cash flow and liquidity through public markets (NAREIT, 2025). Take Blackstone's BREIT as an example, it's a non-listed REIT pooling billions from tens of thousands of investors, spread over offices, industrial assets, multifamily, retail, and hotels. By mid-2022, BREIT managed $320 billion in assets, showing just how much capital these vehicles can handle (Blackstone Real Estate Income Trust, 2022).

That said, some REITs recently faced challenges: payouts sometimes exceeded recurring cash flow, raising concerns about sustainability if acquisitions slow down (Financial Times, 2024). Still, REITs remain critical for market liquidity and transparency, they're the backbone of an efficient CRE ecosystem.

2.1.2 Private Equity Real Estate Funds

Private equity real estate funds work differently. They usually have a closed-end, 7- to 10-year life span. Investors commit capital upfront, then sponsors invest it through opportunistic, value-add, or core-plus strategies. Unlike REITs, these funds can reinvest earnings, striving to maximize value and total returns (Blackstone, 2024).

These funds shine in complex deals, think repositioning properties, public-to-private REIT takeovers, or buying distressed loans. Blackstone's knack for strategic privatizations and repositioning illustrates this approach well: as of end-2023, they managed $337 billion in private real estate, including $125 billion focused on opportunistic plays (Blackstone, 2024).

Capital recycling, the art of reinvesting profits from deals, is key here, letting funds multiply returns over their life cycle and boost value for investors.

2.1.3 Pension Funds, Insurance Companies, and Sovereign Wealth Funds

These institutional giants hold enormous CRE portfolios designed to match long-term liabilities (like pensions and insurance payouts), so they lean toward low-risk, core or core-plus properties. They're also flexible, upping value-add or development exposure during boom cycles (CBRE Investment Management, 2025; Preqin, 2025).

Their capital often comes through separate accounts, large co-investments, or commingled funds. For instance, in 2023, CPP Investments joined Blackstone and Rialto Capital to buy a $16.8 billion FDIC CRE loan portfolio, highlighting the sector's ability to turn distressed assets into opportunities (Blackstone, 2023). Their patient capital and long horizons support mega-projects and take on cyclical risks others avoid.

2.2 Key Processes in CRE Markets

2.2.1 Deal Sourcing and Underwriting

Landing deals requires a mix of brokerage channels, proprietary networks, and being quick to spot inefficiencies. The best sponsors often find deals before they hit the market, leveraging deep relationships and analytics.

Underwriting goes deep. It's about modeling cash flows, rent rolls, operating expenses, and value-add potential, plus stress-testing debt and vacancy risks amid shifting economic conditions (Goldman Sachs Asset Management, 2025; CBRE, 2025).

We're seeing massive growth in CRE debt funds, too. Blackstone's $8 billion real estate debt fund launched in early 2025 is a prime example of targeting cross-continental opportunities with debt strategies (Wall Street Journal, 2025).

2.2.2 Structuring and Capital Recycling

Top-tier dealmakers layer capital stacks to balance risk and boost returns. Senior debt, mezzanine loans, preferred and common equity all stack up to optimize each project.

Capital recycling, reinvesting proceeds from asset sales into new deals, is how sponsors keep the momentum going. Blackstone's privatization of AIR Communities, a massive $10 billion acquisition of 27,385 apartments, is a classic case: they flipped capital from sales back into new value plays (Blackstone, 2024).

2.3 Objectives and Differences Among Investor Types

- **REIT Investors** want reliable income, transparency, and liquidity. Public REIT shareholders demand steady cash flow; non-listed REIT investors accept less liquidity for higher yields (Blackstone Real Estate Income Trust, 2022).
- **Private Equity Investors** chase capital growth through active value creation, paying close attention to IRR, risk, and exit timing.
- **Institutional Investors** like pension funds balance steady income with growth, mixing core holdings with opportunistic bets to meet their long-term needs.

2.4 Case Studies of Leading Global CRE Platforms

2.4.1 Blackstone

By the end of 2023, Blackstone had nearly $337 billion in real estate capital under management worldwide, a massive platform spanning the Americas, Europe, and Asia (Blackstone, 2023). What sets Blackstone apart is its multi-pronged, dynamic strategy:

- **Debt:** Blackstone's real estate debt platform is a major force. Their 2023 purchase of a $16.8 billion loan portfolio from the FDIC is a prime example of how they move decisively in distressed and debt-heavy sectors, showing real agility in markets where others hesitate.
- **REIT Privatization:** The firm has led roughly 15 public-to-private REIT transactions totaling about $180 billion, demonstrating sharp capital deployment aimed squarely at creating value by taking public companies private, revamping them, and extracting profit (CRE Analyst, 2024).
- **Income Vehicles:** Blackstone's income-focused products, like BREIT, attract a broad base of retail investors seeking steady payouts. Though there are occasional questions about sustainability, especially when dividends outstrip cash flow, the appeal remains strong (Financial Times, 2024).

Blackstone's ability to recycle capital quickly, operate at massive scale, and change strategies on the fly puts it right at the top as a trendsetter and powerhouse in global CRE.

2.4.2 Brookfield

Brookfield Asset Management takes a patient, value-oriented approach to CRE. Faced with tough industry headwinds like U.S. office market oversupply and the lasting effects of remote work, Brookfield shifted gears toward sectors with strong growth prospects, industrial, logistics, data centers, and alternative assets (Reuters, 2024). This shift isn't random; it reflects careful risk management and strategic repositioning to stay ahead of changing macroeconomic trends (Brookfield Asset Management, 2025).

Their long-term horizon and nimble allocation underscore an approach focused on resilience and steady growth.

2.4.3 KKR

KKR's real estate business has quietly but steadily expanded by blending private equity with credit strategies. Although they're less public about details compared to others, KKR's strength lies in close partnerships with sovereign wealth funds, pensions, and a host of global co-investors. This network lets them tap into both equity and debt opportunities spread across various sectors and regions, allowing for a diversified and flexible approach.

2.4.4 Carlyle

Carlyle runs a global private equity platform that's all about diversification and opportunism. They mix traditional development, value-add transformations, and core investment vehicles to chase top-tier properties and platforms worldwide. Their edge comes from deep-rooted sponsor relationships and patient co-investment capital, which gives them the ability to compete strongly for premium deals while riding out market cycles.

2.4.5 Family Offices and Ultra-High-Net-Worth (UHNW) Investors

Family offices have become one of the fastest-growing capital sources in global CRE, especially since the market shocks and liquidity squeezes of 2020 (PwC, 2025; RSM US LLP, 2024). Real estate now takes up about 39% of the average family office portfolio, a clear shift toward tangible, inflation-resistant assets that can protect wealth while offering strategic independence (PwC, 2025).

What's driving this rise? It's not just a hunt for stability, but also a growing appetite for co-investments, more operational control, and direct property ownership. These are defining traits of the UHNW investment mindset (Ho & Singh, 2025). Family offices aren't just looking to park money, they're building legacy portfolios they can manage hands-on and pass down generations.

2.5 Market Trends and Broader Dynamics

Let's talk about the big forces shaping commercial real estate right now, because understanding these trends helps you stay ahead of the curve.

First up: **global capital flows**. Cross-border CRE investment rebounded sharply in 2024, with $37 billion pouring into North America, Europe, and Asia-Pacific, a solid 31% jump from the previous year (CBRE, 2025). What's driving this surge? Investors like you are looking beyond borders, chasing diversification and growth where capital and opportunity align. It means you're competing in a truly global marketplace, and staying plugged into how and where capital moves is crucial to spotting your next big win.

Next, a trend reshaping ownership structures: the **convergence between private equity and public REITs**. Private equity sponsors have been aggressively acquiring public REITs, taking advantage of pricing inefficiencies while recapitalizing portfolios to unlock hidden value (CRE Analyst, 2024). This wave creates new dynamics in liquidity and asset management strategies, and if you're investing today, you need to understand how this shift could impact deal flow, pricing, and competition in your target sectors.

Then, there are the **macro-level changes** influencing everything, from how deals get sourced to which assets you favor. The recent cycle of rising interest rates, persistent inflation, and escalating geopolitical tensions has investors recalibrating. What are we seeing? A clear pivot toward defensive property types, think industrial warehouses, healthcare, and essential retail, and a growing emphasis on assets that can generate strong organic income growth (Governance structures in CRE funds Asset Management, 2025). In other words, chasing yield alone won't cut it anymore; you've got to factor in stability and resilience into your investment thesis.

When you combine these global capital movements, structural shifts in ownership, and macroeconomic pressures, it becomes clear: the commercial real estate landscape isn't just shifting, it's evolving in ways that demand a sharper, more strategic perspective. So whether you're sourcing deals locally or managing a sprawling portfolio, staying on top of these broader dynamics is what separates reactive investors from those who shape the market.

2.6 How Deals Are Sourced

Sourcing commercial real estate deals today involves a complex blend of institutional pipelines, deep-rooted local connections, and strategic collaborations—each playing a distinct role depending on the asset type and the investor's risk profile.

At the forefront are brokerage pipelines, which dominate transactions involving stabilized assets and large-scale portfolio deals, especially those crossing borders. Global firms like CBRE leverage their extensive networks and proprietary data platforms to bridge buyers and sellers efficiently, creating transparency in pricing and market availability. For 2025, CBRE predicts this channel will remain the primary source for high-quality, institutional-grade deals, driven by its ability to consolidate market intelligence and match global capital to prime assets.

However, when investors pivot to value-add or distressed opportunities, they often turn to off-market networks. These are cultivated through long-term relationships with local brokers, property owners, lenders, and operators, providing early or exclusive access to assets before they hit the broader market. CRE Analyst's 2024 research highlights that off-market sourcing not only helps avoid highly competitive bidding but also uncovers hidden gems that might be mispriced or overlooked in public listings. This approach requires significant local market knowledge and trust, making it a favored tactic of private equity firms and opportunistic investors seeking alpha.

Developer joint ventures (JVs) form another critical source, particularly for large-scale development projects. These partnerships blend the capital strength of institutional investors with the technical expertise and local market insight of developers, enabling risk-sharing and access to early-stage projects. JVs allow investors to enter growth assets on favorable terms and participate in value creation from construction through stabilization.

Lastly, sale-leaseback transactions have emerged as a growing avenue, with $30 billion of U.S. deals closed in 2023 alone (RSM US LLP, 2024). Through these transactions, corporations sell their real estate holdings to unlock capital while continuing to occupy the properties via leases. For investors, sale-leasebacks offer stable, long-term cash flows anchored by high-credit tenants, making them attractive in sectors like retail, logistics, healthcare, and industrial.

Effective deal sourcing is therefore a multi-channel strategy, aligning different pipelines with specific asset classes and investor risk appetites. Successful investors invest time and resources into building diverse, adaptable sourcing networks, balancing access to high-profile, auctioned deals with discreet off-market opportunities and strategic partnerships, to stay ahead of the market curve.

2.7 Underwriting and Risk Assessment

Underwriting commercial real estate demands a rigorous, data-driven process that combines a deep understanding of market fundamentals with robust financial modeling. It's about more than just numbers, it's about painting a comprehensive picture of an asset's potential performance and vulnerabilities.

Market Analysis is the foundation. We analyze key economic indicators like absorption rates, supply-demand dynamics, local employment trends, and competitor development pipelines to validate rent and occupancy projections. According to JLL's 2025 market outlook, understanding how new supply aligns with demand,

and where market tightness exists, is critical to setting realistic assumptions and avoiding overoptimism.

Next comes financial modeling. This involves constructing detailed cash flow forecasts that incorporate operating income, capital expenditures, and financing structure. Metrics like debt service coverage ratio (DSCR), internal rate of return (IRR), and equity multiples are stress tested under various rent growth and expense inflation scenarios, as highlighted by Goldman Sachs Asset Management's recent methodologies. This multi-scenario approach reveals how sensitive returns are to shifts in market conditions, helping investors gauge risk tolerance accurately.

For value-add or repositioning opportunities, capital expenditure (CapEx) assessment is pivotal. Evaluating renovation costs is more than ticking boxes, it entails estimating timelines, budget contingencies, and the potential uplift in asset value post-renovation. Clarion Partners (2024) emphasizes that a well-executed CapEx strategy can unlock significant hidden value and improve market positioning.

But smart underwriting also means preparing for the unexpected. Stress testing via worst-case scenarios examines the resilience of an asset if cap rates widen, vacancies rise, or interest rates spike. MSCI Real Assets' 2024 guidelines recommend simulating downturns to understand downside risk and capital preservation thresholds thoroughly.

Finally, exit planning is integral to underwriting. The analysis doesn't stop at acquisition; multiple exit strategies, whether a sale, refinance, or recapitalization, are modeled to align with evolving market environments and investor objectives. CBRE Investment Management's 2025 framework highlights the importance of flexible exit paths as market dynamics shift.

Investor priorities deeply influence underwriting approaches. Public REITs typically focus on stable cash flows and diversification to satisfy income investors. Private equity firms pursue higher total returns through active management and asset repositioning. Family offices prioritize long-term wealth preservation, often with a conservative risk profile. Pension funds weigh downside protection heavily, integrating ESG factors into underwriting models, as detailed by PwC's 2025 institutional investor report.

In essence, underwriting and risk assessment form the backbone of disciplined commercial real estate investing, an iterative process anchored in rigorous data analysis, thoughtful scenario planning, and alignment with strategic investor goals.

2.8 Structuring Transactions

CRE deals stack capital in layers tailored to risk and return needs. Here's a quick snapshot from Table 2.1 showing typical return targets and characteristics by tranche:

Table 2.1 CRE Capital Stack and Risk-Return Characteristics

Tranche	Targeted Return (%)	Characteristics
Common Equity	12-22+	Highest risk/returns, capital gain
Preferred Equity	8-12	Fixed/floating; downside protection
Mezzanine Debt	10-16	Secured by equity pledges
Senior Debt	5-7 (typical)	Largest, lowest risk tranche

Adapted from Preqin, 2024; JLL Capital Markets, 2025; MSCI Real Assets, 2024

Take Hudson Yards in NYC, it's a $25 billion mega-project combining senior bank loans, pension fund equity (like Ontario Teachers'), common equity sponsors, and EB-5 mezzanine capital from foreign investors, showcasing how layered financing tackles mammoth developments (Oxford Properties, 2024).

2.9 Transition to Chapter 3: Divergent Investor Objectives and Strategic Implications in CRE

Next, we'll dig into how different capital sources, the big public REITs, nimble private equity funds, patient pension funds, and nimble family offices, each bring a unique lens to CRE investing. Their goals, risk tolerance, and timelines shape everything from deal structure to asset strategy and exit plans. To bring it all alive, we'll zoom in on four heavyweights, Blackstone, KKR, Brookfield, and Carlyle, showing how distinct capital strategies help them stay resilient and successful in this complex market.

References

Blackstone. (2023). *Blackstone Real Estate 2023 capital markets update* [Investor report]. https://www.blackstone.com

Blackstone. (2024). *Blackstone completes privatization of AIR Communities.* https://www.blackstone.com/news/press

Blackstone Real Estate Income Trust. (n.d.). *Blackstone Real Estate Income Trust, Inc. public filings and supplemental materials.* https://breit.com

Bloomberg. (2024, December 30). *Bloomberg U.S. aggregate bond index: 2024 performance summary.* https://www.bloomberg.com

Brookfield Asset Management. (2025). *2025 annual report.* https://www.brookfield.com

CBRE. (2025). *Global capital flows H2 2024.* https://www.cbre.com/insights

CBRE. (2025). *Market outlook report.* CBRE Group.

CBRE Investment Management. (2025). *Global outlook 2025.* https://www.cbreim.com

Clarion Partners. (2024). *The ongoing outperformance of U.S. industrial real estate.* https://www.clarionpartners.com/research

CRE Analyst. (2024). *Public-to-private REIT transaction study.* https://www.creanalyst.com

CRE Analyst. (2024). *U.S. commercial real estate sourcing trends.* CRE Insights Publishing.

Credaily. (2025). *Family office real estate survey.* https://www.credaily.com

Financial Times. (2024). *BREIT payout scrutiny.* https://www.ft.com

Goldman Sachs Asset Management. (2025). *Real estate investment 2025 outlook.* https://www.goldmansachs.com

Ho, S., & Singh, D. (2025). *Patient capital: Ultra-high-net-worth and family office strategy trends.* (Publisher unavailable; web report).

JLL Capital Markets. (2025). *CRE capital stack outlook.* https://www.us.jll.com/en/trends-and-insights/research

MSCI Real Assets. (2024). *CRE debt volume tracker.* https://www.msci.com

Nareit. (2025). *REIT sector annual review 2024.* https://www.reit.com

Oxford Properties. (2024). *Hudson Yards: Financing structure report.* https://www.oxfordproperties.com

Preqin. (2024). *Global private equity real estate report.* https://www.preqin.com

PwC. (2025). *Global family office survey.* https://www.pwc.com

Reuters. (2024, March 13). *Brookfield pivots from office.* https://www.reuters.com

RSM US LLP. (2024). *Global family office survey.* https://rsmus.com

RSM US LLP. (2024). *Real estate industry outlook.* RSM.

U.S. Census Bureau. (2024). *Sun Belt urbanization trends.* https://www.census.gov

Wall Street Journal. (2025). *Blackstone closes $8B global CRE debt fund.* https://www.wsj.com

CHAPTER 03

Divergent Investor Objectives and Strategic Implications in Commercial Real Estate

Introduction

When you look at commercial real estate (CRE), you're not just seeing buildings, you're seeing a whole spectrum of investors with wildly different goals, styles, and timelines. From giant public REITs to family offices quietly making moves across generations, each one plays a very specific game. And those differences aren't just trivia, they literally shape where capital flows, how deals get done, and how markets behave over time.

In this chapter, we unpack how your investor type changes your whole approach, what properties you chase, how you structure deals, and when you decide to exit. We'll take a close look at four of the biggest global players, Blackstone, KKR, Brookfield, and Carlyle, showing how their distinct strategies and capital deployment styles help them deliver steady results. Plus, we'll talk about family offices, those long-game players who focus on wealth preservation and flexibility, shaping the CRE landscape in ways you might not expect.

By understanding these different investor profiles and strategies, you'll be better prepared to see the trends coming, align your own allocations smarter, and confidently navigate the growing complexities of CRE investing. And heads up, this leads right into Chapter 4, where we dive into market cycles and the analytics that help you time your moves just right.

3.1 Investor Profiles: Objectives, Horizons, and Risk Appetite

What drives you, and how much risk you're willing to take, really shapes your whole approach to CRE investing. Let's break down the main types of investors, what they focus on, how long they typically hold their assets, and the risks they're comfortable with. Table 3.1 lays out a clear snapshot of these key differences across capital sources.

Table 3.1 Investor Profiles in Commercial Real Estate

Investor Type	Primary Goal	Time Horizon	Risk Appetite
Real Estate Investment Trusts (REITs)	Income stability; dividend consistency	Long-term	Low to moderate
Private Equity Funds	Total return: income plus appreciation	7–10 years (finite)	Moderate to high
Pension Funds & Insurance Companies	Liability matching; steady income	Very long	Low to moderate
Family Offices	Wealth preservation; tax efficiency; flexibility	Indefinite	Wide-ranging

Note. Adapted from Blackstone Real Estate Income Trust (2022), Ho and Singh (2025), and Preqin (2024).

For example, if you're a REIT, your main play is low-risk assets that generate reliable income, like office towers or big logistics hubs with solid tenants. You want liquidity and dividend consistency, no surprises (Prologis, 2024). Now, if you roll with a private equity fund, you've got a ticking clock, usually 7 to 10 years to get your money back with a bang. That means going for value-add or opportunistic deals, think rehabs, upgrades, and hands-on management to juice both income and property appreciation, then selling at peak value (Blackstone, 2024).

Pension funds and insurers have to think even longer term, matching assets to liabilities decades out, so they keep to core, high-grade properties with long leases. ESG considerations are creeping in here too, environmental and social factors increasingly shape what they buy (CPP Investments, 2023).

And what about family offices? These players bring a very different flavor. Their horizons might be multigenerational, focusing on preserving wealth, cutting tax burdens, and staying flexible. They often dive into niches others overlook, like medical offices or boutique hotels, and prefer direct ownership where they can steward assets for the long haul (Ho & Singh, 2025).

3.2 How Goals Shape CRE Strategies and Underwriting

What you want and when you want it drives everything, the mix of properties in your portfolio and how you crunch the numbers on each deal.

If you're a REIT, your deal pipeline includes assets that get you steady cash flow without hiccups, think properties with long-term tenants and strong lease profiles, minimizing vacancy risks. Liquidity matters here, so they steer clear of anything that needs lengthy lease-ups or has volatile cash flow (Prologis, 2024).

Private equity funds? Their clock pushes them toward higher risk and higher reward. They're hunting for properties ripe for repositioning, renovation, or a total operational overhaul. Their underwriting tends to be on the optimistic side, projecting strong rent growth and cost efficiencies to make the numbers work (Blackstone, 2024).

On the more conservative end, pension funds and insurers use cautious underwriting, lower loan-to-value ratios, and long-term fixed-rate debt. Their focus is on assets that can hold steady for decades, providing stable income to match long-term payouts (CPP Investments, 2023).

Family offices break the mold a bit by playing with flexible hold periods, sometimes indefinitely. They look at opportunities across sectors and often appreciate the perks of specialized asset classes, like tax benefits combined with legacy value (Ho & Singh, 2025).

3.3 Divergent Deal Structures and Portfolio Implications

These differences don't just stay abstract—they show up in how deals get built and financed. To give you a clearer picture, think about how a pension fund approaches a core office building: steady, cautious, and focused on long-term stability. Now, compare that to a private equity sponsor tackling a value-add multifamily project, a much more hands-on, higher-risk, high-reward play.

Table 3.2 breaks down these contrasts in a practical way, highlighting how their strategies and risk comfort levels shape everything from loan terms to hold periods and exit plans.

Table 3.2 Underlying Deal and Financing Characteristics by Capital Source

Dimension	Example: Pension Fund Core Office	Example: Private Equity Value-Add Multifamily
Loan-to-Value Ratio (LTV)	40–55%	70%+
Debt Type	Long-term, fixed-rate senior debt	Higher leverage including mezzanine debt
Lease Profile	Long-duration leases, high-credit tenants	Moderate-term leases, active lease-up
Rent Growth Assumptions	Conservative, stable	Aggressive, pro forma driven
Hold Period	10–20+ years	3–5 years
Exit Strategy	Hold or refinance	Sale or recapitalization

Note. Synthesized from Goldman Sachs Asset Management (2025) and JLL Capital Markets (2025).

Pension funds rely on longer-term, senior debt with lower leverage to keep things stable. Private equity? They pack on more leverage and mezzanine layers to push returns higher, aiming to flip or recapitalize after driving value (Goldman Sachs Asset Management, 2025; JLL Capital Markets, 2025).

3.4 Profiles of Leading Global CRE Sponsors and Their Strategic Differentiation

Let's get specific. When you look at four of the biggest players in CRE, you see how very different strategies take shape on a massive scale. Here's the rundown on what they focus on, how much capital they manage, the types of investment vehicles they use, and where they operate around the world.

Table 3.3 lays out the key traits and strategic moves that set these major CRE firms apart, showing how their size, asset focus, and geographic reach influence their success.

Table 3.3 Key Characteristics of Major Global CRE Firms

Dimension	Blackstone	Brookfield	KKR	Carlyle
Primary Focus	Logistics, opportunistic, Core+	Diversified real estate and infrastructure	Real estate credit and structured finance	Opportunistic and core across US, Europe, Asia
Real Estate AUM (2025)	$339B	$272B (nearly $1T firm-wide)	$35B+ real estate credit	Multi-billion global platform
Capital Vehicles	Opportunistic funds, BREIT, Core+	Listed partnerships, preferred units, co-investment	Real estate credit funds (ROX series)	Closed-end funds, regional strategies
Capital Recycling	$1B+ S. Florida industrial disposals	Tens of billions across sectors	Loan refinancing and credit exits	Multifamily/ industrial sales to REITs/ institutions
Geographic Reach	N. America, Europe, Asia	30+ countries	N. America, Europe	U.S., Europe, Asia
Competitive Advantage	Scale with logistics focus	Multi-platform integration	Yield-focused credit	Global sourcing, flexible exits

Note. Consolidated from public disclosures (Blackstone, 2025; Brookfield, 2025; KKR, 2025; Carlyle, 2025).

Blackstone stands tall with logistics, focused aggressively on capital recycling, selling mature assets in big metros and plowing money into fast-growth corridors fueled by e-commerce and supply chain changes. Their $339 billion real estate pile benefits from this nimble cycle approach (CBRE, 2024; The Real Deal, 2025).

KKR carves out a niche in real estate credit, managing $35 billion in senior and mezzanine debt products that aim for solid returns around 8–12%. With banks tightening, their flexible credit offerings bridge the gap for transitional assets, offering investors less volatility and shorter duration alternatives to pure equity plays (KKR, 2025; Simpson Thacher, 2025).

Brookfield rides scale and diversification, nearly $1 trillion firm-wide, with $272 billion in real estate, and leverages operational expertise plus multi-asset integration across 30+ countries. Their layered capital vehicles and flexible exit options help them pivot with shifting markets, delivering reliable, long-term yield (Brookfield, 2025).

Carlyle blends opportunistic breadth with geographic diversity and creative exits, selling to REITs, IPOs, and more, making the most of global networks and developer partnerships to unlock value across US, Europe, and Asia (Carlyle, 2025).

3.5 Comparative Insights: Themes Across Sponsors

What's the secret sauce that ties heavyweights like Blackstone, Brookfield, and Carlyle together? It's capital agility, their ability to recycle capital efficiently by taking profits from mature assets and redeploying that cash into hotter, higher-growth opportunities.

Look at Figure 3.1, where we map how these powerhouses prioritize this agility in practice. Blackstone, for example, recently sold a portfolio of stabilized office buildings in primary U.S. markets at peak valuations, locking in gains north of 15% IRR. They didn't sit on that cash, they swiftly redeployed it into emerging sectors like life sciences labs and data centers, where early-stage demand is skyrocketing.

Brookfield's strategy leans heavily on refinancing. In 2024, they refinanced core assets in Europe during a favorable rate window, pulling out significant equity without disrupting operations. They used that liquidity to back high-conviction redevelopment projects in urban logistics hubs, where supply-demand imbalances promised outsized returns.

Carlyle took a more opportunistic tack, rotating out of retail assets hit by structural headwinds and redirecting capital into multifamily developments in fast-growing Sun Belt cities. This nimbleness helped them avoid longer-term asset decline and capture growth where population trends and housing demand are strongest.

What these examples show is that it's not enough to just buy and hold. You've got to be ready to move, selling, refinancing, and redeploying capital, sometimes within months, sometimes over a few years, to sharpen returns and stay ahead of market cycles.

So, when you think about your own portfolio, ask yourself: Are you maximizing your capital's agility? Or are you leaving value on the table by holding too long or moving too slow? The market won't wait, and neither should you.

Figure 3.1 Capital Recycling Activity Among Major CRE Sponsors, 2024–2025

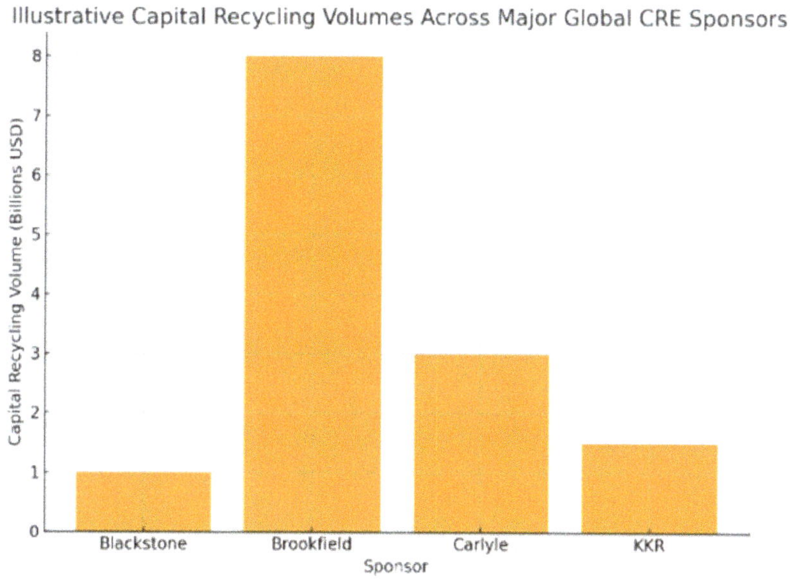

Note. *Approximate volumes based on qualitative industry reports (Blackstone, 2025; Brookfield, 2025; Carlyle, 2025; The Real Deal, 2025).*

3.5 Transition to Chapter 4: The CRE Market Cycle

Up next, we dive deep into the CRE market's rollercoaster ride, the cycles shaped by economic forces, investor moods, and property fundamentals. Expansion, hypersupply, recession, and recovery all shift rents, vacancies, investor appetite, and valuations. Spotting where you are in the cycle means you can manage risk smarter and pounce on opportunities faster. We'll even break down how property types diverged through recent upheavals, multifamily stood strong against office and retail disruptions from 2020 to 2023 (CBRE, 2023; OECD, 2022). And we'll ground it all with real-world case studies to show you how cycle theory gets put into practice in CRE investing.

References

Blackstone. (2025). Corporate real estate assets under management report.
https://www.blackstone.com/

Brookfield Asset Management. (2025). Annual report: Global real assets portfolio.
https://bam.brookfield.com/

Carlyle Group. (2025). Global private equity and real estate fundraising update.
https://www.carlyle.com/

CBRE. (2024). Global e-commerce and logistics real estate report.
https://www.cbre.com/

CRE Analyst. (2024). Blackstone's platform acquisition strategies.
https://www.creanalyst.com/

Financial Times. (2024). Growth of private credit in CRE.
https://www.ft.com/

Ho, J., & Singh, R. (2025). Family office real estate investment.
https://www.foinsights.com/

JLL Capital Markets. (2025). Debt and equity market conditions.
https://www.us.jll.com/

KKR. (2025). Real estate opportunistic credit fund closing.
https://www.kkr.com/

Preqin. (2024). Global real estate investment outlook.
https://www.preqin.com/

Prologis. (2024). Annual report and portfolio performance metrics. https://www.prologis.com/

The Real Deal. (2025). Blackstone industrial asset sales. https://therealdeal.com/

Mueller, G. R. (2023). Real estate market cycle analysis. https://www.cyclemonitor.com/

J.P. Morgan. (n.d.). Global commercial real estate outlook. https://www.jpmorgan.com/

CPP Investments. (2023). Sustainable real asset strategies. https://www.cppinvestments.com/

OECD. (2022). Commercial property cycles and risk. https://www.oecd.org/

CHAPTER

04

The CRE Market Cycle

Introduction

The commercial real estate (CRE) market doesn't just wander aimlessly, it moves through clear, distinct cycles shaped by big-picture forces: macroeconomics, capital markets, and the nuts and bolts of the properties themselves. Think of it like equity or commodity markets; CRE has its own patterns that sway investor moods, risk appetite, and ultimately asset performance. Most experts, from Mueller (2023) to J.P. Morgan, point to four main phases: Expansion, Hypersupply, Recession, and Recovery.

Why does this matter to you? Knowing exactly where we are in this cycle means you can spot opportunities earlier, mitigate risks better, and tweak strategies around development, refinancing, or rotating your portfolio with more confidence. Just remember, cycle timing isn't uniform, it shifts by geography and property type. Between 2020 and 2023, for example, multifamily properties in the U.S. and Western Europe showed surprising resilience compared to office and retail, thanks to demographics, limited supply, and policy moves (CBRE, 2023; OECD, 2022).

This chapter walks you through these four phases in detail, points out the key indicators you should monitor to catch cycle turns, and shares real-world case studies showing how investors have adapted smartly in recent cycles.

4.1 Four Phases of the CRE Market Cycle

To navigate CRE investment effectively, you've got to understand the cycle. Every phase leaves its mark, not just on prices but on how you manage risk and shape strategy. Let's break it down:

4.1.1 Expansion

Expansion is the time when everything feels upbeat. The economy's growing, unemployment is falling, businesses are hungry for space, and rents are climbing. Interest rates tend to be low or moderate, credit's flowing, and investor enthusiasm heats up, perfect for new development and value-add projects.

Look back to 2016-2019 in the U.S.: GDP grew around 2.5% per year, unemployment dipped close to 3.5%, and you saw record construction, especially in industrial and multifamily sectors (U.S. Bureau of Labor Statistics, 2020). J.P. Morgan highlights how this phase fuels developers with cheap financing and strong leasing demand. Take the industrial market in places like Los Angeles and Chicago from 2010 to 2018, rents surged over 50%, propelled by the e-commerce boom and upgraded supply chains (Prologis, 2019).

4.1.2 Hypersupply

Hypersupply hits when all that new construction overshoots leasing demand. Vacancy creeps up, and rent growth slows, even if it doesn't stop completely. Mueller (2023) identifies this as cycle points 11–14, where vacancy rises but rents still inch up or stay flat.

2023 was a hypersupply year in the U.S., with 480,000 new multifamily units delivered, the highest since the 1980s. In fast-growing metros like Austin and Atlanta, vacancy jumped by 1.5% points, dialing down rent growth despite continued underlying demand (RealPage, 2023). Europe saw similar issues: Dublin and Berlin added lots of dense housing stock, which outpaced absorption and pushed landlords into concessions, even with housing shortages (Knight Frank, 2023).

4.1.3 Recession

Downturn alert. Recession phases bring declining rents, swelling vacancies, cash flow tightness, fewer transactions, and little to no new construction. This often follows economic slowdowns, interest rate hikes, or credit squeezes.

Think back to the 2007-2009 Global Financial Crisis, when U.S. commercial property prices dropped roughly 28% in the first year and 35% by the second (FDIC, 2021). Office and retail spaces took the hardest hits thanks to tenant struggles and weak leasing. Fast forward to 2022-2024, rising interest rates increased distress in office markets, defaults and loan maturities piled up, with distress eclipsing $38 billion, even surpassing GFC levels (MSCI Real Assets, 2024). Meanwhile, essentials like retail and multifamily showed comparatively stronger footing.

What do investors do? They turn defensive, stretching debt terms, bulking reserves, renegotiating leases, or hunting for discounted distressed assets.

4.1.4 Recovery

This phase starts when occupancy and values hit bottom, and then slowly rise again. New construction stays limited because lenders stay cautious, and costs are high. Mueller (2023) maps this phase to cycle points 1-3, where vacancy falls and rents start trending positive again.

After COVID, industrial and multifamily sectors in the U.S. bounced back fast: industrial rents grew over 10% annually between 2021 and 2022, powered by e-commerce and reshoring moves (CBRE, 2022). Investors who bought during that uncertain 2020 period saw strong gains as cap rates tightened. Similarly, European multifamily markets in Finland and Austria showed rent rebounds beating office and retail after 2021 (Eurostat, 2022).

4.2 Macroeconomic and Property-Level Indicators You Should Track

To really time your moves well and manage risk, you'll want to monitor both the big-picture macro signals and the on-the-ground property data.

4.2.1 Macroeconomic Indicators

GDP Growth: When GDP ticks up, leasing demand and rents often follow. Between 2016 and 2019, the U.S. saw roughly 2.5% annual GDP boosting industrial net absorption by 250+ million square feet yearly (CBRE, 2020).

Employment & Unemployment: More jobs mean more space needed. After that unemployment spike in April 2020, it slid quickly to around 3.9% by December 2021, driving rebounds in multifamily and industrial (BLS, 2022).

Interest Rates & Credit: Low rates invite new projects and deals. When rates climb, borrowing tightens and deals slow. The Fed's hikes in 2022–2023 coincided with a 54% drop in CRE transactions as borrowing costs doubled (MSCI Real Assets, 2024).

Capital Flows & Transactions: The volume of deals shows market liquidity. Global transactions plunged 39% in 2020 but bounced back strongly in 2021, with fundraising topping $200 billion, an indicator of renewed investor faith (Preqin, 2022).

4.2.2 Property-Level Indicators

Vacancy Rates: This is often your first tip-off to shifting tides. For example, the U.S. office vacancy hit a record 18.6% in 2023 (CBRE, 2024), a signal that supply outpaced demand.

Rent Growth & Net Absorption: Look for steady rent gains and strong absorption to confirm healthy demand. Industrial rents jumped 11.3% in 2022, fueled by e-commerce logistics needs (Prologis, 2023).

Construction Pipeline: Pipeline data shows what's coming soon. Nearly 480,000 multifamily completions in 2023 tipped some markets into oversupply, creating leasing competition (RealPage, 2023).

Capital Expenditures (CapEx): When CapEx climbs, it often means owners are upgrading or repositioning properties. U.S. office landlords boosted CapEx by 18% in 2023 to stay competitive (JLL, 2023).

Refinancing Risk: Watch closely here, debt maturing soon can expose you to rate shocks. Between 2024 and 2026, $1.2 trillion in U.S. CRE loans mature, with about a quarter tied to floating rates, making this a serious risk (Morgan Stanley, 2024).

4.3 Case Example: Multifamily Resilience During the 2020–2023 Downturn

Multifamily proved its mettle amid widespread CRE challenges, buoyed by steady housing demand, affordability pressures, and investor interest.

4.3.1 U.S. Multifamily Performance

Between 2020 and 2021, U.S. CRE transaction volume doubled to $809 billion, with multifamily making up 43%, the largest share (CBRE & Econometric Advisors, 2022). Vacancies ticked up to 6.7% in early 2023 (NAR, 2023), but rents stayed positive in many spots. Mortgage rates surged nearly 70% by 2023, pushing more households toward renting (Redfin, 2023). By mid-2024, vacancies stabilized near 7.8%, while rent growth held at about 1.1%, supported by demographics (CNBC, 2024).

4.3.2 European Multifamily Trends

Meanwhile, offices in the UK, Germany, and France stumbled under remote work and financing hurdles (Savills, 2024). Residential gained ground as a defensive asset (Financial Times, 2025). Places facing housing shortages, Netherlands, Ireland, Germany, saw steady or rising rents (Eurostat, 2023).

4.3.3 Why Multifamily Stayed Strong

Here's why multifamily held up:

- Steady household formation, especially millennials and Gen Z moving out or living independently, keeps demand robust (Pew Research Center, 2022).
- Mortgage rates climbing over 7% in 2023 shrunk the pool of buyers, boosting renters (Freddie Mac, 2023).
- Supply constraints in key metros because of regulatory hurdles, labor shortages, and high building costs keep vacancies down.
- Institutional investors love the relative income reliability and stability multifamily offers, especially when other sectors feel shaky.
- Many multifamily owners locked in low-rate refinancings before rates spiked, improving cash flow and resilience.

Put it all together, and multifamily outperformed peers through volatile times, and remains a favorite for investors across cycles.

4.4 Risks, Challenges, and Strategic Considerations

Navigating these cycles means staying alert to timing, refinancing, regulatory, and valuation pitfalls.

Timing risk: Jumping in too late into hypersupply or too early into recession can crush returns. Office assets bought near the pre-2020 peak shed about 35% in value during the pandemic (Green Street, 2023). Studies show that buying within a year before downturns can cost you 20–30% in the long run (FDIC, 2021).

Refinancing risk: Debt maturing amid rising rates creates liquidity risks. With over $1.2 trillion of U.S. CRE debt coming due between 2024 and 2026, and a quarter exposed to floating rates, owners face big refinancing challenges. Multifamily loan special servicing tripled in 2023, and some office buildings were even handed back due to failed refinancing (Trepp, Wall Street Journal, 2023).

Regulatory and macro shifts: Interest rate changes, green building mandates, and banking regulations impact costs and project feasibility (Federal Reserve, 2023; NYC Mayor's Office, 2023; PwC, 2025).

Valuation swings: Prices can swing wildly, sometimes 20–30%, when moving between cycle phases. Office appraisals diverged widely from 2022 to 2024 amid uncertainty, offering both risks and chances (JLL, 2024; Green Street, 2023).

4.5 Strategic Implications for CRE Investors

Staying competitive in commercial real estate goes far beyond spotting the right assets. The top performers track where we are in the economic cycle and shift their portfolio strategy in real time, adjusting allocations, risk, and deployment to keep an edge.

Success hinges on **tactical capital allocation** that matches the moment. During expansion, it's about leaning in: ramp up investment, pursue development, and secure advantageous long-term financing while the wind is at your back. But as markets tip into hypersupply, the approach gets more defensive, pivoting to stabilized assets that throw off reliable income and weather softening demand. In recession, capital preservation becomes the name of the game; smart investors hunt for distressed bargains but temper risk, holding resources back until signals turn. When the cycle turns toward recovery, opportunity knocks, deploying capital ahead of the crowd can lock in gains before prices snap back. This phase-based approach to allocation is common among blue-chip names like Blackstone, Brookfield, and KKR, who have built playbooks for every stage of the market (Blackstone, Brookfield, KKR, 2025).

Diversification is another core principle. By mixing property types and regions, investors insulate themselves from sector-specific disruptions, a lesson learned between 2020 and 2023, when multifamily and industrial outperformed the struggling office sector. Global diversification extends this cushion: it spreads risk across economies, making a single local shock less likely to derail portfolio performance (MSCI, Savills, 2024).

Market timing isn't about educated guessing; it's a matter of synthesizing data at every level. Smart investors read both the big signals, GDP, employment, interest rates—and on-the-ground realities like rent growth and absorption rates. For example, the rate hikes of 2023 presaged a slowdown in deal activity, while improving absorption rates in multifamily by 2024 pointed to an earlier rebound in that segment (RealPage, 2024). Viewing the landscape through both macro and micro lenses helps clarify when to reposition or double down.

Robust stress testing is now non-negotiable. Top institutional players run scenarios that model hits from cap rate jumps, plunging rents, rising vacancies, and escalating expenses. This risk discipline is foundational in the post-pandemic world, protecting portfolios from shocks both foreseeable and unexpected (Moody's, 2023).

And then there's **liquidity**. Flexible capital, think undrawn credit lines and cash reserves, lets investors pounce when market dislocations create uncommon value. Those best positioned with "dry powder" can seize assets on favorable terms, just as Blackstone did with its $1 billion industrial portfolio recycling in South Florida, a classic example of the power of ready capital to capture returns when the tide turns (The Real Deal, 2025).

Altogether, the lesson is clear: strategic success in CRE means actively managing capital with cycle-driven discipline, sharp data analysis, portfolio resilience, and liquidity to stay agile. The winners aren't just picking assets, they're actively steering the ship through whatever the market throws at them.

4.6 Investor Behavior Case Studies by Cycle Phase

Expansion: From 2014-2019, Prologis ramped up industrial development aggressively, adding 40 million square feet yearly and snapping up $25 billion in assets, all while keeping vacancy super low. They rode e-commerce's wave perfectly, locking tenancy and pricing power ahead of tougher times (Prologis, 2019).

Hypersupply: Between 2021-2023, Southeast U.S. multifamily saw a delivery boom that outpaced demand. Investors got cautious, leasing concessions rose, and the focus shifted toward keeping tenants rather than chasing new ones (Yardi Matrix, 2023).

Recession: Office markets plunged in 2022-2024; distress soared. Opportunists like Oaktree Capital swooped in to buy deeply discounted debt and assets. More conservative REITs held back to see how the storm passed (MSCI, 2024). Risk tolerance separated winners from others.

Recovery: Hotels bounced back fast post-pandemic. Big funds like KKR and Blackstone jumped in early, betting on rising occupancy and RevPAR, positioning for strong gains as travel picked back up (STR, 2023).

Adjusting strategy in step with the market cycle is crucial for success in commercial real estate, as these case studies demonstrate. As shown in Figure 4.1, hypothetical CRE investment volumes fluctuate across different cycle phases. Table 4.1 provides a summary of each phase, outlining major risks, typical investor responses, and recommended strategies.

Figure 4.1 Hypothetical CRE Investment Volumes Across Cycle Phases

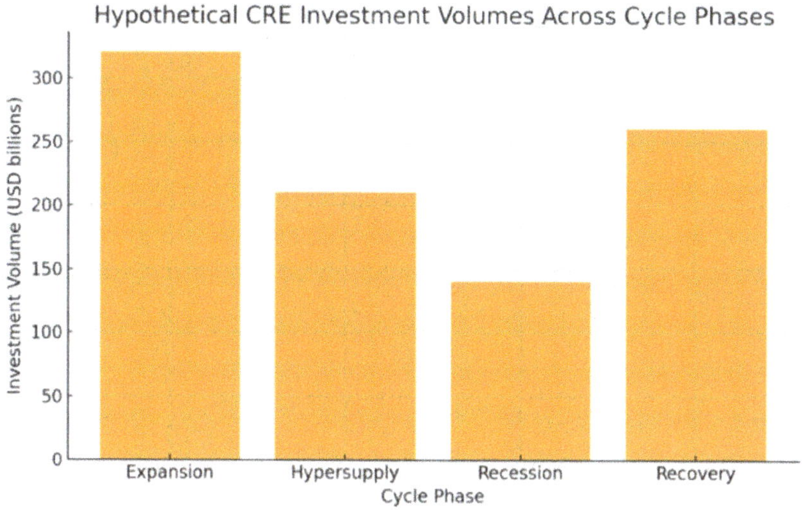

Note: Investment volumes peak during Expansion, contract during Recession, and rebound in Recovery, though the details vary by market and asset.

Table 4.1 Risks and Strategies Across CRE Cycle Phases

Cycle Phase	Key Risks	Representative Investor Behavior	Recommended Strategies
Expansion	Overpaying for assets; construction cost inflation	REITs and PE funds increase development and acquisitions	Pursue value-add and development; lock in long-term financing
Hypersupply	Vacancy increases; slowing rent growth	Institutional investors shift to income-oriented assets	Prioritize stabilized assets; reduce speculative development
Recession	Valuation declines; refinancing stress	Distressed investors pursue note purchases and recapitalizations	Preserve liquidity; pursue opportunistic distressed acquisitions
Recovery	Uncertain timing; uneven market recovery	Private equity re-enters markets: REITs stabilize portfolios	Acquire discounted assets; refinance legacy debt; reposition underperforming assets

4.7 Transition to Part II: Evaluating Markets and Opportunities

Understanding the cycle gets you part of the way there, but the next step is knowing where to put your money and which property types are best suited for each phase.

Part II will take you through:

- ☐ How to assess market fundamentals
- ☐ Comparing metros and submarkets effectively

- ☐ Evaluating asset classes like multifamily, office, industrial, retail, hotel, and mixed-use
- ☐ Using data, forward-looking analytics, and structural drivers to spot high-potential investments

By connecting the dots between big-picture cycles and detailed market and asset data, you'll build a powerful toolkit for disciplined, data-driven real estate decisions.

That's your blueprint for making sense of the CRE market cycle, and, more importantly, how to use it to your advantage. Ready to dive deeper?

References

Blackstone. (2025). *Annual report 2025*. Blackstone Group. https://www.blackstone.com

Brookfield. (2025). *Global real estate outlook*. Brookfield Asset Management. https://www.brookfield.com

CBRE. (2020). *U.S. industrial market report*. CBRE Research. https://www.cbre.com/insights

CBRE. (2022). *U.S. industrial market report*. CBRE Research. https://www.cbre.com/insights

CBRE. (2023). *Multifamily market trends and outlook*. CBRE Research. https://www.cbre.com/insights

CBRE. (2024). *U.S. office vacancy and leasing report*. CBRE Research. https://www.cbre.com/insights

CBRE, & Econometric Advisors. (2022). *U.S. commercial real estate transaction volume analysis*. CBRE. https://www.cbre.com/insights

CNBC. (2024). *Rental market data and trends*. CNBC Real Estate. https://www.cnbc.com/real-estate

Eurostat. (2022). *European housing market statistics*. Eurostat. https://ec.europa.eu/eurostat

Eurostat. (2023). *Rent growth and housing indicators in Europe*. Eurostat. https://ec.europa.eu/eurostat

FDIC. (2021). *Commercial real estate during the 2007–2009 financial crisis*. Federal Deposit Insurance Corporation. https://www.fdic.gov

Federal Reserve. (2023). *Monetary policy and impacts on real estate*. Federal Reserve Board. https://www.federalreserve.gov

Financial Times. (2025). *European commercial real estate outlook*. Financial Times. https://www.ft.com

Freddie Mac. (2023). *Mortgage trends and their impact on renting*. Freddie Mac Research. https://www.freddiemac.com/research

Green Street. (2023). *Office market valuation update*. Green Street Advisors. https://www.greenstreet.com

IMF. (2021). *Global commercial real estate capital flow report*. International Monetary Fund. https://www.imf.org

J.P. Morgan. (n.d.). *Commercial real estate market cycle analysis*. J.P. Morgan Asset Management. https://am.jpmorgan.com

JLL. (2023). *Capital expenditures in office real estate 2023*. JLL Research. https://www.jll.com/research

JLL. (2024). *Office valuation uncertainty and market disruption*. JLL Research. https://www.jll.com/research

Knight Frank. (2023). *Europe residential market insight Q1 2023*. Knight Frank Research. https://www.knightfrank.com/research

Moody's Analytics. (2023). *CRE risk modeling and stress testing*. Moody's Analytics. https://www.moodysanalytics.com

Morgan Stanley. (2024). *U.S. CRE debt maturity and refinancing risk report*. Morgan Stanley Research. https://www.morganstanley.com

MSCI Real Assets. (2024). *Global commercial real estate market update*. MSCI. https://www.msci.com/real-assets

NAR. (2023). *Multifamily vacancy and rent report*. National Association of Realtors. https://www.nar.realtor

OECD. (2022). *Housing market trends in Western Europe.* Organisation for Economic Co-operation and Development. https://www.oecd.org

Preqin. (2022). *Commercial real estate fundraising statistics.* Preqin. https://www.preqin.com

Prologis. (2019). *Logistics real estate trends and forecasts.* Prologis. https://www.prologis.com/research

Prologis. (2023). *Industrial rent growth analytics.* Prologis. https://www.prologis.com/research

RealPage. (2023). *U.S. multifamily construction and vacancy report.* RealPage. https://www.realpage.com/analytics

RealPage. (2024). *Multifamily market recovery insights.* RealPage. https://www.realpage.com/analytics

Redfin. (2023). *Housing affordability and rental market shifts.* Redfin Housing Analytics. https://www.redfin.com/news

Savills. (2024). *European office and residential market report.* Savills Research. https://www.savills.com/research

STR. (2023). *Hotel sector recovery and investment trends.* STR. https://str.com

The Real Deal. (2025). *Industrial asset recycling case study.* The Real Deal. https://www.therealdeal.com

Trepp. (2024). *Multifamily loan special servicing statistics.* Trepp LLC. https://www.trepp.com

U.S. Bureau of Labor Statistics. (2020). *Employment and unemployment data.* U.S. Department of Labor. https://www.bls.gov

U.S. Bureau of Labor Statistics. (2022). *Labor market recovery post-COVID*. U.S. Department of Labor. https://www.bls.gov

Wall Street Journal. (2023). *Office property distress and refinancing issues*. Wall Street Journal. https://www.wsj.com

Yardi Matrix. (2023). *Southeast U.S. multifamily construction report*. Yardi Matrix. https://www.yardimatrix.com

PART II

Evaluating Markets and Opportunities

OVERVIEW

In this section, we're arming you with the frameworks, data tools, and evaluation techniques you need to pinpoint markets and property types that offer strong risk-adjusted returns. Building on what we covered in Part I, we shift gears from understanding how commercial real estate works to figuring out where and why the best opportunities pop up, whether across cities, sectors, or even countries.

Today, you're swimming in data and transparency like never before. The challenge? Avoiding that overwhelm and knowing what actually matters. That's exactly where Part II comes in. We'll guide you through assessing market fundamentals, distinguishing between property sectors, and comparing regional prospects on both national and global scales. Whether you're scoping out a single acquisition or spreading capital across borders, this part helps you turn raw data into clear, confident decisions.

Through three focused chapters, we cover the essentials of opportunity evaluation: (1) understanding the core market fundamentals and using data analytics effectively, (2) digging deep into sector-specific drivers and long-term trends, and (3) comparing markets across U.S. cities and global regions to find the best fit for your strategy.

Overview of Chapters

Chapter 5 – Market Fundamentals and Data Analysis

Here, we break down the key economic and property-level metrics that actually move the needle in CRE, things like employment growth, demographic shifts, supply-demand balance, absorption rates, vacancies, and rent trends. You'll get how these indicators behave through cycles and learn to plug them into systematic market scoring models that spotlight cities and submarkets with sustainable outperformance. We'll also walk you through the best data sources, from government reports to private platforms, and show how predictive analytics and scenario planning can sharpen your investment decisions. The chapter wraps up with real-world examples that show you how market rankings are built from the ground up.

Chapter 6 – Property-Type Deep Dives

This chapter takes you inside the DNA of each major CRE sector: office, industrial, retail, multifamily, and hospitality. Plus, we highlight exciting emerging niches like life sciences, data centers, student housing, and build-to-rent single-family homes. For each property type, you'll learn the key performance drivers, lease terms, capital needs, tenant demand patterns, and how macro trends play a role. This side-by-side look helps you line up your property choices with your portfolio goals, risk appetite, and market themes.

Chapter 7 – Comparative Market Analysis

Time to zoom out. We move from individual markets to a macro view, comparing Tier 1, Tier 2, and Tier 3 metros across the U.S. based on liquidity, volatility, growth potential, and capital appreciation. You'll see how demographics, infrastructure, business climates, regulations, and economic diversity shape these differences. Then we cross borders, exploring investment landscapes in Europe, Asia-Pacific, and beyond. This chapter also unpacks how cross-border capital flows, policy, currency shifts, and geopolitical trends impact market attractiveness. Real-world examples bring this global perspective to life, helping you build diversified, multi-regional holdings.

Key Takeaways from Part II

- ☐ Using data-driven market evaluation is your best shot at finding regions and sectors with strong risk-adjusted returns.
- ☐ Core fundamentals, employment, absorption, vacancy, rent growth, demographics, are the building blocks of solid market analysis.

- ☐ Knowing the specifics behind each sector lets you tailor your asset choices to your strategy, risk tolerance, and bigger macro trends.
- ☐ Comparing markets across tiers and borders uncovers important structural differences that help you target and diversify your capital smarter.
- ☐ Sticking to a disciplined analytical framework lets you cut through short-term noise and focus on lasting opportunity.

CHAPTER

05 Market Fundamentals and Data Analysis

Introduction

Understanding market fundamentals is essential for us to accurately evaluate commercial real estate (CRE) opportunities and forecast future performance. You, as an investor or professional in this space, rely on a combination of macroeconomic indicators, demographic trends, leasing activity, and price signals to assess the health of any given market. Over the past decade, the emergence of high-frequency datasets, predictive analytics, and machine-learning-enabled forecasting has transformed how we, as CRE professionals, evaluate opportunities.

Together, we integrate a diverse range of data sources, from public economic statistics to proprietary market intelligence and alternative datasets, to develop a comprehensive view of supply and demand dynamics. It's indicators like job growth, net absorption, vacancy rates, and rent growth that give you the power to forecast future cash flows, pinpoint outperforming metropolitan areas, and anticipate market turning points ahead of traditional reports.

In this chapter, we'll walk through the key market fundamentals and datasets you should know, introduce predictive scoring methods you can apply, and wrap up with a practical exercise that helps you build a comparative market dashboard using real-world data.

5.1 Primary Data Sources and Their Uses

5.1.1 Bureau of Labor Statistics (BLS)

The U.S. Bureau of Labor Statistics (BLS) is a cornerstone source of monthly and annual labor-market data, everything from payroll employment and unemployment rates to hours worked and wage trends. This information forms the backbone of the demand forecasting we all depend on in CRE. In particular, sector-specific employment growth is a powerful predictor: when professional and business services expand, you can expect corresponding office demand, while growth in transportation and warehousing payrolls usually drives industrial leasing activity (Bureau of Labor Statistics, 2025).

You'll find, as we do, that employment increases within specific sectors tend to precede space absorption by 6 to 18 months. For example, between 2015 and 2024, metros with strong employment growth, Austin with a 45% increase in tech jobs, Phoenix's 28% growth in construction and logistics, and Miami's 22% rise in professional services, also saw above-average rent growth in multiple property sectors (Bureau of Labor Statistics, 2025).

5.1.2 Brokerage Research

Leading brokerage firms such as CBRE, JLL, and Cushman & Wakefield provide in-depth market reports that are indispensable tools for you and me as CRE professionals (CBRE, 2025a; JLL, 2025; Cushman & Wakefield, 2024). Unlike broader macroeconomic data, these reports drill down into specific asset classes, office, industrial, retail, and multifamily, and cover more than 60 U.S. markets. They deliver granular information on vacancy and availability rates, net absorption, effective rent growth, leasing velocity, tenant migration trends, and the development pipeline.

Take CBRE's latest industrial report, which pointed to a fascinating trend: despite annual net absorption exceeding 250 million square feet, speculative construction also pushed U.S. industrial vacancy rates up from 3.8% in 2022 to 5.2% by the end of 2024 (CBRE, 2025a). Alongside data like cap rate analyses and submarket narratives, you get the detailed story required for precise underwriting and for benchmarking assets or locations. JLL's and Cushman & Wakefield's reports now increasingly incorporate ESG and tenant experience metrics, helping us factor evolving occupier preferences into investment decisions (JLL, 2025; Cushman & Wakefield, 2024).

5.1.3 Proprietary Platforms

Beyond public data, proprietary platforms deliver even greater granularity and real-time intelligence that we can use to sharpen market analysis. CoStar, for example, aggregates an expansive database on inventory, leasing comparables, ongoing construction, and historical rent trends, equipping you to analyze submarkets and assets on a granular level (CoStar, 2025). RealPage focuses heavily on multifamily, tracking daily rent movements, lease renewals, and concession trends across thousands of properties. By detecting sudden surges in concessions or anomalous rent reversals, you and we can spot important market shifts early.

Real Capital Analytics (now part of MSCI) tracks institutional sales transactions, capital flows, pricing benchmarks, and liquidity indices, giving us a window into market sentiment and liquidity (MSCI, 2025). For instance, RealPage data showed that supply pressures in Sun Belt markets pushed effective rent growth negative from 2023 to 2024 as concessions exceeded 12% of asking rents, a nuance you might not catch with slower, less frequent data (RealPage, 2024).

The power of these platforms, especially when combined with techniques like hedonic rent modeling and scenario analysis, is that they allow you, and us, to anticipate inflection points, stress test assumptions, and benchmark portfolios in near real time.

5.1.4 Alternative Data Sources

Non-traditional data has become a vital early warning system in our toolkit. Foot traffic data from companies like Placer.ai helps you quantify visitation patterns to shopping centers or neighborhoods, silent signals that often presage major shifts in retail fortunes or spotlight pockets of resilience (Placer.ai, 2025).

Employment data mined from online job boards like LinkedIn and Indeed provide another lens, tracking surges or drops in job postings well before official payroll statistics are published. Mobility data from anonymized cell phone tracking enables us to model changes in commuting and remote work trends that are vital in the post-pandemic office market environment.

For sectors like data centers, near-real-time electricity consumption data tracks capacity growth and tenant activity. JLL's 2025 report noted a 20% annual increase in U.S. data center capacity between 2023 and 2025, insights that pair powerfully with leasing and construction data to identify emerging risks or opportunities (JLL, 2025b).

Using these alternative datasets, you can stay ahead, spotting changes in foot traffic, tenant behavior, or commuting patterns months before traditional quarterly reports arrive. This early insight positions you to act strategically and confidently.

5.2 Key Market Indicators: Their Meaning and Importance for You

5.2.1 Employment

Employment stands as one of the most reliable leading indicators of CRE demand. By developing sector-specific employment predictors, such as tech job growth driving office or lab demand, or transportation jobs signaling industrial growth, you can forecast shifts with 6 to 18 months lead time (Bureau of Labor Statistics, 2025).

5.2.2 Net Absorption

Net absorption, measuring the change in occupied space over a period, signals how much leasing activity is underway. Positive absorption generally leads to rent growth, while negative absorption warns of market easing. For example, CBRE documented record multifamily absorption after the pandemic, linked directly to household formation trends (CBRE, 2025a).

5.2.3 Vacancy Rate

Vacancy reveals the balance (or imbalance) between supply and demand. Low vacancy hints at landlord pricing power; rising vacancy may indicate oversupply or weakening demand. But interpret vacancy rates carefully: spikes can reflect new deliveries rather than sustained softness (CBRE, 2024; CBRE, 2025a).

5.2.4 Rent Growth

Rent growth is the clearest signal of market pricing trends. Sustained increases suggest supply constraints and strong demand. That said, national averages can hide local variability, as seen in Sun Belt metros where multifamily rent growth moderated in 2023–2024 amid surging deliveries (CBRE, 2024).

5.3 Building a Predictive Market-Scoring System: How You Can Bring Structure to Your Decisions

Adopting a predictive market-scoring system lets you synthesize complex data, producing ranked lists of metros or submarkets. This approach streamlines everything from deal sourcing and portfolio construction to thematic investing, targeting, for example, regions benefiting from nearshoring or life sciences concentration (JLL, 2025a).

5.3.1 Step 1: Select Variables

Start with carefully chosen variables covering demand, supply, capital markets, and quality of life. You might focus on 12-month employment growth (both overall and sector-specific), net absorption per 1,000 residents, vacancy changes, trailing rent growth, and construction pipeline relative to stock.

5.3.2 Step 2: Normalize the Data

To compare apples to apples, normalize your metrics, through z-scores or min-max scaling, so no single indicator skews the results due to differences in scale.

5.3.3 Step 3: Apply Weights

Assign weights based on what matters most to your strategy. Many investors prioritize demand strength (around 30%), followed by supply risk (25%), capital activity (20%), fundamental rent trends (20%), and macro or livability factors (5%). Tailor this based on sector specifics, industrial models might overweight logistics employment; multifamily scoring may lean heavily on renter demographics (JLL, 2025a).

5.3.4 Step 4: Create Composite Scores

Calculate a composite score for each market by aggregating weighted, normalized data. Present scores with risk bands or confidence intervals to communicate uncertainty and assist in decision-making.

5.3.5 Step 5: Backtest

You want to validate the model by backtesting, checking if your top-ranked markets historically outperformed on NOI growth, capital appreciation, or total returns. Use rolling three-year periods with annual rebalancing to smooth cycles, and assess both rank stability and absolute performance. This gives you confidence that your scoring truly captures winning markets over time.

5.4 Sector-Specific Adjustments: Tailoring What You Track

Each CRE sector has unique dynamics. Adjust scoring variables and weights accordingly to sharpen your insights.

- ☐ **Office:** Watch growth in professional services jobs, sublease inventory, and hybrid work patterns (CBRE, 2025a). Divide by property class and location for nuance.
- ☐ **Industrial:** Weight logistics employment, port volume, and inventory turnover heavily (JLL, 2025).
- ☐ **Retail:** Focus on foot traffic, wage growth, and tourism data (Placer.ai, 2025).
- ☐ **Multifamily:** Emphasize household formation, mortgage rates, and supply pipeline (CBRE, 2024).
- ☐ **Life Sciences & Data Centers:** Track biotech employment, R&D funding, power availability, and prelease rates (JLL, 2025a; JLL, 2025b).

5.5 Practical Exercise: Build a Comparative Market Dashboard

Objective

Our goal here is to develop a comprehensive dashboard that lets you compare 8 to 12 U.S. metropolitan areas across key real estate performance indicators. This tool will help you identify which metros show the strongest near-term fundamentals, empowering you to make more informed investment decisions and portfolio adjustments.

Required Data

To build a robust and meaningful dashboard, you'll need data from various public and proprietary sources. For broad economic health indicators, collect metro-level employment growth using BLS APIs like the Local Area Unemployment Statistics (LAUS) or the Current Employment Statistics (CES) metro datasets. For core real estate fundamentals, net absorption, vacancy changes, and rent growth, leverage quarterly reports from major brokerage firms such as CBRE and JLL. If available, incorporate high-frequency datasets from platforms like CoStar and RealPage. Don't forget to pull pipeline data (such as new construction as a percentage of existing inventory), sourced from developers, brokers, or proprietary reports.

Steps

1. **Data Ingestion:** Begin by pulling the latest metro employment figures from BLS's LAUS or CES APIs. Simultaneously, gather net absorption, vacancy, and rent growth data from CBRE, JLL, or your preferred proprietary sources.

2. **Cleaning:** Standardize your data by aligning all metros under common definitions, preferably using Core-Based Statistical Areas (CBSAs). Sync all data to the same timeframe (e.g., Q1 2025). Where needed, convert raw counts to per-capita or per-1,000-residents figures to properly normalize for metro size.

3. **Normalization:** Apply statistical normalization methods such as z-scores to bring your indicators onto a comparable scale, limiting outlier influence. Alternatively, use percentile ranks if you prefer an intuitive 0-to-1 scale.

4. **Weighting:** Assign weights to each metric based on your sector focus and strategic priorities. For example, focus on household formation and pipeline metrics in multifamily, while emphasizing employment growth in business services and net absorption more for office.

5. **Composite Score:** Combine the weighted, normalized metrics to calculate a composite score for each metro. This ranked list will highlight which markets are strongest overall.

6. **Visualization:** Use tools like Excel, Tableau, or Power BI to turn your data into clear visualizations, bar charts, heatmaps,

and time series plots showing how metros compare across individual metrics and how their rankings evolve over time.

7. **Interpretation:** Dive into your dashboard outputs to spot top and underperforming metros. Analyze the underlying drivers and document any caveats, such as missing or lagging data, so your evaluation remains transparent and actionable.

8. **Deliverables**
   The final product you build should be an interactive dashboard that lets you filter by sector, timeframe, or specific metrics. Include tooltips to explain each data point and provide an appendix detailing your data sources, normalization and weighting choices, and any backtesting you've conducted to validate your methodology. This tool not only identifies today's highest-potential markets but also demonstrates a repeatable process you can apply as market conditions evolve.

5.6 Case Studies

5.6.1 Multifamily Oversupply in the Sun Belt (2024–2025)

We saw record multifamily deliveries in Sun Belt metros over 2024-2025, raising vacancy and tempering rent growth despite robust population increases. This is a textbook case where construction front-runs near-term demand (CBRE, 2024; CBRE, 2025a). If your scoring system overweighs near-term pipeline data without factoring in multi-year absorption capacity, you risk unfairly penalizing these high-growth markets.

5.6.2 Data Center Resilience in North America (2024–2025)

JLL's mid-2025 report highlighted record construction and impressive prelease rates across North American data centers, though emerging bottlenecks in power transmission created new challenges (JLL, 2025b). Markets with recent grid upgrades and strong hyperscale tenant activity, like Northern Virginia's Ashburn and Dallas, consistently scored highest and demonstrated strong leasing resilience.

5.7 Common Analytical Pitfalls

When you're knee-deep in data, it's easy to fall into a few traps that can skew your analysis and lead you down the wrong path. Let's break down some of the most common mistakes we see, and how you can steer clear of them.

Overreliance on a Single Source

We get it, sometimes that BLS table or a glossy brokerage report feels like the last word. But leaning too heavily on one source is a recipe for bias. Always, always triangulate. Compare statistics from the Bureau of Labor Statistics with what brokerage shops are seeing on the ground. Then layer in your own proprietary data for extra context. When you constantly cross-check, you'll catch the stories buried between the lines, and those inconsistencies are where real insights hide.

Ignoring Pipeline Data

It's tempting to anchor your forecasts on what's already out there, but the pipeline tells a deeper story. If you don't factor in all the new construction underway, including projects nearing delivery, you risk getting your vacancy and rent forecasts all wrong. A wave of freshly built units can tip a balanced market into oversupply before you even spot it in the headlines. So, make pipeline data a regular stop in your analysis, not just an afterthought.

Confusing National Trends with Local Realities

It's easy to quote national figures, but in real estate, the local picture almost always wins. If you try to make decisions based only on big-picture stats, you'll miss what's actually driving your neighborhood or submarket. Drill deep, look at city-level, or even zip code-level, trends. Two metros a hundred miles apart might respond very differently to the same national headwinds. By getting granular, you'll stay ahead of the curve when the broader trends miss the nuances right in front of you.

Mixing Different Inventory Types

Not all inventory is created equal, and treating it that way can throw off your projections for both rents and NOI. Lease-up properties, stabilized assets, and secondary market deals each perform differently. So, slice your data, model each group separately. When you segment leased, lease-up, and stabilized properties, you spot true trends sooner, instead of getting lost in averages that don't tell the full story.

If you stay alert to these common analytical pitfalls, and keep questioning your assumptions, you'll be far better equipped to draw reliable conclusions from your data. We're all learning as we go, but a little vigilance here pays off in the insights you'll unlock.

5.8 Transition to Chapter 6: Property Type Deep Dives

Now that we've built a solid framework for data-driven market evaluation and predictive scoring, we're ready to zoom in on specific property types. The next chapter explores operating fundamentals, demand drivers, and industry trends across major CRE sectors, office, industrial, retail, multifamily, hospitality, and specialized niches like life sciences and data centers. Here, you'll see how these market insights translate directly into smarter underwriting and operational strategies.

With these tools, data, and processes at your disposal, you're well-equipped to make confident, informed decisions that navigate today's complex CRE landscape, and prepare you for what's coming next.

References

Bureau of Labor Statistics. (2025). *Metropolitan area employment and unemployment* (Monthly news release). U.S. Department of Labor. https://www.bls.gov/news.release/metro.htm

CBRE. (2024). *Sun Belt Multifamily MarketView*. https://www.cbre.com

CBRE. (2024). *U.S. real estate market outlook: 2024-2025*. CBRE Research. https://www.cbre.com/insights/books/us-real-estate-market-outlook-2024

CBRE. (2025a). *Quarterly market insights and U.S. real estate market outlook: 2025 updates*. CBRE Research. https://www.cbre.com/insights

CBRE. (2025b). *U.S. Industrial MarketView Q4 2024*. https://www.cbre.com

CBRE. (2025c). *U.S. Office Market Trends Q1 2025*. https://www.cbre.com

CoStar. (2025). *Market Analytics Database*. https://www.costar.com

Cushman & Wakefield. (2024). *Quarterly U.S. CRE market reports*. https://www.cushmanwakefield.com

JLL. (2025a). *Industrial & Logistics Real Estate Outlook*. https://www.us.jll.com

JLL. (2025b). *Life sciences market dynamics & outlook*. JLL Research.

JLL. (2025c). *Life Sciences Real Estate Outlook*. https://www.us.jll.com

JLL. (2025d). *North America data center report – Midyear 2025*. Jones Lang LaSalle IP, Inc. https://www.jll.com/en-us/insights/market-dynamics/north-america-data-centers

JLL. (2025e). *North America Data Center Report.* https://www.us.jll.com

JLL. (2025f). *Data Center Real Estate Outlook: Capacity, Power, and Tenant Trends.* https://www.us.jll.com

JLL. (2025g). *U.S. Real Estate Market Insights, Q1 2025.* https://www.us.jll.com

LinkedIn. (2025). *Workforce Insights: U.S. Hiring Trends.* https://www.linkedin.com

MSCI. (2025). *RCA U.S. Capital Trends.* https://www.msci.com

MSCI Real Assets. (2024). *U.S. capital markets report: Transaction volume and liquidity trends.* MSCI.

Placer.ai. (2025). *Retail Foot Traffic Insights.* https://www.placer.ai

RealPage. (2024a). *Multifamily market analytics and rent index.* RealPage Market Intelligence.

RealPage. (2024b). *U.S. Market Intelligence: Multifamily Update.* https://www.realpage.com

CHAPTER 06

Property-Type Deep Dives

Introduction

When you invest in commercial real estate (CRE), your long-term performance ultimately comes down to two things: sector-specific fundamentals and structural trends. Macroeconomic and metro-level indicators certainly shape *where* you invest, but it's the property-type fundamentals that tell you what to invest in and how an asset will generate income, attract tenants, and grow in value over time.

That's why, in this chapter, we walk together through the major CRE property types, office, industrial, retail, multifamily, and hospitality, along with rapidly expanding specialty sectors like life sciences and data centers. As you move through each section, you'll see how demand drivers, supply conditions, operating metrics, technological influences, and long-term shifts all combine to reshape competitiveness within each sector.

To cap things off, we take you through a real-world example of a strategy you'll encounter more often: converting underperforming suburban office buildings into life sciences facilities, a direct response to the post-pandemic reset in office demand.

6.1 Office

6.1.1 Demand Drivers

If you focus on the office sector today, you're operating in the middle of a deep structural reset. Three forces matter most: labor market composition, return-to-office patterns, and tenant space requirements.

First, professional services and technology employment remain the backbone of office demand, and you can quantify that effect. According to the U.S. Bureau of Labor Statistics (2025), every 1% increase in professional services employment typically yields a 0.5% to 0.7% increase in office occupancy. From 2010 to 2019, the sector expanded nearly 24%, fueling one of the strongest office cycles in recent memory. But this momentum reversed sharply: between 2022 and 2024, tech hiring dropped 10–14% in hubs like San Francisco and Seattle, pushing vacancy rates up and flooding markets with sublease space. In 2023 alone, firms such as Meta, Salesforce, and Amazon released over 4 million square feet in San Francisco, driving the city's sublease vacancy above 35%, nearly double the national trend (JLL, 2025a).

Second, return-to-office behavior still varies widely. According to Kastle Systems (2025), physical attendance has plateaued at 50–60% of pre-pandemic norms, though metros diverge: New York sits near 65%, Houston around 62%, Los Angeles at 52%, and San Francisco at only 45%. Even as mandatory RTO policies among large corporations climbed from 36% in 2022 to 54% in 2024, hybrid work remains the dominant model, especially in professional services.

Third, and perhaps most consequential for you as an investor, space efficiency has fundamentally changed. Large employers today allocate roughly 120 square feet per employee, down from 175–225 square feet pre-2020 (JLL, 2025a). That's a 30–40% reduction, a structural headwind transforming the demand landscape. Companies like Deloitte, PwC, and Accenture reduced footprints by similar magnitudes, contributing to elevated vacancy across gateway markets.

6.1.2 Supply Conditions

If you've been watching the office market these past few years, you know just how dramatically the supply landscape has shifted. We're in the middle of one of the sharpest slowdowns in new office development that anyone in the industry can remember. According to CBRE (2025a), construction starts for new office buildings have plunged more than 55% since 2019, dropping to their lowest level in a decade by 2024. Why the slowdown? It comes down to a triple threat: high interest rates making borrowing more expensive, lenders getting skittish about project risk, and this cloud of uncertainty looming over future office demand, especially with so many companies still figuring out their long-term workplace strategies.

So, what does this supply drought actually look like on the ground? The market has split cleanly into two very different lanes.

First, there's the Class A+ and trophy segment. These are the top-of-the-line, amenity-heavy buildings in the best submarkets, think downtown financial districts or thriving mixed-use urban cores. These assets are still holding their ground, mostly bucking the vacancy trend. In the best locations, they're posting occupancy rates between 80% and 95%, and tenants are paying serious premiums, sometimes 20-30% above average market rents. Tenants looking for the best addresses and the highest wellness ratings are actually competing for these spaces.

On the flip side, we're seeing persistent struggles among Class B and C buildings. Vacancy rates here often hover between 25% and 35%, and the pressure isn't easing up. These older offices aren't just competing for tenants, they're also staring down bigger bills to stay relevant. Rising capital requirements, whether it's retrofitting for better energy efficiency, upgrading HVAC for modern air quality standards, or redesigning floorplates to meet changing work patterns, are making it even harder for these buildings to find a path forward.

But all is not lost for these underperforming assets. Take Chicago's LaSalle Street corridor as an example. There, city leaders and private owners got creative, launching a major initiative to convert outdated Class B and C office towers into vibrant mixed-use and residential projects. After redevelopment, occupancy surged and stabilized around 90%. It's proof that with the right vision, and a willingness to invest, adaptive reuse can give new life to struggling office buildings and turn them into assets that actually meet today's demand.

So, as you evaluate the office market, keep in mind that the headline supply shortage isn't hitting all assets equally. The best-in-class buildings are mostly weathering the storm, while Class B and C properties, unless they evolve, risk falling further behind. The split will only grow if the capital and creativity don't catch up. We're in a new era, and how you respond to these shifts on the supply side could make all the difference.

6.1.3 Operating Fundamentals

Let's talk about the day-to-day reality of owning or operating office buildings right now, because by 2024-2025, the landscape has gotten tough, even by the standards of veteran owners who remember the dot-com bust and the aftermath of the Great Recession. Across the country, we're staring at numbers we haven't seen in more than 30 years. National office vacancy rates hit 19% (CBRE, 2025a), that's not just a blip, it's a structural challenge that's redefining how we have to think about leasing, tenant retention, and value preservation.

And it's not just one or two cities driving up the averages. Some markets have blown right past the national figure, hitting almost unimaginable levels. Let's break down a few standouts. San Francisco is facing 32% vacancy, almost a third of office space sitting empty. That's a stunning turnaround for a city that, not long ago, had companies scrambling for space. Over in Washington D.C., vacancy hovers around 21%, and Dallas isn't far behind at roughly

24%. These aren't just statistics, they're a clear sign you can't count on traditional demand drivers to bail you out in a pinch.

Figure 6.1 (which you'll want to study closely) gives you the play-by-play: from 2021 to 2025, you can see vacancy climbing year after year, with the gap between cities getting wider, not narrower. This isn't just about remote work or a couple of corporate relocations, there's a fundamental mismatch between the space companies want and what's actually available in most markets.

So, what does all this mean if you're on the ground, trying to lease up a building or pitch an asset to potential investors? We're in an environment where you have to work twice as hard for every signed lease. Tenants are in the driver's seat, they know they have options and they're shopping around for the best deals, incentives, or the freshest buildouts.

We're in a moment where being reactive just won't cut it. To thrive, or even just to hold ground, you need to track occupancy and leasing activity by building class, submarket, and even by floorplate. We can't rely on broad averages anymore. The differences between a trophy tower in a CBD and an aging property in a secondary node are huge, both in terms of vacancy risk and rent trajectories.

Bottom line: These fundamentals have forced all of us to rethink property strategy from the ground up. Staying close to the data, market by market, block by block, is the only way to spot opportunities or risks before everyone else.

Figure 6.1 Office Vacancy Rates, 2021–2025

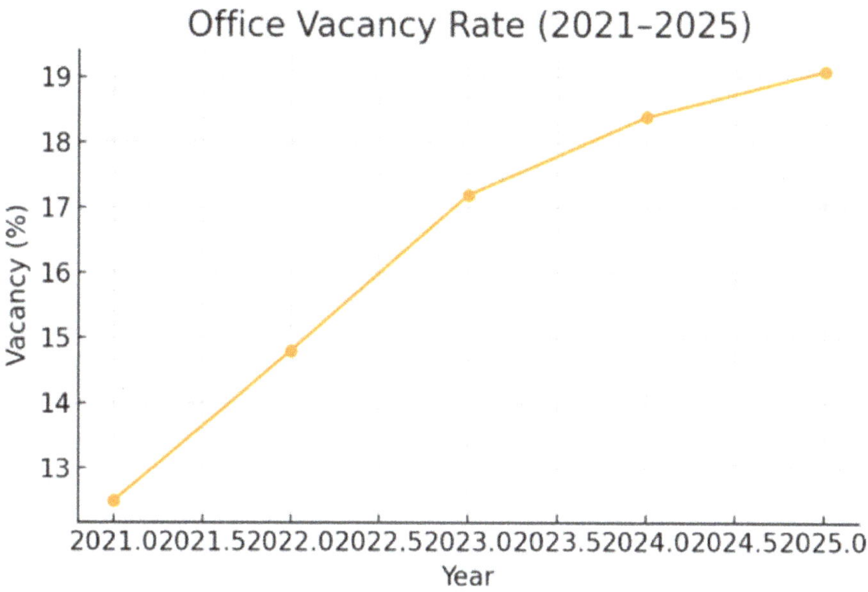

Note. Vacancy approached 32% in San Francisco, 21% in Washington, D.C., and 24% in Dallas in 2025. Source: CBRE (2025a).

Even though asking rents held relatively steady, effective rents fell because landlords leaned heavily on concessions. In major metros, tenant improvement allowances ran $100–$150 per square foot, often with 6–12 months of free rent on 10-year leases. If you're negotiating deals today, expect longer cycles, now averaging 9+ months, and more collaborative landlord offerings like design assistance and flexible expansion options.

6.2 Industrial & Logistics

6.2.1 Demand Drivers

If you're looking for the most resilient asset class in CRE, industrial continues to lead the pack. The biggest driver remains e-commerce, which the U.S. Census Bureau (2025) expects to surpass 25% of retail sales by 2027. Each 1% increase in e-commerce equates to an estimated 35-40 million square feet of new industrial demand.

You're also seeing accelerating nearshoring and reshoring. Manufacturing-linked markets like Phoenix, Dallas-Fort Worth, and Columbus have expanded rapidly, and nearshoring in Mexico saw a 38% jump in foreign investment in 2024, boosting logistics demand along the Texas border.

Retailers' shift from just-in-time to just-in-case inventory practices increased the national inventory-to-sales ratio by 14% between 2022 and 2024. This shift supports strong demand for large distribution centers, particularly automated facilities like Walmart's $2+ billion investment program, which raised throughput efficiency by up to 30%.

6.2.2 Supply and Development Trends

After a historic boom delivering more than 700 million square feet between 2021 and 2023, construction moderated sharply due to higher financing costs and zoning restrictions. Industrial starts fell about 40% from the 2022 peak.

Vacancy ticked up to 6% in 2025, still below the long-term average of 7%. Figure 6.2 illustrates how vacancy has stabilized despite a cooling development pipeline.

Figure 6.2 Industrial Vacancy Rates, 2021-2025

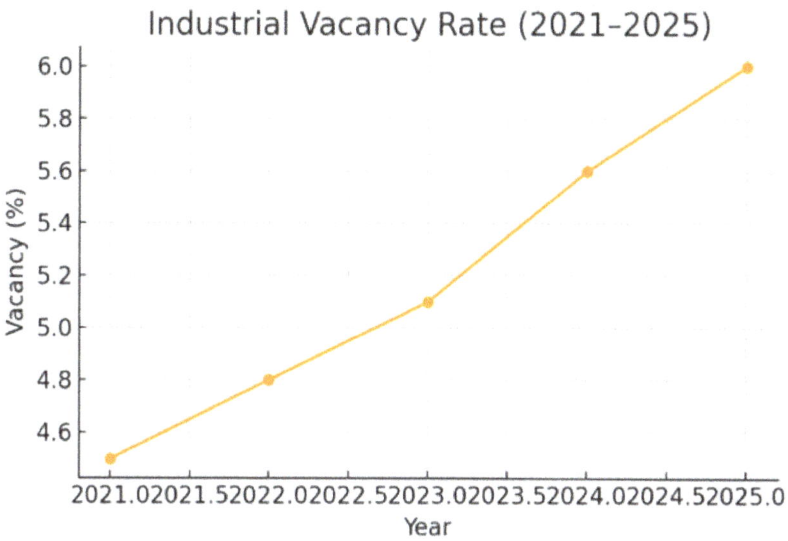

Note. Industrial vacancy stabilized around 6 percent nationally despite construction moderation. Source: CBRE (2025b).

In dense urban markets like Seattle, Brooklyn, and San Francisco, you're seeing more multistory warehouses, which command a 15-25% rent premium and serve last-mile delivery providers such as Amazon and UPS.

6.2.3 Operating Fundamentals

Rents rose 6-8% annually in 2023-2024 before moderating in 2025. But even with that slowdown, national industrial rents remain 35% higher than in 2019. The most competitive markets include West Coast port cities, inland hubs like Dallas-Fort Worth and Indianapolis, and cross-border logistics centers backed by strong freight activity.

Tenants are increasingly prioritizing 40-foot clear heights, automation readiness, and ESG-compliant buildings, along with proximity to labor and transportation networks.

6.3 Retail

6.3.1 Demand Drivers

Retail surprised many analysts by staging one of the strongest post-pandemic recoveries. Consumer spending grew steadily thanks to wage gains and low unemployment (McB Real Estate, 2024). Retail sales rose about 3.2% annually through 2024-2025.

What may matter most to you is that new retail construction remains extremely limited, only about 0.3% inventory growth per year since 2018. Simultaneously, the demolition of older retail properties removed over 155 million square feet from supply (JLL, 2025a).

Retailers have shifted their mindset too: stores now operate as last-mile nodes, return centers, and experiential hubs, increasing foot traffic through services like click-and-collect and ship-from-store.

6.3.2 Operating Fundamentals

Not all retail performs equally. Grocery-anchored and neighborhood centers dominate thanks to necessity-driven trips and consistent cash flow. National vacancy fell to 5.3% in 2024, one of the tightest readings in 20 years (Buxton, 2025). Experiential concepts, including fitness, entertainment, food-and-beverage, and medical tenants, are now driving leasing momentum.

6.3.3 Structural Trends

Underperforming malls continue to be converted into mixed-use districts, logistics facilities, medical campuses, or multifamily projects. You'll also notice rising tenant improvement allowances as landlords compete for long-term credit tenants in a supply-constrained environment.

6.4 Multifamily

6.4.1 Demand Drivers

If you've been paying attention, you've probably noticed that the demand for multifamily housing didn't just recover after the pandemic, it took off in a way that surprised a lot of people. What happened? As we moved into the post-pandemic world, household formation picked up steam again. People who had doubled up or moved in with family got their own places, and suddenly, the apartment market sprang back to life.

But there's more at play than just post-COVID energy. Sky-high mortgage rates started locking out would-be homebuyers, sending more people into rentals and keeping them there longer. Instead of stretching for a house, many decided to wait out the rate storm, which funneled even more demand toward apartments.

Then, there are the generational shifts you and I can't ignore. Right now, we're watching the largest wave of U.S. renters in history roll through the market, Millennials and Gen Z are calling the shots. Their tastes? Flexibility over permanence, and amenities over yardwork. They want professionally managed buildings, pet amenities, built-in WiFi, and a sense of community, all wrapped up in attractive urban neighborhoods or "15-minute" suburban enclaves. You see this in both the biggest cities and fast-growing suburbs; the story is playing out nationwide (MMCG Invest, 2025).

6.4.2 Supply Dynamics

With all that demand, the industry responded by ramping up new construction, big time. In 2023, developers delivered 416,500 new apartments, and in 2024, that number swelled to roughly 450,000. That's over a million new units added across just two years (CBRE), which would've seemed unimaginable not that long ago.

But when the pipeline gets that full, some markets inevitably feel the strain. Oversupply has started to crop up, especially in certain Sun Belt metros where everyone rushed in at once. We've watched vacancy rates in those hot spots jump by 1.5 to 2.5 percentage points, as new units came online faster than they could be leased. It's a classic case of capital chasing last year's wins.

At the same time, rising interest rates and tighter lending forced a slowdown in new project starts by late 2024. As a result, we expect the pace of new deliveries to drop below 400,000 units for 2025, offering some breathing room for markets that have become oversaturated. This pullback should help keep fundamentals from tipping too far into the red.

6.4.3 Operating Fundamentals

Despite the tidal wave of new supply, absorption kept up, and then some. Through 2024 and the first quarter of 2025, enough renters snapped up new apartments to keep national vacancy rates moving in the right direction. By Q1 2025, vacancy dipped to 4.8%, a level that's actually tighter than what we usually see over the long term.

Let's walk through the numbers for a clearer picture (all from Table 6.1). New deliveries climbed from 416,500 in 2023 to nearly 450,000 in 2024, before cooling in Q1 2025 with just over 70,000 new units. Over that same stretch, vacancy steadily shrank—from 5.4% in 2023 to 4.9% the next year, finally settling at 4.8% in early 2025. Absorption numbers tell an even more dramatic story: in Q4 2023, 84,800 units were leased up, but by Q4 2024 that number rocketed to 183,600 units, more than doubling in just one year. Q1 2025 kept the momentum with 100,600 units absorbed.

What about rents? Growth has returned to earth, but it's still ticking up. Year-over-year rent growth was a modest 0.4% in 2023 and rose to 0.5% in 2024, before reaching 0.9% by Q1 2025. It's not the double-digit increases from a couple years ago, but it's solid, steady progress. Class A buildings in cities seeing the most construction is still offering concessions to keep their units occupied, but overall, the market remains fundamentally healthy.

So, if you're deep in this market, buying, developing, or just investing, the message is clear: demand isn't the problem, and the recent supply rush is already starting to cool as developers hit the brakes. Our challenge now is to keep tracking the pace of absorption and stay ahead of the next supply wave, so we don't get blindsided again. The fundamental story, for now, still looks positive, especially if you're able to zero in on the right submarkets and keep a close watch on the numbers.

Multifamily demand surged post-pandemic as household formation rebounded and high mortgage rates kept would-be buyers in the rental market. Millennials and Gen Z, now the largest renter cohorts in U.S. history, prefer flexible, professionally managed living environments in urban and suburban centers (MMCG Invest, 2025).

Table 6.1 Multifamily Key Fundamentals (2023-2025)

Multifamily Key Fundamentals (2023-2025)	2023	2024	Q1 2025
New Units Delivered	416,500	~450,000	70,600
Vacancy Rate	5.4%	4.9%	4.8%
Net Absorption	84,800 (Q4)	183,600 (Q4)	100,600
Rent Growth (YoY)	0.4%	0.5%	0.9%

Note: Data sources include CBRE (2024; 2025a; 2025b).

6.5 Hospitality

6.5.1 Demand Drivers

By 2024, hospitality fully regained its footing, with RevPAR surpassing 2019 levels by about 5% (STR, 2025). Both leisure and business travel grew, as convention and group travel rebounded in major metros. Younger travelers, especially Millennials and Gen Z, pushed lifestyle, boutique, and wellness-focused hotels into faster growth trajectories.

6.5.2 Operating Trends

Urban luxury hotels performed well but unevenly across markets depending on convention bookings and international arrivals. Select-service and extended-stay hotels remained the most stable performers thanks to lower operating costs and steady business-traveler demand.

Labor shortages and rising insurance costs pressured margins, leading more operators to adopt tech-enabled efficiencies like mobile check-in, dynamic staffing models, and streamlined service offerings.

To help you visualize wider trends, Table 6.2 summarizes hospitality momentum across RevPAR, group travel, experiential lodging, segment resilience, and cost pressures. Rather than leaving the figure isolated, we integrate it here as a narrative summary:

Table 6.2 Hospitality Demand and Operational Trends (2024-2025)

Trend	Description
RevPAR Recovery	Approximately 5% above 2019, strong Q1 2025 performance (STR, 2025; CBRE, 2025)
RevPAR Recovery	Approximately 5% above 2019, strong Q1 2025 performance (STR, 2025; CBRE, 2025)
Group Travel	Rebound in convention demand in major metros (CBRE Hotels Research, 2025)
Experiential Lodging	Growth in boutique, wellness, design-focused properties (STR, 2025)
Segment Resilience	Strong cash flow in select-service & extended-stay segments (CBRE Hotels Research, 2025)
Cost Pressures	Rising labor and insurance costs mitigated with technology (CBRE, 2025)

Across 2024-2025, RevPAR continued lifting above prepandemic performance, convention travel rebounded, and experiential lodging grew rapidly. Select-service hotels maintained strong cash flow, while rising labor and insurance costs pushed operators to adopt technology-driven efficiencies.

Markets such as Miami and Fort Lauderdale illustrate these dynamics, with projected RevPAR increases of 0.8% and 2.4%, respectively (CBRE, 2025).

6.6 Life Sciences

Let's talk about life sciences real estate, a sector that continues to punch above its weight, thanks to powerful tailwinds from both public and private capital. If you're tracking the numbers, the scale of investment is eye-popping: In fiscal year 2024, the National Institutes of Health (NIH) poured $36.9 billion into external grants alone, fueling research that stretches well beyond the lab. For every dollar NIH spends, over $2.56 in economic activity is generated, resulting in more than 400,000 direct and indirect jobs supported nationwide (Harvard Gazette, 2025; Nietzel, 2025).

And it's not just federal dollars driving growth. Venture capitalists are still writing big checks, especially when it comes to cutting-edge fields like cell therapy, gene editing, and precision medicine. Even in a tighter funding environment, the appetite for breakthrough science remains strong, keeping demand resilient for specialized lab and biomanufacturing space.

If you've spent any time analyzing this sector, you know the core markets, Boston-Cambridge, San Diego, and the Bay Area, are in a league of their own. These clusters have what you can't buy: deep talent pools, anchor institutions, and world-class infrastructure. Unsurprisingly, vacancy rates are still low at 4–6%, holding firm even as new projects deliver to the market (JLL, 2025a).

There's also a strategic pivot happening that you'll want to note: high construction costs are pushing investors to get creative. In many cases, rather than go through the pain and expense of a ground-up build, they're converting older office buildings, often left vacant post-pandemic, into modern, lab-ready facilities. This approach isn't just faster; it's also much more capital-efficient and lets you plug directly into the networks that make life sciences clusters thrive.

So, if you're considering deploying capital here, focus on three things: prioritize adaptive reuse over new construction, zero in on cluster markets where demand is deepest, and make sure your projects offer the kind of flexible, specialized lab systems today's growing biotech firms need. If you can deliver on those, we think you'll be well-positioned no matter how the broader market moves.

6.7 Data Centers

Now, let's turn to data centers, a sector completely transformed by the twin forces of cloud computing and artificial intelligence. If you've tried to get into a new project recently, you already know that hyperscale clients like AWS, Google Cloud, and Microsoft Azure are driving the market. In fact, these three account for a staggering 70–80% of all preleasing activity in top U.S. data center regions (JLL, 2025b).

The big shift for investors? It's no longer about finding land. Your toughest challenge is securing power, full stop. In leading Tier 1 markets like Northern Virginia, we're seeing power interconnection queues that stretch out for years. This single bottleneck is reshaping how and where new construction happens, often causing risk and timeline headaches even for the most experienced players. Despite these delays, the global market isn't slowing down: construction activity reached about 4.5 gigawatts worldwide for 2024–2025, showing just how much demand there is, even if the supply chain keeps complicating the rollout.

The U.S. map for data centers still centers on heavy hitters: Northern Virginia, Phoenix, Dallas, and Chicago. But if you're looking for the next wave, secondary markets are having their moment. Cities like

Atlanta, Salt Lake City, and Columbus are picking up steam, offering lower costs, less power congestion, and shorter project timelines thanks to more available utility infrastructure.

As shown in Table 6.3, hyperscaler preleasing remains exceptionally strong at 70–80%, while global new construction activity totals approximately 4.5 GW. Power constraints continue to represent the most significant risk, particularly within Tier 1 markets. At the same time, secondary markets such as Atlanta, Salt Lake City, and Columbus are emerging as increasingly attractive alternatives due to faster interconnection timelines and notable cost advantages.

Table 6.3 Key Conditions in the Current Data Center Development Environment

Factor	Current Conditions
Hyperscaler Preleasing	Extremely high, averaging 70–80% prior to delivery
New Construction Pipeline	Approximately 4.5 GW of capacity under development globally
Primary Market Constraints	Power availability remains the largest limiting factor, particularly in Tier 1 markets
Emerging Secondary Markets	Cities such as Atlanta, Salt Lake City, and Columbus gaining traction due to faster interconnection timelines and lower development costs

Note. Table summarizes major trends influencing data center development and market selection.

6.8 Case Example: Suburban Office-to-Life Sciences Conversion

Given all the turbulence in the suburban office world, adaptive reuse is quickly becoming every savvy investor's go-to play. One project that really stands out is the transformation of a plain vanilla, Class B office building from the 1980s in Waltham, Massachusetts, just outside Boston, right in the heart of New England's biotech cluster.

Instead of letting the property languish, investors turned the building into a GMP-certified life sciences facility. By leaning into the existing infrastructure and proximity to world-class research centers, the renovated asset filled up quickly. Not only did this approach dodge the higher costs and long lead times of starting from scratch, it generated a significant boost in asset value almost immediately. It's a real-world demonstration of how, in this market, adaptability and location-awareness can outpace even the best speculative builds. If you're mapping out your next move, conversions like these deserve a long, hard look.

6.9 Strategic Implications for CRE Practitioners

As you look ahead, here's where you can capture the most strategic value:

- ☐ **Hospitality:** Focus on luxury urban markets, convention-centric metros, and flexible-stay formats.
- ☐ **Life Sciences:** Target lab-ready conversions within innovation clusters.
- ☐ **Data Centers:** Pursue secondary markets where power risk, permitting delays, and interconnection queues are more manageable.

- ☐ **Adaptive Reuse:** Strengthen your toolkit by converting underutilized offices and hotels into labs, experiential hospitality, or mixed-use spaces.
- ☐ **Infrastructure Risk:** Integrate power, grid reliability, and ESG requirements into underwriting, especially for data centers and life sciences.
- ☐ **ESG & Resiliency:** Prioritize sustainability and resiliency across all development types, from lab infrastructure to hospitality operations.

6.10 Transition to Chapter 7: Comparative Market Analysis

Now that you and I have walked through the fundamentals shaping each major property type, from office and industrial to life sciences and data centers, it's time to widen our lens. Understanding the dynamics within each asset class is essential, but real estate performance is also deeply shaped by place.

In Chapter 7, we shift the conversation to a broader comparative market analysis. We'll explore how Tier 1, Tier 2, and Tier 3 metros differ in resilience, demand drivers, demographic trends, and investment performance. Then we take this analysis global, stepping into key markets across Europe and Asia-Pacific to help you understand how talent ecosystems, infrastructure investment, and policy shape market opportunity.

By the end of the next chapter, you'll have a stronger foundation for choosing where to allocate capital, not just what to invest in, helping you design portfolios that perform across cycles and geographies.

References

AEW. (2024). *Multifamily market overview.* https://www.aew.com

Buxton, M. (2025). *Retail vacancy trends.* https://www.buxtonco.com

CBRE. (2024). *U.S. multifamily construction analysis.* https://www.cbre.com/insights

CBRE. (2025a). *U.S. office market outlook.* https://www.cbre.com/insights

CBRE. (2025b). *Industrial sector trends and statistics.* https://www.cbre.com/insights

CBRE Hotels Research. (2025). *Hospitality market insights.* https://www.cbrehotels.com

Cushman & Wakefield. (2024). *Multifamily market report.* https://www.cushmanwakefield.com

JLL. (2025a). *Office and life sciences market report.* https://www.us.jll.com

JLL. (2025b). *Data center market analysis.* https://www.us.jll.com

JLL. (2025c). *Retail market trends.* https://www.us.jll.com

Kastle Systems. (2025). *Workspace occupancy data.* https://www.kastle.com/safety-wellbeings/return-to-work-barometer

Lee & Associates. (2025). *Retail real estate supply constraints.* https://www.lee-associates.com

McB Real Estate. (2024). *Consumer spending and retail market report.* https://www.mcbrealestate.com

MMCG Invest. (2025). *Multifamily rental sector analysis.* https://www.mmcginvest.com

Nietzel, M. (2025). *Economic impact of NIH funding. Harvard Gazette.* https://news.harvard.edu

STR. (2025). *Hospitality performance report.* https://str.com

U.S. Bureau of Labor Statistics. (2025). *Employment statistics.* https://www.bls.gov

United for Medical Research. (2025). *NIH funding impact* (as cited in *Harvard Gazette*). https://unitedformedicalresearch.org

CHAPTER 07

Comparative Market Analysis

Introduction

When you're sizing up real estate opportunities, just looking at price tags or city names won't cut it. You need a way to compare apples to apples, one that takes into account how mature an economy is, what demographics are doing, how plugged-in the infrastructure is, and what kind of risk you're betting on. That's exactly what Comparative Market Analysis (CMA) does. By breaking down U.S. markets into Tier 1, Tier 2, and Tier 3, and then extending that lens globally across Europe and Asia-Pacific, you get a clear view of how things like regional fundamentals, innovation hubs, and policies shape real estate outcomes long-term. In this chapter, we'll build you a solid framework to compare markets by tier, diving into sector examples, data-driven insights, and the risk-return tradeoffs you need to know.

7.1 Understanding Market Tiers in the U.S.

When you hear "market tiers," don't just think city size or popularity. These tiers give you a picture of economic maturity, capital availability, and how stable those cash flows really are. Institutional investors often bucket metros into three tiers:

- **Tier 1** markets are the giant gateways, think New York, Los Angeles, San Francisco, Boston, Washington, D.C. These places have deep capital pools and steady, reliable cash flows thanks to broad, diversified economies.

- **Tier 2** markets, like Denver, Atlanta, Seattle, Charlotte, Phoenix, and Dallas-Fort Worth (DFW), are growth powerhouses with more affordable development costs and good balance between risk and reward.
- **Tier 3** markets, such as Raleigh, Boise, Tucson, Huntsville, and Greenville, are more about emerging opportunity. There's rapid growth potential but with thinner capital markets and elevated long-term risk.

7.1.2 Tier 1 Markets: High Liquidity, Global Gateways

Tier 1 cities bring the big guns: massive economies mixing finance, tech, biotech, and creative industries. The global capital flow here is no joke, supported by mature infrastructure like airports, transit, and universities.

Take New York City's metro area, that's nearly 8% of the entire U.S. GDP (Moody's, 2023). Over in Boston, recognized as a global biotech hub, life sciences lab space is booming but going through a rough patch. By late 2024, over 16 million square feet of lab space stood vacant, with an especially high 29.7% vacancy rate in Q2 2025 (Bisnow, 2025; HereBoston, 2025a, 2025b). The mix of overbuilding and some funding hiccups means you need to tread carefully here.

Entry prices are steep across all property types, office, multifamily, labs, you name it. But the sheer scale and liquidity tend to tame volatility. Regulatory hurdles and ESG requirements around zoning and sustainability bump up development complexity and costs. Still, stability and global connectivity keep Tier 1 markets attractive. Smart moves here include deep due diligence on asset fit and exploring opportunistic plays like converting underused office space into life science incubators or creative labs.

7.1.3 Tier 2 Markets: Growth Engines with Balanced Risk

Moving down a tier, you find metros thriving with population inflows and robust job creation. Think Denver, Atlanta, Seattle, Charlotte, Phoenix, DFW. These cities blend logistics, tech, finance, and corporate relocations while keeping development costs way friendlier than Tier 1. More institutional capital is flowing here, but it hasn't overwhelmed the market yet, so there's still room to grow.

Dallas-Fort Worth is a star example, it added about 152,000 residents in 2023, ranking among the fastest-growing U.S. metros (Dallas News, 2024; Ebby Halliday Realtors, 2024). Domestic migration and business expansions in corporate services and logistics are driving demand for multifamily, industrial, and office spaces alike. Essentially, Tier 2 gives you scalable upside with more flexible capital deployment options, backed by strong fundamentals.

Of course, it's not all smooth sailing. Compared to Tier 1, these markets have tighter liquidity. Rapid growth strains infrastructure, and competition for buildable land tightens, presenting challenges.

7.1.4 Tier 3 Markets: Emerging but Riskier Upside

At the riskiest end, Tier 3 markets show early signs of outsized returns, but you have to be patient. Cities like Raleigh, Boise, Tucson, Huntsville, and Greenville shine with affordability, spiking population growth, and lower land costs, but with limited institutional capital pools and higher volatility.

Boise, for instance, saw rapid net in-migration spiking between 2020 and 2022, fueled by remote work and quality of life appeals (CBRE, 2024). Multifamily rents briefly surged over 12% annually before supply caught up. Early institutional entrants here chase value-add opportunities, but they also wrestle with liquidity constraints and concerns about infrastructure keeping pace with growth.

7.1.5 Comparative Risk-Return Trade-Offs

Comparative Risk-Return Analysis Across Three Market Tiers

When you break down investments over the long haul, understanding how risk and return dance together is key. Looking at 20 years of data, from 2005 to 2024, three distinct market tiers show how these dynamics play out: bonds, developed-market equities, and emerging-market equities (Curvo, 2024).

Tier 1: Bonds (Bloomberg U.S. Aggregate Index)

This is the low-risk zone. The Bloomberg U.S. Aggregate Bond Index returned an annualized 3.02% with a volatility (standard deviation) of 7.95% over the 20 years (Curvo, 2024). It's the reliable, steady-as-she-goes asset class that investors turn to when they want capital preservation and consistent income. Its returns mainly bounce with interest rates, credit quality, and liquidity.

Tier 2: Developed Equities (S&P 500 Index)

Here's where growth comes knocking. The S&P 500 brought in a much higher annualized return of 11.02%, though with more ups and downs, a volatility of 15.26% (Curvo, 2024). Investors get broader exposure to big, developed market companies, balancing risk and reward. It's a favorite for those who want solid growth but aren't keen on sky-high swings.

Tier 3: Emerging Market Equities (MSCI Emerging Markets Index)

The wild card. The MSCI Emerging Markets Index churned out an annualized 10.02%, just shy of Tier 2's return, but with a volatility soaring to 21.00% (Curvo, 2024). This tier's pumped by economic shifts, political risks, currency swings, and less market depth. Patient investors aiming for bigger growth take the bumps in stride here.

What the Scatterplot Tells Us

Plotting these on a risk-return scatterplot reveals a textbook picture: the higher the expected returns, the bumpier the ride. You see Tier 1 settling in the lower-left corner, low risk, low returns. Tier 2 shifts up and to the right, showing that good balance of risk and opportunity.

Tier 3 pushes out farthest right, the highest risk but with the chance to capture growth that few others can.

Keep in mind, small changes in the indexes selected or the time span studied can tweak these numbers, especially for volatile markets like emerging economies (Curvo, 2024). But the core insight stands: you pick your tier based on how much risk you can stomach and how patient you want to be.

To sum it up:

- Tier 1 shines with lowest risk and steady cash flows.
- Tier 2 offers moderate risk for those craving solid growth.
- Tier 3 is for the patient who wants to chase outsized returns despite high volatility.

Figure 7.1 Comparative Returns by Market Tiers

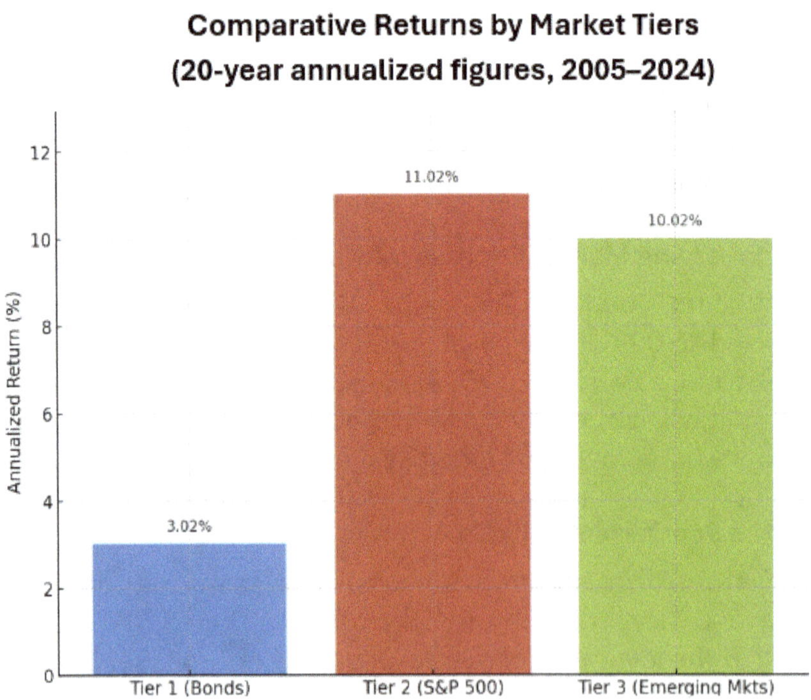

Note. This scatterplot illustrates the trade-off between risk (volatility) and return for bonds (Tier 1), developed equities (Tier 2), and emerging market equities (Tier 3) using annualized data from 2005 to 2024. Data source: Curvo (2024).

7.1.6 Cross-Border Extensions: Europe & Asia-Pacific

Now, this U.S.-centric framework doesn't work in a vacuum. Europe's gateway cities, London, Paris, Frankfurt, feel like Tier 1 equivalents, with policy frameworks like ECB mandates shaping the CRE climate (European Commission, 2024). Tier 2 and 3 here include cities like Madrid, Milan, Lisbon, and Prague.

Jump over to Asia-Pacific, and Singapore, Hong Kong, and Sydney slot into Tier 1, Seoul and Tokyo into Tier 2, and emerging inland cities to Tier 3. Innovation clusters, demographics, infrastructure spending, and political risks add layers to the picture (JLL, 2024). Adding global diversification smooths risk but invites currency and regulatory complexity.

7.1.7 Practitioner Checklist: Applying Comparative Market Analysis

Putting this into practice means:

- ☐ Clarifying what you want (income, growth, geographic spread)
- ☐ Quantifying how much risk you can stomach
- ☐ Gathering and benchmarking data on demographics, economics, and capital markets
- ☐ Stress-testing scenarios and exit plans
- ☐ Partnering with local pros who really know the sub-markets

7.1.8 Case Study: An Institutional Portfolio Comparison

Imagine you're managing a $2 billion U.S. real estate portfolio focused on multifamily and life sciences across these tiers. You allocate 20% of multifamily and 40% of life sciences exposure to Tier 1 metros like Boston and NYC for stability and barriers to entry. Tier 2 metros,

DFW and Atlanta, get 40% multifamily and life sciences to chase growth with lower costs. Tier 3, using Boise and Raleigh, takes on 40% multifamily and 20% life sciences for opportunistic plays.

Looking out 10 years, Tier 1 delivers stable but lower volatility returns. Tier 2 gives a solid balance of risk and growth. Tier 3 shows higher IRR potential but demands patience and an appetite for volatility.

7.2 Comparing U.S. Markets Across Key Dimensions

When you compare markets, you need to look through many lenses, demographics, economic drivers, infrastructure, and policies.

Population trends, especially migration, are huge. From 2020 to 2023, Texas, Florida, Arizona, and the Carolinas stole the show, capturing over 70% of net U.S. domestic migration (U.S. Census Bureau, 2024). Texas is powering multifamily and industrial growth; Florida's pull on retirees and companies fuels multifamily and hospitality; Arizona and the Carolinas benefit from affordability driving households to form.

Economic clusters deepen the story. Seattle's tech giants like Amazon and Microsoft grew nearly three times faster than the national average between 2015 and 2024, holding multifamily occupancy and rent steady even with tech layoffs elsewhere (CBRE, 2025). Table 7.1 shows leading markets' dominant industries and how they affect CRE.

Table 7.1 Key U.S. Markets and Dominant Drivers of Commercial Real Estate Performance

Market	Primary Drivers	Impacts on CRE
Texas	Strong in-migration; diversified economy	Expanding multifamily and industrial development
Florida	Retiree and corporate migration; tax advantages	Growth in multifamily and hospitality sectors
Arizona	Affordability; population inflow	Increased household formation; expanding housing demand
Carolinas	Affordability; sustained in-migration	Growth across multifamily and industrial segments
Seattle	Strong tech cluster (Amazon, Microsoft)	Stable multifamily rents and occupancy despite sector volatility
Inland Empire	Proximity to major ports; logistics infrastructure	Elevated industrial demand; vacancy below 3%
Charlotte	Airport expansion; financial services growth	Attracts corporate relocations and finance-sector employment

Note. Population migration data from 2020–2023 indicate that Texas, Florida, Arizona, and the Carolinas accounted for more than 70% of net U.S. domestic migration (U.S. Census Bureau, 2024). Tech sector growth in Seattle averaged nearly three times the national rate from 2015–2024 (CBRE, 2025). Industrial vacancy in the Inland Empire remained below 3% due to logistics advantages (CBRE, 2024).

Sources: U.S. Census Bureau (2024); CBRE (2024, 2025).

Infrastructure plays a crucial role in market strength. Take the Inland Empire, for example, a sprawling Southern California region east of Los Angeles, covering Riverside and San Bernardino counties. It's one of the nation's top logistics and warehousing hubs, sitting right along major highways and rail lines that connect directly to the bustling Ports of Los Angeles and Long Beach. That prime location keeps its industrial market incredibly tight, with vacancy rates below 3% (CBRE, 2024). Meanwhile, in Charlotte, recent airport upgrades are driving growth by attracting finance firms and corporate headquarters, boosting the local economy

Policy and regulation often shape how easy it is to build or invest. For example, Florida's absence of a state income tax turbocharges growth, whereas California's longer permitting and higher costs slow development but still attract huge demand because of sheer scale. Table 7.2 breaks down these pros and cons market by market.

Table 7.2 Policy Environment Pros and Cons Across Major U.S. Markets

Market	Policy / Regulatory Pros	Policy / Regulatory Cons
Florida	No state income tax; business-friendly regulatory environment; streamlined permitting	Rapid growth strains infrastructure; insurance costs rising in coastal counties
Texas	Favorable tax structure; predictable permitting process	Local zoning differences create variability across metros; property taxes relatively high
Arizona	Generally efficient permitting; pro-growth stance toward development	Water-resource constraints may slow long-term development capacity
North & South Carolina	Competitive tax incentives; supportive environment for corporate relocations	Infrastructure catching up to population growth; uneven zoning regulations among municipalities
California	Large, diverse economy; strong state incentives for green building and tech	Lengthy permitting timelines; higher regulatory costs; stringent environmental requirements
Washington (Seattle)	Innovation-driven incentives; supportive funding for technology and sustainability	Higher taxes and regulatory complexity; increasing compliance obligations for development
Illinois (Chicago)	Robust transit system; established planning frameworks	Higher tax burdens; budget pressures create uncertainty for long-term investment

Note. Policy advantages and disadvantages reflect market-level regulatory conditions that influence commercial real estate investment, development, and operational feasibility. States such as Florida and Texas offer business-friendly environments that accelerate growth, whereas California and Illinois often present higher regulatory and tax burdens that can slow development despite strong economic demand.

Sources: CBRE (2024, 2025); U.S. Census Bureau (2024).

7.3 Global Comparisons: Europe and Asia-Pacific

Europe's markets bring stability and transparency, but supply is tight, and stringent ESG mandates like the EU's Energy Performance of Buildings Directive push expensive upgrades (European Commission, 2024). London dominates with over $25 billion in cross-border CRE investment yearly (MSCI Real Assets, 2024). Table 7.3 profiles European hubs along these lines.

Asia-Pacific blends strong demographics with mixed risk. Singapore, Tokyo, Sydney top the Tiers; Vietnam and India punch above their weight but face regulatory and currency uncertainties. Singapore's Grade A office vacancy dropped below 4% in 2023, driven by multinational expansion (JLL, 2024).

Table 7.3 Global Comparisons: Europe and Asia-Pacific

Region / City (Hub)	Key Strengths / Features	Vacancy / Supply Conditions (or Market Tightness)	Key Risks / Challenges
Europe, London **(UK)**	Large volume of cross-border CRE investment; high liquidity and investor demand (CBRE, 2024).	Among top European investment hubs; core markets generally see faster supply equilibrium compared to secondary cities (PwC, 2024a).	Stringent ESG and regulatory requirements (e.g., energy-performance and building-upgrade mandates) increase upgrade costs (European Commission, 2024).
Europe, Other **major hubs (Munich, Paris, Amsterdam, Frankfurt)**	Stable, transparent, institutional-quality markets; moderate-to-strong investment interest post-2023 (PwC, 2024b).	Office supply growth slowed; prime office rents rising due to supply shortages vs. demand in many cities (Aberdeen Investments, 2024).	ESG/upgrade costs; need to retrofit or reposition older buildings to meet tenant expectations and regulations (European Commission, 2024).
Asia-Pacific, **Singapore**	Strong demographics, multinational expansions, stable institutional investment; well-located Grade-A office stock (Aberdeen Investments, 2024a).	Grade-A office vacancy low, about 5.3% in Q1 2024 (Aberdeen Investments, 2024a).	Mixed macro, currency, and regulatory risk; supply growth pressures lower-quality submarkets (CBRE, 2024a).

Region / City (Hub)	Key Strengths / Features	Vacancy / Supply Conditions (or Market Tightness)	Key Risks / Challenges
Asia-Pacific, **Tokyo (Japan)**	Mature commercial market with stable demand; expansion and upgrades fueling prime office demand (CBRE, 2024b).	Grade-A office vacancy in prime submarkets around 2.4% in late 2023; some peripheral submarkets weaker (Cushman & Wakefield, 2024a).	New supply entering market and some submarket weakness (Cushman & Wakefield, 2024a).
Asia-Pacific, **Seoul (South Korea)**	Strong investor demand and stable fundamentals; among tightest office markets in APAC (Cushman & Wakefield, 2024b).	Vacancy expected below 5-5.5% through forecast horizon (Cushman & Wakefield, 2024b).	Risks include oversupply in lower-quality stock, ESG/building upgrades, regulatory and macro uncertainties (Cushman & Wakefield, 2024b).
Asia-Pacific, **Emerging/High-Growth Markets (India, Vietnam)**	Large populations, growth potential, rising demand for office and logistics, expanding CRE investment (CBRE, 2024a).	Mixed supply-demand balance; rising demand but supply increases and uneven quality cause varying vacancy (CBRE, 2024a).	Regulatory risk, currency fluctuations, policy uncertainty, infrastructure gaps, and uneven ESG standards (CBRE, 2024a).

7.4 Case Example: Migration-Driven Demand in the U.S. Sun Belt

The Sun Belt cities like Austin, Nashville, Phoenix, Tampa, and Charlotte are booming thanks to affordable living, tax benefits, corporate relocations, and growing logistics. CBRE (2025) reports record-setting multifamily deliveries and leasing from 2023-2025. Phoenix's industrial sector skyrocketed following TSMC's semiconductor plant opening and expanding distribution (CBRE, 2024). Austin's population has grown over 30% since 2010, pushing up multifamily absorption and rent growth alongside office and logistics development (U.S. Census Bureau, 2024).

7.5 Practical Framework for Comparative Market Selection

Here's how you approach market selection like a pro:

- ☐ Start with your goals, income, value-add, growth, or diversification.
- ☐ Screen markets for solid population and job growth, rent trends, vacancy rates, and construction pipelines.
- ☐ Stack qualitative factors: regulatory climate, landlord-tenant laws, infrastructure, political stability.
- ☐ Align sectors with markets, logistics in Inland Empire, life sciences in Boston, for example.
- ☐ Do a risk-adjusted check on volatility, liquidity, cap rates, supply, and policy exposure to finalize the best picks.

7.6 Transition to Part III: Financial Analysis and Valuation for Investors

With this comparative market groundwork behind us, we're ready for the next phase: the financial mechanics of investing. Part III dives into the investor's toolkit, valuation and due diligence, and capital structuring. Chapters 8 through 10 will take you from understanding markets to mastering the numbers and deal architecture that make real estate investing work.

References

Aberdeen Investments. (2024a). *Asia Pacific real estate market outlook Q3 2024.* https://www.aberdeeninvestments.com/en-gb/intermediary/insights-and-research/asia-pacific-real-estate-market-outlook-q3-2024/

Aberdeen Investments. (2024b). *European real estate market outlook Q4 2024.* https://www.aberdeeninvestments.com/en-sg/investor/insights-and-research/european-real-estate-market-outlook-q4-2024/

Bisnow. (2025). *Boston lab vacancy soars to 16M sf.* https://www.bisnow.com/boston/news/life-sciences/boston-lab-vacancy-soars-to-16m-sf-127446

CBRE. (2024). *H2 2024 global real estate capital flows.* https://www.cbre.com/insights/reports/h2-2024-global-real-estate-capital-flows

CBRE. (2024a). *Office | Asia Pacific real estate market outlook 2024.* https://www.cbre.com/insights/books/asia-pacific-real-estate-market-outlook-2024/office

CBRE. (2024b). *U.S. industrial market outlook.* https://www.cbre.com

CBRE. (2024c). *U.S. real estate market outlook 2024.* https://www.cbre.com

CBRE. (2025). *U.S. multifamily midyear outlook.* https://www.cbre.com

Cushman & Wakefield. (2024a). *Office Marketbeat Report: Japan.* https://www.cushmanwakefield.com/en/japan/insights/japan-marketbeat/office-marketbeat-report

Cushman & Wakefield. (2024b). *Asia Pacific office outlook 2025.* https://www.cushmanwakefield.com/en/insights/asia-pacific-office-outlook

Dallas News. (2024, March 14). *D-FW leads all metro areas in population growth, adding 152,000 new residents.* https://www.dallasnews.com/business/2024/03/14/d-fw-leads-all-metro-areas-in-population-growth-adding-152000-new-residents/

Ebby Halliday Realtors. (2024, March 15). *D-FW leads all metros in population growth.* https://www.ebby.com/blog/2024/03/15/d-fw-leads-all-metros-in-population-growth/

European Commission. (2024). *Energy Performance of Buildings Directive.* https://commission.europa.eu

HereBoston. (2025a). *Boston's life sciences sector faces unprecedented downturn.* https://www.hereboston.com/boston-life-sciences-sector-challenges/

HereBoston. (2025b). *Greater Boston's life sciences market shows resilience.* https://www.hereboston.com/greater-boston-life-sciences-resilience/

JLL. (2024). *Asia-Pacific office market report.* https://www.jll.com

PwC. (2024a). *Emerging Trends in Real Estate Europe 2025, Press release.* https://www.pwc.ie/media-centre/press-releases/2024/emerging-trends-in-real-estate-europe-2025.html

PwC. (2024b). *Emerging Trends in Real Estate Europe 2024.* https://www.pwc.com/gx/en/asset-management/emerging-trends-real-estate/assets/emerging-trends-in-real-estate-europe-2024.pdf

PART III

Financial Analysis and Valuation for Investors

OVERVIEW

Now that we know where to look and why opportunities exist, it's time to get precise about how you evaluate those opportunities. Part III delivers the quantitative backbone you need to make smart investment decisions. In today's competitive, data-heavy market, you've got to analyze income streams clearly, value properties under different scenarios, and measure risk-adjusted returns with confidence and transparency.

This section puts the financial modeling and valuation tools used by institutional investors, private equity, lenders, and savvy private buyers right in your hands. Over three focused chapters, we take you step-by-step through calculating key return metrics, modeling cash flows, valuing properties rigorously, and structuring capital stacks that align interests and optimize your returns. With these skills, you'll compare deals objectively, stress-test assumptions, and underwrite with confidence.

Overview of Chapters

Chapter 8 – The Investor's Financial Toolkit

Here's where we get into the nuts and bolts of CRE finance. You'll master essential metrics and modeling techniques like:

- ☐ Calculating Net Operating Income (NOI)
- ☐ Understanding how cap rates relate to risk, growth, and pricing
- ☐ Building discounted cash flow (DCF) models
- ☐ Measuring returns with IRR, equity multiple, and yield-on-cost
- ☐ Running sensitivity and stress tests to see how changes ripple through your model

- ☐ Evaluating leverage, how debt can boost returns but also amplify risks

Real-world examples show how small tweaks in rents, expenses, exit cap rates, or financing terms can dramatically shift your investment's outcome. By the end, you'll be crafting and analyzing models with the rigor of the pros.

Chapter 9 — Valuation and Due Diligence

Next, we move beyond the numbers to how professional investors zero in on value using three classic valuation approaches:

- ☐ Income Approach (using NOI, cap rates, and DCF)
- ☐ Cost Approach (accounting for replacement costs, land value, and depreciation)
- ☐ Sales Comparison Approach (looking at comps, transaction speed, and price discovery)

We also dig into tenant credit quality, lease terms, capital expenditure needs, and property condition to refine valuations. Plus, you get a comprehensive due diligence checklist, covering lease audits, operating expenses, environmental and structural reviews, legal title, and market positioning, to help you spot any hidden risks or overlooked upside before you commit.

Chapter 10 — Structuring the Capital Stack

Finally, this chapter unpacks how the layers of your capital stack shape your returns, risks, and governance rights. We break down:

- ☐ Senior debt
- ☐ Mezzanine debt
- ☐ Preferred equity
- ☐ Common equity

You'll see how cash flow is distributed, control is allocated, and downside protections are layered across these parts. We also cover promote (carry) structures, waterfalls, co-investments, and recapitalizations/refinancings. By mastering capital stack design, you'll learn to optimize returns, align incentives across partners, and build resilience through market swings. Real-world cases demonstrate how different stacks perform when things go right, and when they don't.

Key Takeaways from Part III

- ☐ Financial modeling is your foundation for disciplined, precise CRE investing, measuring risk, return, and value clearly.
- ☐ Knowing how to calculate NOI, interpret cap rates, and run DCF valuations keeps your property pricing consistent across sectors and markets.
- ☐ Solid valuation combines multiple methods, all backed by thorough due diligence and property fundamentals.
- ☐ How you structure your capital stack can make or break investor outcomes, balancing debt and equity layers carefully.
- ☐ Mastering these financial tools puts you in the driver's seat, helping you spot mispricing, compare deals fairly, and build strong, durable portfolios.

CHAPTER

08

The Investor's Financial Toolkit

Introduction

If you want to succeed in commercial real estate (CRE) investing, you can't just rely on gut feelings or neighborhood hype. You need a firm framework, one that's all about financial modeling, understanding capital markets, and sizing up risk with real numbers. Over the past 20 years, this landscape has twisted and turned a lot. After the 2008 Global Financial Crisis, commercial lending practically dried up, dropping nearly 80%, with CMBS issuance plunging from $230 billion in 2007 to below $30 billion by 2009 (FDIC, 2011). Then, for over a decade, ultra-low interest rates fueled property prices across almost every type of asset.

From 2011 through 2019, cap rates tightened as big institutional players like pension funds and sovereign wealth funds ramped up their real estate stakes (PwC, 2024). When the pandemic hit, e-commerce took off, industrial leasing surged, and prime U.S. market cap rates even dipped under 4% for the first time ever (CBRE, 2024). But the rapid interest-rate hikes in 2023-2024 shook things up again, pushing borrowing costs higher, expanding bid-ask spreads, and forcing a big reset on how properties are priced.

In this whirlwind, you need a sharp set of analytical tools to evaluate deals, size income streams, discount risk, and measure returns. This chapter is your guide through those essentials, NOI, cap rates, discounted cash flow, IRR, and sensitivity analysis. We'll dive into real numbers and scenarios, including a full Chicago industrial acquisition example modeled with leverage and exit numbers. These tools will help you navigate today's shifting landscape with confidence.

8.1 Net Operating Income (NOI): The Foundation of CRE Analysis

8.1.1 Definition and Importance

Think of NOI as the property's pure economic engine, what it earns after operating expenses but before debt, taxes, or big repairs come into play:

NOI = Effective Gross Income – Operating Expenses

NOI is critical because it:

- ☐ Determines value under the cap-rate valuation method
- ☐ Helps lenders figure out how big a loan they'll offer (using debt-service coverage ratios)
- ☐ Shows you the property's stabilized income, without being clouded by how you finance it

Operating expenses usually eat up about 30% to 45% of gross income, depending on the type of property (CBRE, 2024). Multifamily and retail are higher due to more staff and utilities, while industrial often operates leaner. Thanks to triple-net (NNN) leases, where tenants pay property taxes and maintenance, industrial properties hold up well, even when offices and retail took hits during the pandemic (JLL, 2024).

8.1.2 Real-World Example: Chicago Industrial Property

Picture this: a 100,000 sq. ft. light-industrial warehouse in metro Chicago leasing at $12 per sq. ft. on an NNN basis. That's $1.2 million in gross rent. With minimal landlord expenses, say $100,000 in operating costs, your NOI is: $1,200,000 - $100,000 = $1,100,000

This $1.1 million shapes the whole story, valuation, returns, financing, you name it.

8.2 Understanding Capitalization Rates (Cap Rates)

8.2.1 Definition and Market Use

Cap rates are the shorthand way investors relate income to price:
Cap Rate = NOI / Value

They help you quickly estimate price, compare yields across cities or property types, and gauge market sentiment compared to safe investments like bonds. But cap rates aren't a physical quality of your building; they're a reflection of what's happening in the broader capital markets, interest rates, credit availability, capital flows, and supply-demand balance.

When industrial cap rates fell below 4% in 2021-2022, institutional demand for logistics was off the charts (CBRE, 2024). By 2023-2024, rising interest rates pushed cap rates up around 5% to 6% in many Midwest markets (JLL, 2024).

8.2.2 Historical Perspective: Cap Rates Over Cycles

Here's how cap rates have moved with the economic tides over 20 years:

- Early 2000s: Credit was flowing, and cap rates compressed
- 2008-2010: Markets crashed, and cap rates jumped 150-300 basis points (FDIC, 2011)
- 2011-2019: Low rates brought cap rates to historic lows across core markets

- 2020–2022: Pandemic logistics boom sent industrial cap rates below 4% (CBRE, 2024)
- 2023–2024: Fed rate hikes reversed the trend, swelling cap rates especially where debt dependence is high (JLL, 2024)

8.2.3 Current Market Context (2024–2025)

In today's market, industrial cap rates hover between:

- National average: 5.0%–6.0%
- Chicago: 5.5%–6.25% depending on building age and tenant (JLL, 2024)
- LA / Northern New Jersey: 4.5%–5.0%
- Indianapolis, Kansas City, Columbus: 6.0%–7.0%

For example, a 150,000 sq. ft. Class A warehouse in Joliet leased to a 3PL sold at a 5.6% cap in early 2024. Meanwhile, a 20-year-old Schaumburg flex building traded near 6.4%, reflecting more risk from upcoming lease rollovers.

Table 8.1 Typical U.S. Industrial Cap Rates by Period

Year	Economic Environment	Typical Industrial Cap Rate	Market Dynamics
2019	Stable pre-pandemic	5.2%–6.0%	Balanced conditions
2020	Pandemic disruption	5.0%–5.5%	Supply-chain reshoring
2021	E-commerce surge	3.75%–4.5%	Institutional buy-in frenzy
2022	Inflation spike	4.0%–5.0%	Rising rates
2023	Fed tightening	5.0%–6.0%	Cap-rate expansion
2024	High-rate plateau	5.5%–6.5%	Price discovery

Sources: CBRE, 2024; JLL, 2024; Marcus & Millichap, 2024

8.2.4 Cap Rate Example: Valuing the Chicago Warehouse

With that $1.1 million NOI, if you value at a 6.0% cap, the property is worth about $18.3 million. Raise the cap to 6.5%, and it drops to roughly $16.9 million. That half-percent swing cuts about $1.4 million off the value, showing just how sensitive pricing is to market shifts (Marcus & Millichap, 2024).

8.3 Case Example: Current Market Pricing

Look at a recent sale in Chicago's O'Hare submarket:

- 85,000 sq. ft. shallow-bay warehouse leased to FedEx Ground
- Eight years left on an NNN lease
- NOI: roughly $1.2 million
- Cap rate: 5.5%
- Price: $1,200,000 ÷ 0.055 ≈ $21.8 million

This deal underscores several market truths: strong credit tenants command premium pricing, airport-adjacent industrial spots keep outperforming, and even with rising rates, quality logistics assets stay in high demand.

8.4 Discounted Cash Flow (DCF) Modeling

8.4.1 Definition and Purpose

DCF takes you beyond that single snapshot of value from cap rates and looks at the full story, projecting cash flows over the next 5 to 10 years and discounting those back to today's value using a rate reflecting risk and opportunity cost (Geltner et al., 2021).

When do you need DCF? When rents change, leases expire at different times, you're planning capital projects, or just want a detailed, long-term view. Since the early 1990s, institutional investors have demanded this level of detail to make smarter decisions.

8.4.2 Example: Simplified 5-Year DCF

Say Year 1 NOI is $1.1 million, growing 2.5% annually, discounted at 9%, with an exit cap of 6.25%. Your Year 5 NOI is about $1.18 million, and your exit value sits near $18.9 million. Discount all cash flows and sale proceeds back, and the DCF value lands around $17.8 million, very close to the cap-rate estimate.

8.5 Discounted Cash Flow (DCF) Modeling: Valuing Future Income

8.5.1 Purpose and Rationale

DCF respects money's time value, market shifts, and terminal value, often 50% to 70% of total returns (Geltner et al., 2021). This is why leading investors like Blackstone use DCF models to compare risks across markets and capital structures.

8.5.2 Structure of a CRE DCF Model

1. Projection Period: Usually a 10-year hold, matching typical pension or private equity timelines.

2. Annual Cash Flows include base rent, reimbursements, vacancy, credit loss, operating expenses, tenant improvements, leasing commissions, and capital expenditures. Industrial tenants often lease shorter (5-7 years), so rollover risk matters more here (JLL, 2024).

3. Terminal Value: Calculated as Year 11 NOI divided by an exit cap usually a bit higher than entry due to aging and income risk.

4. Discount Rate varies by strategy: Core industrial sits at 7-9%, core-plus at 9-10%, value-add at 10-14%, opportunistic 14-20% (JLL, 2024).

8.5.3 Real-World Example: 100,000 sq. ft. Chicago Warehouse

Entry NOI $1.1 million, 2% annual growth, 6.5% exit cap, 8% discount rate, held for 10 years. Terminal value works out to about $20.6 million. Discounted cash flows plus terminal value sum to roughly $18.7 million, matching your earlier cap-rate valuation and showing consistency for a stable, triple-net property.

If you want a clear, step-by-step guide to performing Discounted Cash Flow (DCF) analysis, check out **Appendix**. It takes you through the whole process using a commercial real estate acquisition example, from setting your assumptions and building pro forma financials to calculating free cash flow, selecting your discount rate, and arriving at a solid valuation. This manual will give you practical, hands-on detail to apply DCF modeling confidently alongside the concepts covered here.

8.6 Internal Rate of Return (IRR): Measuring Investment Performance

8.6.1 Definition and Application

IRR is your go-to return metric, it's the discount rate that sets the net present value of your cash flows to zero. It accounts for timing, sale proceeds, and leverage and makes it easy to stack up different deals (Fisher & Martin, 2023).

But watch out, IRR can be misleading if early cash flow is low but sale profits balloon. Leverage can artificially boost IRR, and some cash flow patterns throw up multiple IRRs. Remember, it's a rate, not the total dollar gain.

8.6.2 Example: Projected IRR for the Chicago Industrial Property

Using $18.3 million purchase price, 60% loan at 6.25% interest-only, and 10-year cash flows, you get a levered IRR of about 12.5%. That's right in line with recent industrial deals, where core returns hover 9–11% and value-add chase upper teens (Marcus & Millichap, 2024).

8.7 Leverage: Enhancing Returns, and Risks

8.7.1 Understanding Financial Leverage

Leverage can pad your returns by letting you put less cash down and lock in fixed financing costs, but it also can deepen losses. Remember 2008? Highly leveraged deals crumbled when cap rates shot up (FDIC, 2011). And lately, office spaces are struggling due to rising rates and occupancy declines (CoStar, 2024).

8.7.2 Real Example: Effect of Leverage on Cash-on-Cash Returns

For the Chicago warehouse: $1.1 million NOI, debt service around $686,000, leaves about $414,000 to equity, translating into a 5.65% cash-on-cash return on $7.32 million equity. If NOI grows 9% to $1.2 million, cash-on-cash jumps 24%, to 7.02%. Leverage is your friend when things go up, but your enemy when they go down.

8.8 Sensitivity Analysis: Navigating Market Uncertainty

8.8.1 Why Sensitivity Modeling Matters

Markets are unpredictable. Running the numbers against changes in cap rates, interest rates, rents, expenses, and vacancy helps you foresee best- and worst-case results, and avoid overpaying or over-leveraging yourself (ULI, 2024).

8.8.2 Cap-Rate Sensitivity Table

Here's how your $1.1 million NOI warehouse's value shifts when cap rates move:

Table 8.2 Cap-Rate Sensitivity Table

Cap Rate	Property Value
5.0%	$22,000,000
5.5%	$20,000,000
6.0%	$18,333,333
6.5%	$16,923,077
7.0%	$15,714,286

See how moving from 6% to 7% cuts value 14%? That's enough to wipe out equity in a leveraged deal.

8.9 Combined Case Study: Leveraged Industrial Acquisition in Chicago

Let's put it all together:

- ☐ NOI: $1.1M
- ☐ Entry cap: 6.0%
- ☐ Purchase price: $18.3M
- ☐ Debt: 60% at 6.25%
- ☐ NOI growth: 2% annually
- ☐ Exit cap: 6.5%

Your DCF value is about $18.7 million with a levered IRR near 12.5%. Cash-on-cash returns range from 5.6% to 7.1%, and equity multiples near 1.9x. This matches real deals in Chicago and nearby markets like Cincinnati and Columbus during 2023-2024, where high-quality warehouses remained solid despite rate hikes (JLL, 2024).

8.10 Advanced Modeling Techniques

Today's tools let you do way more than simple valuations; you can quantify risk and understand uncertainties deeply.

8.10.1 Sensitivity Analysis

Change variables like cap rates, rents, expenses, or exit prices to see which ones matter most (Figure 8.1). It's crucial in rising-rate climates when cap rates can move fast (JLL, 2024).

Figure 8.1 Cap Rate Sensitivity Analysis

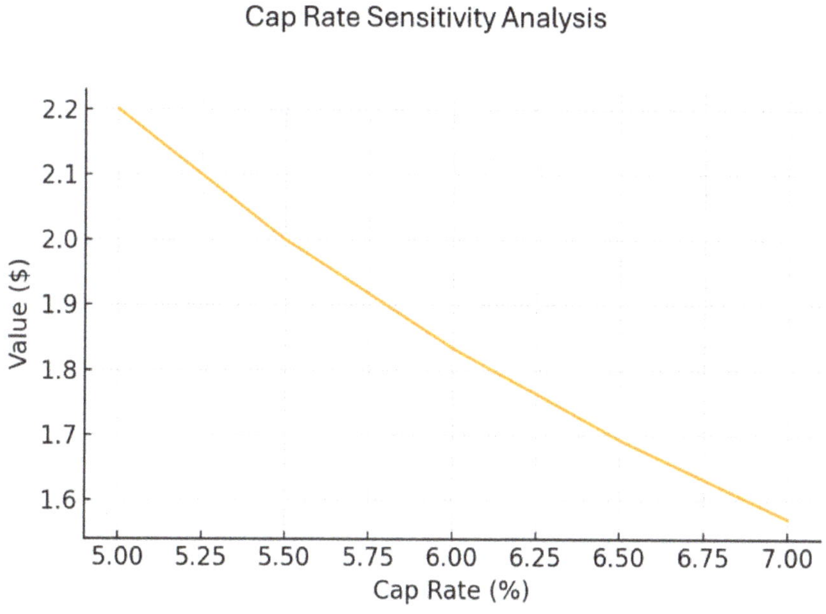

Note. This consideration is especially important in rising-rate environments, where cap rates may adjust rapidly (JLL, 2024).

8.10.2 Scenario Analysis

Look at entire paths like base case (2% rent growth), upside (4%), or downside (0%). Perfect for complicated multi-tenant industrial setups with staggered lease terms.

8.10.3 Monte Carlo Simulation

This crunches thousands of possible futures, showing averages, risks, probabilities of loss, and value-at-risk. Big institutional players lean on Monte Carlo to make data-backed decisions (PwC, 2024).

8.10.4 Real Options Analysis (ROA)

ROA lets you value flexibility like redevelopment, expansions, or conversions, think office to industrial or residential. It's popular in urban mixed-use and logistics corridor projects.

8.10.5 Debt and Capital Structure Modeling

Crunch amortization, fixed vs. floating debt, DSCR tests, lender covenants, preferred equity, and mezzanine layers. For example, with a $20M purchase, 60% loan at 6.5%, and $1.2M NOI, your levered cash-on-cash can hit 15% while unlevered runs 6%. Leverage works both ways.

8.10.6 Risk-Adjusted Performance Metrics

Sharpe ratios, Sortino ratios, VaR, expected shortfall, and Capital at Risk formulas help compare projects not just on return but also volatility and downside risk. Two deals yielding the same IRR might look very different once you factor in risk.

8.11 Transition to Chapter 9: Valuation and Due Diligence

Now that you've got the financial toolkit navigating income, valuation, and returns, it's time to root those numbers in reality. Chapter 9 shows how professional investors combine income, cost, and sales-comparable approaches with tenant credit checks, lease analyses, physical inspections, and legal due diligence. We'll wrap up with a checklist to help you avoid costly surprises.

References

CBRE. (2024). *U.S. industrial market outlook*. CBRE Research. https://www.cbre.com

CBRE. (2024). *U.S. Real Estate Market Outlook 2024*. CBRE Research.

CBRE. (2024). *U.S. Real Estate Market Outlook 2024: Industrial & Logistics*. CBRE Research.

CoStar. (2024). *Industrial market analytics and transaction volume report*. CoStar Group.

CoStar. (2024). *State of the U.S. commercial real estate market*. CoStar Group.

Cushman & Wakefield. (2024). *Capital markets risk assessment report*.

FDIC. (2011). *Crisis and response: An FDIC history, 2008–2013*. Federal Deposit Insurance Corporation. https://www.fdic.gov

FDIC. (2011). *The value of the Savings and Loan Crisis: A 20-year retrospective*. Federal Deposit Insurance Corporation.

Federal Reserve. (2024). *Senior loan officer opinion survey on bank lending practices*. https://www.federalreserve.gov

Fisher, J., & Martin, R. (2023). *Real estate finance and investments* (18th ed.). McGraw-Hill Education.

Fisher, D., & Martin, P. (2023). Investment performance measures in commercial real estate. *Journal of Real Estate Finance*.

Geltner, D., Miller, N., Clayton, J., & Eichholtz, P. (2021). *Commercial real estate analysis and investments* (4th ed.). OnCourse Learning.

JLL. (2024). *Industrial capital markets insight report*. Jones Lang LaSalle. https://www.jll.com

JLL. (2024). *Industrial real estate: Operating benchmarks and expense ratios.* Jones Lang LaSalle.

JLL. (2024). *U.S. industrial outlook.* Jones Lang LaSalle.

JLL. (2024). *U.S. Industrial Outlook 2024.* Jones Lang LaSalle.

JLL. (2024). *U.S. Industrial Outlook Q1 2024.* Jones Lang LaSalle.

Marcus & Millichap. (2024). *2024 national industrial investment forecast.* Marcus & Millichap Research Services.

Marcus & Millichap. (2024). *Industrial investment forecast 2024.* https://www.marcusmillichap.com

Marcus & Millichap. (2024). *Industrial National Report 2024.* Marcus & Millichap Research Services.

MSCI Real Assets. (2024). *Global capital trends report.* https://www.msci.com

NAREIT. (2024). *Historical returns and risk-adjusted performance across U.S. real estate sectors.*

Prologis Research. (2023). *Industrial real estate demand and performance outlook.*

PwC. (2024). *Emerging trends in real estate 2024.* PricewaterhouseCoopers. https://www.pwc.com

PwC, & Urban Land Institute. (2024). *Emerging trends in real estate 2024.* PwC/ULI.

ULI. (2024). *Real estate risk and scenario planning report.* Urban Land Institute.

ULI. (2024). *Risk and return expectations in commercial real estate.* Urban Land Institute.

CHAPTER 09

Valuation and Due Diligence

Introduction

When you're investing in commercial real estate (CRE) at an institutional level, valuation and due diligence aren't just checkboxes, they're your analytical backbone. They guide everything from acquisition pricing to portfolio strategy and capital deployment. Over the last century, valuation methods have evolved from simple rent multipliers and land-value heuristics in the early 1900s (Geltner et al., 2021) to today's sophisticated mix of income, cost, and sales comparable approaches.

By the 1970s and 1980s, as institutional money flooded into CRE, the focus shifted squarely onto the income approach and market comparables. The 1990s brought a technological leap: Excel allowed analysts like us to build multi-year discounted cash flow (DCF) models, considering rollover risk, inflation, and reinvestment. Post-2008 Global Financial Crisis (GFC), everyone realized relying on one method was risky. That crisis exposed frailty in overleveraged deals and underscored the need to integrate multiple valuation methods for defensible, transparent pricing (FDIC, 2011).

Jump forward to the 2020s, and major disruptions like hybrid work, surging e-commerce, inflation in construction costs, and rapid monetary tightening forced another reckoning. Now, no one ignores multi-method valuation or rigorous due diligence (PwC & ULI, 2024).

Last chapter, we covered essentials like NOI, cap rates, DCF, IRR, and sensitivity analysis. Now, we delve deeper into the core valuation approaches including the cost approach, where replacement risk and functional obsolescence come into play, and we'll further cement understanding with a Chicago industrial acquisition example, complete with leverage and exit numbers. Ready? Let's take a closer look.

9.1 Core Valuation Approaches

9.1.1 Income Approach: Measuring Cash Flow Durability and Growth

You'll find the income approach remains the go-to for valuing income-generating assets because it zeroes in on cash flow's durability, timing, and growth potential.

Think about how this has evolved:

- In the 1980s, underwriting mostly used direct capitalization, basically, a quick snapshot, because we lacked strong forecasting tools.
- Come the 1990s, with Excel spreading like wildfire, institutional investors (including us) got serious about 5- and 10-year DCF models, which let us factor in rollover risk, inflation, and capital reinvestments (Geltner et al., 2021).
- From 2000 on, DCF got more sophisticated, think vacancy probabilities, debt terms, Monte Carlo simulations, option-value analysis, and even AI-driven rent forecasting.

When is direct capitalization your friend? It works best for stabilized assets where rents climb predictably, rollover risk is low, expenses steady, and tenants have solid credit. Take the example of Class A industrial portfolios owned by the likes of Prologis. Their long-term NNN leases and strong market fundamentals make direct capitalization a fit (Prologis Research, 2023).

But when you're looking at value-add or development plays, with lease turnovers, varied capex, and uncertain future rents, DCF is king. It lets you incorporate re-tenanting probabilities, market rent growth, capital expenses like tenant improvements or system upgrades, and thoughtful exit cap assumptions.

A quick glance at office cap rate trends shows how volatile valuations can get. After the GFC in 2010, office cap rates averaged 6.8%, reflecting shaky markets and tough credit. Between 2015-2019, those rates compressed to 4.5%-5.0%, thanks to low interest rates and solid demand (CBRE, 2024). But more recently, from 2023 into 2024, rates popped back up to 6.0%-6.5%, a cocktail of remote work, banking sector jitters, and a hawkish Federal Reserve hiking rates by more than 500 basis points (Federal Reserve, 2024).

According to a 2024 survey by the Pension Real Estate Association (PREA), 78% of institutional investors now rely primarily on 10-year DCF models, with direct capitalization mostly used to reconcile or sanity-check those results (PREA, 2024).

9.1.2 Cost Approach: Replacement Risk and Functional Obsolescence

Now, the cost approach may not often headline your valuation process, but it's a crucial backstop. It calculates value based on what it would cost to replace the property, land plus construction, minus depreciation.

Historically, this approach stepped up when construction costs were jumping. For instance, inflation in the 1970s drove materials and labor prices up by 50% or more in many markets. After the GFC, slow recovery and supply chain issues created bottlenecks and skilled labor shortages (Turner & Townsend, 2024). More recently, the pandemic caused global shipping delays and labor crunches, pushing construction costs nationally up 31% from 2020 through 2024 (Turner & Townsend, 2024).

Why does this matter? In Midwest metros like Chicago, Minneapolis, and St. Louis, replacement costs now often outpace rents for Class A office buildings. That means building new isn't always economically viable, giving existing properties solid valuation support despite weaker leasing (JLL, 2024).

You'll find the cost approach especially helpful when you're dealing with specialty assets, think cold storage, data centers, life sciences labs, where custom infrastructure soars above typical market norms. It's also your go-to method in markets where supply is tapped out due to zoning restrictions or geography (like infill industrial near LA's port). And of course, for insurance valuation or early-stage ground-up feasibility studies, cost remains key.

9.1.3 Comparable Sales Approach: Market Sentiment and Liquidity Signals

You know that sales comparables are the classic appraisal tool, relying on recent transactions as guides. Before 2000, this was often the dominant way to value. Today, its reliability hinges heavily on market liquidity.

Check out recent CRE transaction volumes (MSCI Real Assets, 2024):

- ☐ 2010: $420 billion in transactions
- ☐ 2021: peaked at $680 billion, driven by ultra-low interest rates and abundant global capital
- ☐ 2023: plummeted to $330 billion, a 52% drop, marking the slowest deal flow since the GFC
- ☐ 2024: slight liquidity rebound, but still historically constrained due to expensive financing

Figure 9.1 visualizes this trend, showing the steep rise to 2021 followed by sharp contraction through 2023.

Figure 9.1 CRE Transaction Volume Trend (2010-2024)

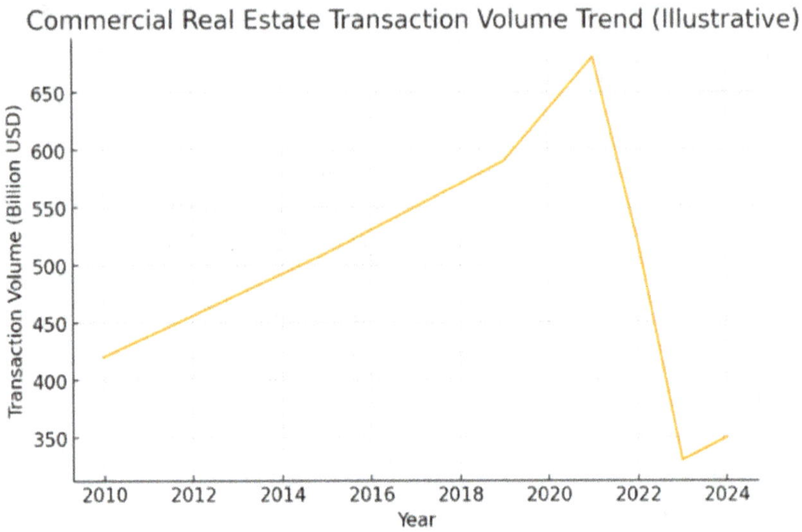

Note. This figure illustrates peak liquidity in 2021 and rapid contraction in subsequent years, underscoring the challenges of relying solely on sales comparables in times of tight financing.

When liquidity dries up, you have to stretch comparables by adjusting for micro-location factors (like distance to logistics hubs), building age and efficiency, tenant quality, rollover risk, and capital needs. If the market's distressed, qualitative judgment often beats statistical matching. You'll see this play out in retail with tricky co-tenancy provisions and unit sales variability.

9.2 Integrating Tenant and Lease Analysis

9.2.1 Tenant Creditworthiness

Nothing holds more sway over your property's income durability than who's paying rent. MSCI's 2024 distress survey sure drives this home: 68% of asset underperformance ties back to tenant credit issues rather than physical problems or rent drops (MSCI Real Assets, 2024). In multi-tenant buildings, the top five tenants typically command 60-80% of rental income. So even one weak tenant can rattle the whole deal (JLL, 2024).

High-credit tenants, think investment-grade firms or national brands, bring lower risks of early lease termination, steadier rent hikes, and longer leases. That translates into cap rates 30-75 basis points tighter compared to local or sub-investment-grade tenants (Marcus & Millichap, 2024). On the flip side, smaller businesses weather economic storms poorly, as we saw during the 2020-2021 pandemic when national chains bounced back faster than independents (CoStar, 2024).

To help you measure tenant credit, here's a common scorecard, see Table 9.1:

Table 9.1 Typical Institutional Underwriting Metrics for Tenant Evaluation

Category	Metric	Example Rating	Underwriting Implication
Financial Strength	Debt/EBITDA	3.5×	Moderate leverage; stable cash flow
Liquidity	Current Ratio	1.8×	Adequate operating buffer
Profitability	3-year CAGR	+4.2%	Positive but slow growth
Lease Performance	On-Time Payments	100%	Strong compliance history
Industry Risk	Sector Volatility	Low	Defensive sector (e.g., grocery, healthcare)

Note. This reflects typical institutional underwriting metrics for tenant evaluation.

Assets crowded with sub-investment-grade tenants usually see cap rates expand 30-100 basis points, reflecting jumpier default risk and shorter leases (CBRE, 2024). Beware sectors prone to structural risk: apparel and restaurants face 3-5% annual bankruptcy rates on average, versus below 1% in stable sectors like medical offices or groceries (ULI, 2024).

9.2.2 Lease Structure and Cash Flow Quality

Lease terms shape the reliability of your cash flow. You want to scrutinize:

- ☐ Lease duration and rollover risk (a tower where 60% of space expires in 2 years is a different beast than one with staggered expirations)
- ☐ Rent escalations (fixed, CPI, or flat)
- ☐ Expense responsibilities (NNN leases minimize landlord risk, while gross leases put expenses on you)
- ☐ TI and LC burdens
- ☐ Renewal and termination rights
- ☐ Co-tenancy provisions, especially in retail

Consider this retail case: in 2023, several open-air centers took 15–25% NOI hits when anchor tenants exercised early termination. Co-tenancy clauses triggered cascading rent drops for many inline tenants, hammering valuations (ICSC, 2024).

When you're dealing with a lease expiration schedule that's heavily front-loaded, expect a few challenges to pop up. Your negotiating power shrinks, downtime between tenants increases, tenant improvement and leasing commission costs can balloon, and lenders often respond by tightening loan terms because the risk profile worsens.

Let's look at how different lease types influence the allocation of operating expenses and, ultimately, valuation. Table 9.2 breaks this down clearly:

Table 9.2 Lease Types, Expense Responsibility, Typical Sectors, and Impact on Valuation

Lease Type	Operating Expense Responsibility	Typical Sectors	Impact on Valuation
NNN	Tenant pays taxes, insurance, CAM	Industrial, single-tenant retail	Highest NOI durability; premium pricing
Modified Gross	Partial landlord reimbursement	Office, flex	Moderate income variability
Full-Service Gross	Landlord pays all operating expenses	Office	Highest expense risk; typically, lower valuation

Note. Investors generally favor NNN leases because they reduce expense volatility, driving more stable returns. Combining a sub-investment-grade tenant with a full-service gross lease creates a risky scenario where the landlord shoulders both credit and rising expense risks.

9.3 Property Condition and Physical Due Diligence

9.3.1 Building Systems and Maintenance Backlog

Knowing your building's health protects you from ugly surprises. You need to assess HVAC, MEP systems, roof condition, fire safety, elevators, environmental contamination risks, and code compliance. The 2023 BOMA survey found:

- Average deferred maintenance for U.S. office buildings topped $4.50 per square foot
- Class B/C buildings averaged over $8.00 per square foot (BOMA, 2023)

This deferred maintenance correlates with lower NOI, higher tenant turnover, bigger capital obligations, and weaker valuation. You definitely want to quantify these costs upfront.

9.3.2 Capital Expenditure (CapEx) Reserve Modeling

CapEx planning acts as your shield against unexpected capital needs down the road. Whether it's replacing roofs, upgrading HVAC systems, or refreshing interiors, skimping on CapEx reserves can artificially inflate asset values by 8 to 12 percent. Typical institutional reserve estimates usually fall in these ranges: industrial properties require about $0.25 to $0.35 per square foot annually; multifamily buildings need $0.50 to $0.75; and office or retail assets typically budget between $1.50 and $2.50 per square foot.

Table 9.3 illustrates a sample 10-year CapEx plan, showing how costs often peak in the early years and then level off.

Table 9.3 Sample 10-Year Capital Expenditure Plan

Category	Year 1	Year 2	Year 3	Years 4–10 Average	Total
Roof Replacement	$0	$0	$650,000	,	$650,000
HVAC Upgrades	$120,000	$80,000	$50,000	$40,000/year	$520,000
Parking Lot	,	$150,000	,	,	$150,000
Interior Refresh	$90,000	$90,000	$90,000	$50,000/year	$510,000
Total	**$210K**	**$320K**	**$790K**	**$90K/year**	**$1.83M**

Note. Front-loaded CapEx requirements significantly impact underwriting, especially in the first few years of ownership.

9.4 Environmental Risk and Sustainability (ESG) Assessment

ESG factors have moved from sidebar considerations to core underwriting elements. Environmental Site Assessments (ESAs), energy efficiency, and carbon footprints now influence everything from insurance premiums to tenant appeal.

Key ESG priorities include:

- ☐ Energy-efficient systems and enhanced insulation
- ☐ Water-saving fixtures combined with leak detection technology
- ☐ Carbon emissions reduction and electrification readiness
- ☐ Indoor air quality improvements and alignment with WELL building standards
- ☐ Climate-related risks such as flooding and wildfire exposure

States like New York and California have enacted laws that impose stiff penalties on buildings that miss carbon emissions targets (Local Law 97; California Emissions Standards, 2024). As a result, poorly performing buildings on ESG measures consistently trade at 4-7% discounts relative to peers (CBRE, 2024).

Imagine your building's ESG profile as a radar chart, pinpointing where you excel, and where vulnerabilities lie, so you can prioritize upgrades and risk mitigation.

Integrating All This into Your Investment Decisions

Valuation isn't just about projecting income; it's about assessing risk-adjusted income. That means asking questions like:

- ☐ Who exactly is paying the rent? (Tenant credit quality)

- ☐ How locked in are those leases? (Lease terms and rollover risk)
- ☐ How well is the property operated? (Operational efficiency)
- ☐ What capital expenditures lie ahead? (CapEx planning)
- ☐ What external risks could affect value? (Environmental and ESG factors)

Institutional investors expect thorough underwriting that combines financial scorecards, scenario stress testing, and triangulates valuation via multiple methods. Your goal: an underwriting package so robust it stands up to the toughest scrutiny.

9.10 Transition to Chapter 9: Structuring the Capital Stack

We've built the valuation and due diligence foundation, now, it's time to use those insights to engineer your deal's capital structure. Chapter 9 will walk you through layering debt, preferred equity, mezzanine, and partnerships to optimize returns, allocate risk, and align incentives. That's the puzzle piece that turns projections into real-world strategy.

References

BOMA International. (2023). *BOMA benchmarking report: Office sector performance and operating expenses.* Building Owners and Managers Association. https://www.boma.org

CBRE. (2024). *U.S. cap rate survey: H1 2024.* CBRE Research. https://www.cbre.com/insights

CoStar Group. (2024). *National retail performance update: Recovery patterns and tenant segmentation.* CoStar Market Analytics. https://www.costar.com

ICSC. (2024). *Retail operations and co-tenancy dynamics report.* International Council of Shopping Centers. https://www.icsc.com

JLL. (2024). *U.S. retail outlook: Tenant performance and capital markets update.* Jones Lang LaSalle Research. https://www.jll.com/insights

Marcus & Millichap. (2024). *Net lease investment report: 2024 outlook.* Marcus & Millichap Research Services. https://www.marcusmillichap.com/research

MSCI Real Assets. (2024). *U.S. property market distress and liquidity trends.* MSCI. https://www.msci.com/real-estate

PREA. (2024). *Institutional investor survey: Valuation practices and risk management.* Pension Real Estate Association. https://www.prea.org

Starbucks Corporation. (2024). *Annual report and U.S. store portfolio update.* Starbucks Investor Relations. https://investor.starbucks.com

Turner & Townsend. (2024). *International construction market survey 2024.* Turner & Townsend Global Research. https://www.turnerandtownsend.com/en/insights

U.S. Census Bureau. (2024). *Population estimates and demographic trends: 2023-2024.* https://www.census.gov/data.html

Urban Land Institute. (2024). *Emerging trends in real estate 2024.* ULI & PwC. https://americas.uli.org/research/emerging-trends-in-real-estate

ULI. (2024). *Retail bankruptcy and risk outlook.* Urban Land Institute Research. https://uli.org

CHAPTER 10

Structuring the Capital Stack

Introduction

When you dive into commercial real estate investing, the capital stack is your blueprint for how money flows into a deal, and just as importantly, how risk, control, and returns flow back out. Think of the capital stack as the skeleton holding the entire investment strategy together. It shapes who gets paid when, how much risk each participant takes on, and what rewards they can expect.

In this chapter, we'll walk through the main layers of the capital stack, senior debt, mezzanine or preferred equity, and common equity, before diving into how sponsor incentives align through promote structures. We'll wrap up with a real-world joint venture case study focused on value-add multifamily properties. Along the way, you'll see market data and tables woven in carefully, so you get a solid feel for how these pieces work together in today's environment.

10.1 Understanding the Capital Stack

When people talk about the "capital stack," they're referring to the hierarchy of funding sources used for acquisitions or development. At the bottom, you've got senior debt, the safest money in the deal, typically the cheapest, backed by first lien security on the property. Above that sit mezzanine debt or preferred equity, taking more risk and therefore demanding higher returns. And then at the top, common equity, which is where you get the biggest upsides, but also the most risk.

To give context to the figures, Table 10.1 summarizes typical return expectations by layer using recent market data.

Table 10.1 Typical Returns by Capital Stack Layer

Layer	Typical Return Range*	Source
Senior Debt	~5%-7% interest	Federal Reserve, 2024
Mezzanine Debt	~10%-14%	CBRE, 2024
Preferred Equity	~12%-16%	JLL, 2024
Common Equity	~14%-25%+	PwC & ULI, 2024

*These ranges are approximations that depend heavily on asset type, market, and deal specifics.

Notice how common equity has the widest range, reflecting its sensitivity to how well value creation and exit timing play out. It's where the real performance magic, or heartbreak, happens.

10.2 Senior Debt: The Foundation of the Capital Stack

Senior debt is your baseline, the foundation everybody leans on. It typically sits in the lowest-risk position, secured by a first mortgage or deed of trust on the property. Because it gets paid first, lenders feel comfortable offering lower interest rates. But that comfort comes with strings attached, strict covenants like loan-to-value (LTV) limits, debt service coverage ratio (DSCR) floors, and controls on key property performance metrics.

In value-add projects, you'll often see senior debt covering between 50% and 70% of the property's value or acquisition cost. Market data from CBRE (2024) shows this range pretty consistently: 50%–

70% LTV for stabilized properties, slightly tighter for value-adds, around 55%-65%.

Take U.S. multifamily loans in 2024, for example. Interest rates have jumped to roughly 6%-7%, almost double from the 3%-4% range in 2021. That squeeze on cheap debt means sponsors are having to either pump more equity in or layer on mezzanine or preferred equity to fill in the gaps.

Table 10.2 provides a snapshot of key senior debt metrics for Q3 2024:

Table 10.2 Senior Debt Metrics, U.S. CRE Market, Q3 2024

Metric	Value	Commentary
Average LTV (originations)	~62.8%	Up from ~61.6% year-over-year (CBRE, 2024)
Debt Yield (average)	~9.9%	Slight increase of about 15 basis points
Agency multifamily fixed rate	~5.8%	Reflects current cost of senior debt for multifamily

What jumps out here? Senior debt remains the workhorse of CRE capital, but shifting rates and underwriting have pushed sponsors toward more creative capital stacks.

10.3 Mezzanine Debt and Preferred Equity: Bridging the Gap

With senior debt's safer slice limited, mezzanine debt and preferred equity step in as the bridge between debt and common equity.

Mezzanine debt hangs just above senior debt on the risk ladder. Since mezzanine lenders collect payment only after senior debt holders are satisfied, mezzanine carries noticeably higher risk and compensation, usually between 8% and 14% or even more. It typically comes with interest payments plus sometimes equity kickers or conversion options. Careful intercreditor agreements define who has rights if things go sideways.

In value-add deals, mezzanine normally amounts to 10%-20% of the stack, giving sponsors extra leverage without pushing senior debt limits too far.

Preferred equity sits in that gray area between debt and common equity, offering fixed preferred returns around 12%-16% in today's markets, and sometimes sharing in the upside beyond the preferred rate. Unlike mezzanine debt, preferred equity often comes with governance rights but fewer lender-like restrictions. Its hybrid nature commands higher cost than debt but less risk than common equity.

Both help fill funding holes, but at a cost in return expectations.

Table 10.3 shows a typical capital stack mix in value-add deals, alongside expected return buckets:

Table 10.3 Typical Capital Stack Composition and Returns in Value-Add Deals

Layer	Approximate % of Stack*	Typical Return Expectation	Risk/Return Profile
Senior Debt	~40%-60%	~5%-7% interest	Lowest risk, lowest return
Mezzanine Debt / Preferred Equity	~10%-20%	~10%-16%	Medium risk, medium return
Common Equity	~20%-60%	~14%-25%+	Highest risk, highest return

*These are broad guidelines; your mileage may vary based on deal specifics.

How these layers interplay will affect everything from deal risk to your flexibility when markets shift.

10.4 Common Equity and Promote (Carried Interest) Structures

Now we hit the top of the stack, common equity. This group takes the residual risk after paying debt and preferred returns, but also captures the largest upside if things go well. Targeted IRRs for common equity in value-add or opportunistic strategies often fall in the mid-teens to above 20%, heavily dependent on execution and market conditions.

Common equity holders include the sponsor (general partner, or GP) and passive investors (limited partners, or LPs). Cash flow trickles down after all other obligations are met, making alignment key.

To help sponsors deliver maximum value, promote (or carried interest) structures are used. Here, LPs get a preferred return hurdle, say 8% IRR, and anything above that triggers the GP's promote, which gradually increases their profits share (commonly 20%, sometimes rising to 30% at higher IRR tiers). This tiered "waterfall" motivates sponsors to push beyond simply meeting minimum returns.

10.5 Joint Venture Case Study: Value-Add Multifamily

Picture a joint venture on a 200-unit garden-style apartment complex in a secondary Sun Belt market. The purchase price is $40 million, with a plan for $3.6 million in stabilized NOI, reflecting a 9% initial cap rate. Renovations and lease-up are set for about two years, with a 5-year hold and a targeted exit cap of 7.5%, projecting a $48 million exit valuation.

Table 10.4 breaks down the capital stack:

Table 10.4 Capital Stack for a Hypothetical Value-Add Multifamily Joint Venture

Layer	% of Total Capital	Amount (USD)	Notes
Senior Debt	60%	$24 million	60% LTV on purchase price
Mezzanine/Preferred Equity	15%	$6 million	Subordinate, higher cost
Common Equity	25%	$10 million	Sponsor and LP equity split

Senior debt interest hovers around 6.5%, dialing in about $1.56 million annually. The mezzanine/preferred layer costs about 12% coupon, roughly $720,000 per year. Once those costs are covered, cash flow accrues to common equity.

At exit, the $48 million proceeds minus $5 million debt paydown leaves $43 million for equity. After repaying debt and mezzanine holders, roughly $13 million flows to common equity, a solid 30% total return over five years (~5.4% annual cash yield plus appreciation). Better-than-expected NOI or tighter cap rates can push IRRs over 20%.

This example shows the protective cushion senior debt provides and how mezzanine/preferred equity lets you leverage equity while paying a higher price for that flexibility.

10.6 Capital Stack Variations by Asset Class: Case Studies

Industry data from CBRE, JLL, and PwC/ULI gives us a window into how capital stacks flex across asset types, influenced by rising debt yields (62.8%) and global dry powder reserves (~$394 billion mid-2024).

Figure 10.1 illustrates capital stack profiles across office, industrial, and multifamily sectors. Figure 10.2 maps expected returns by layer for each asset class, highlighting where risk and reward cluster differently.

Figure 10.1 Capital stack profiles across office, industrial, and multifamily sectors.

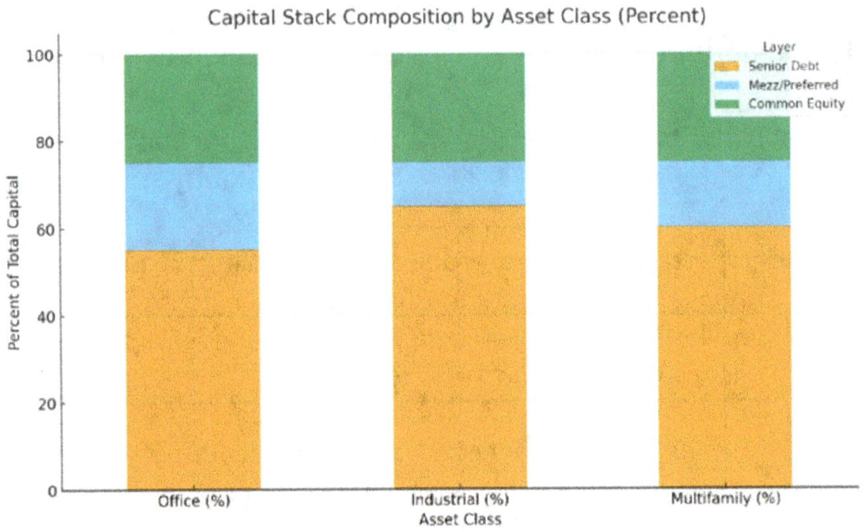

Note: This figure presents representative capital stack compositions for office, industrial, and multifamily real estate assets, including senior debt, mezzanine financing, preferred equity, and common equity. Capital structures reflect elevated financing costs in mid-2024, with senior debt yields averaging approximately 6.2%–6.8%. Differences across asset classes illustrate varying income durability, refinancing risk, and lender risk tolerance. Data are synthesized from industry research published by CBRE, JLL, and PwC/Urban Land Institute.

Figure 10.2 Expected returns by capital stack layer for office, industrial, and multifamily assets, illustrating differences in risk-reward concentration.

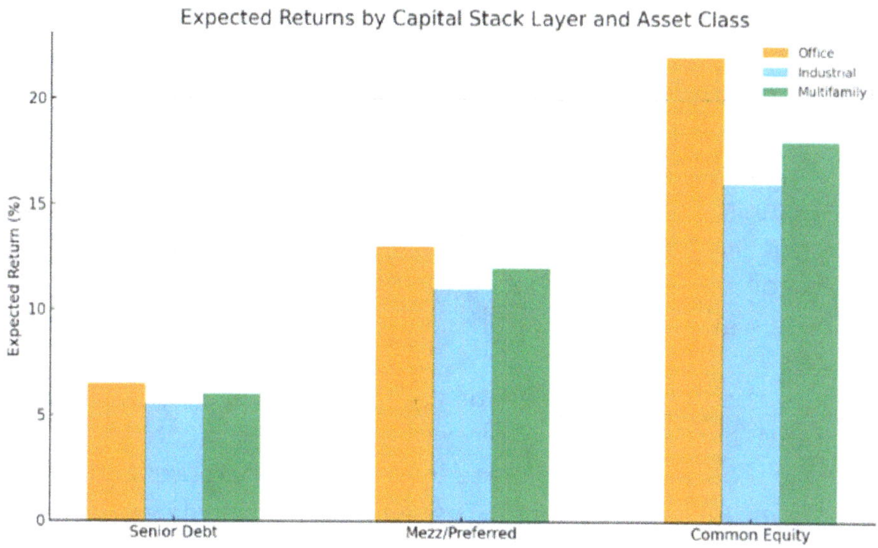

Note: This figure illustrates expected return ranges by position in the capital stack, senior debt, mezzanine debt, preferred equity, and common equity, across office, industrial, and multifamily real estate sectors. Higher return expectations are concentrated in junior capital layers, particularly within office assets, reflecting greater uncertainty related to valuation adjustment, demand shifts, and refinancing conditions. The analysis also incorporates the influence of elevated global private real estate dry powder, estimated at approximately $394 billion in mid-2024. Data are based on aggregated estimates from CBRE, JLL, and PwC/Urban Land Institute.

Office Adaptive Reuse

Let's look at what it takes to turn an outdated downtown office into a future-proof, income-producing asset. Imagine you're working with a 150,000 square foot, Class B office building right in the city core. The plan? Transform it into a flexible mix of office and lab space, designed to appeal to tenants who want adaptive layouts and specialized infrastructure. The numbers are substantial: you're committing to a $45 million acquisition, plus another $6.5 million in capital expenditures planned over a three-year repositioning (JLL, 2025c).

Now, let's break down the capital stack, a term we use to describe how all the funding sources fit together. In this structure, 55% of the capital comes from senior debt, which gives your project leverage but keeps your borrowing costs manageable. Next, 20% is covered by mezzanine or preferred equity, which sits in a riskier spot in the stack but provides flexibility and additional funding. The remaining 25% is common equity, what you and your partners put in, targeted for those higher potential returns.

Because the office sector is still navigating uncertainty, with rising cap rates and undeniable repositioning risk, projects like these typically require a heavier presence of subordinated capital (mezz and preferred) to get financed. That risk, in turn, translates into more ambitious IRR targets. Here, you're aiming for 18% to 25% internal rates of return. Achieving those numbers means executing your repositioning plan with precision, finding the right tenant mix, and staying nimble as the broader office market evolves (JLL, 2025c).

Industrial Last-Mile Logistics

Let's switch gears and talk about industrial, specifically, the "last-mile" distribution centers that have become critical in the age of e-commerce. Picture a recently built, 350,000 square foot distribution facility. It's valued at $78 million, operating at an attractive 8% cap rate. What makes this play appealing is the strength of your tenants—think institutional-grade covenants that help you sleep at night, even when the market gets choppy (CBRE, 2025c).

Debt markets are still quite supportive for deals like these. You can secure senior debt for about 65% of the capital structure at a cost of 5.5%. To round out the stack, you might layer in 10% mezzanine financing at about 11%, and complete the capital base with 25% common equity.

Because industrial assets have proven surprisingly resilient, tight vacancy rates, consistent tenant demand, and minimal obsolescence, your return targets are more conservative but still attractive. For your equity slice, expect to chase IRRs in the 14% to 18% range, which reflects both steady cash flow and strong exit prospects as the logistics sector continues to mature (CBRE, 2025c).

Multifamily Value-Add Garden Apartments

Now, let's zoom in on the multifamily world and explore the value-add playbook, this time with a Sun Belt property, a 220-unit garden apartment complex priced at $44 million. The plan here is straightforward but compelling: invest roughly $6 million into upgrades and renovations aimed at boosting the property's NOI and repositioning it as a market leader.

With a targeted cap rate of 9.1% and a five-year investment horizon, the deal is structured with 60% senior debt (average coupon near 6%), 15% mezzanine or preferred equity (around 12%), and the remaining 25% as common equity.

Why do we like this setup? It gives you leverage without stretching risk too far. Senior lenders get paid first, while the mezz/preferred slice absorbs more risk in return for those higher yields. For equity investors, the IRR goal typically falls between 15% and 22%, but your realized returns will heavily depend on how successfully you execute your renovation program and on the state of the refinancing market when your hold period ends (Berkadia, 2025).

In all three scenarios, the mix of financing structures, risk tolerances, and sector fundamentals tells the story. The common thread: in today's market, a sharp eye for execution and the agility to adapt quickly are what separate the winners from the crowd.

10.7 Practical Notes on Structuring and Governance

Building a winning capital stack means aligning sponsor and investor incentives, stress testing debt covenants, and using hybrid capital wisely. Tiered promotes motivate GP performance, while flexibility in preferred equity coupons helps manage dilution and investor appetite. Market dynamics shift fast: industrial's robust fundamentals justify more senior leverage, but office demands subordinate layers due to leasing uncertainties.

10.8 Summary and Key Takeaways

The capital stack is your playbook for how risk, reward, and control are divvied up on every deal. Senior debt remains your reliable and cheapest layer, but rising rates and tighter underwriting push you to blend mezzanine and preferred equity creatively. Common equity sits where risk and reward peak, with promote structures bringing sponsor incentives into sharp focus. Managing your weighted average cost of capital (WACC) and building cushions with DSCR and debt yield metrics are crucial navigation tools for today's market, characterized by senior debt rates near 5%-7%, debt yields close to 9.9%, and nearly $400 billion in dry powder available globally.

10.9 Transition to Part IV: Portfolio Strategy and Risk Management

With capital stacking dynamics under your belt, it's time to zoom out. Part IV explores portfolio strategy and risk management, revealing how investors diversify across markets and asset classes to weather volatile cycles. You'll see how strategic capital allocation, risk-adjusted returns, ESG, and stress testing keep portfolios resilient and growth-oriented. Chapter 11 kicks things off by unpacking portfolio construction essentials that drive total returns and durability.

References

Apartment Loan Store. (2024). *Multifamily loan rates overview.* https://apartmentloanstore.com

Berkadia. (2025). *Sun Belt multifamily investment strategies.*

CBRE. (2024). *U.S. real estate capital markets update 2024.* CBRE Research. https://www.cbre.com

CBRE. (2025c). *Industrial market outlook: Lending, cap rates, and resilience.*

Federal Reserve. (2024). *Senior loan officer opinion survey on bank lending practices.* https://www.federalreserve.gov

Hopkins, C. (2024, October 23). *Advanced capital stack structuring in private equity real estate to maximize asset liquidity.* https://chopkinsrealestate.com

JLL. (2024). *U.S. multifamily investment trends report.* JLL Research. https://www.jll.com

JLL. (2025c). *U.S. office adaptive reuse: Capital structures and risk.*

Leni. (2025). *Understanding the capital stack: Key concepts and insights.*

MSCI Real Assets. (2024). *Global capital trends report.* https://www.msci.com

PwC, & Urban Land Institute. (2024). *Emerging trends in real estate 2024.* PwC/ULI. https://www.pwc.com

SmartLand. (2022, January 5). *What to know about the capital stack in commercial real estate.* https://smartland.com

Wall Street Prep. (2023). *Capital stack: Real estate investment structure.* https://www.wallstreetprep.com

PART IV

Portfolio Strategy and Risk Management

OVERVIEW

Now that you've got the tools to pick and value individual properties, it's time to think bigger. Part IV shifts the spotlight from single assets to building and managing commercial real estate portfolios that are resilient, high-performing, and built to last. When your holdings grow, success isn't just about finding great properties anymore, it's about crafting portfolios that balance risk and reward, capture long-term growth, and perform steadily through every twist and turn of the market cycle.

In this section, we'll walk you through the strategies used by institutional investors, private equity firms, and savvy family offices to diversify risk, manage volatility, and protect capital. We combine what you've learned about analysis and valuation with a broader, strategic view, covering portfolio construction, risk mitigation, performance boosting, and responsible investing.

Across three detailed chapters, we guide you on how to:

- ☐ Allocate capital smartly across geographies and property types,
- ☐ Identify, measure, and manage risk at both the property and portfolio levels, and
- ☐ Weave sustainability, ESG principles, and responsible investing into your strategy to build lasting value.

Mastering these elements helps you design portfolios that adapt and thrive, while aligning with evolving global expectations.

Overview of Chapters

Chapter 11 – Portfolio Construction

Here, you'll learn how to architect CRE portfolios that weather downturns and tap into structural growth drivers. We dive into:

- ☐ Spreading risk across regions, metros, and submarkets
- ☐ Diversifying across property types and operating models
- ☐ Weighting your portfolio based on risk, expected returns, and how assets correlate
- ☐ Keeping your finger on the pulse with rolling forecasts and key performance indicators
- ☐ Blending real estate with stocks, bonds, and alternatives for a balanced multi-asset approach
- ☐ Using scenario analysis, Monte Carlo simulations, and forward-looking analytics to squeeze the most from your portfolio

You'll see how top managers mix stable core assets with higher-growth value-add and opportunistic plays to keep portfolios strong across market cycles.

Chapter 12 — Risk and Return Analysis

Risk is real, and this chapter arms you with a clear framework to track and manage it on all levels. We break risks into three buckets:

- ☐ Market Risk: think interest rates, economic swings, supply-demand shifts, and cap rate quirks
- ☐ Financial Risk: covering leverage, refinancing, debt structure, and liquidity crunches
- ☐ Operational Risk: tenant credit, lease turnovers, property management, and capital expenses

You'll get practical tools like sensitivity analyses, downside-case modeling, and income/expense stress tests. We also cover hedging strategies with interest rate instruments and insurance, plus how to use performance metrics like Sharpe ratios and risk-adjusted IRR. Real case studies illustrate how disciplined risk management protects your capital and keeps your portfolio durable for the long haul.

Chapter 13 – ESG, Sustainability, and Responsible Investing

Sustainability isn't just buzz, it's a must-have in CRE today. This chapter digs into why integrating environmental, social, and governance (ESG) factors is good for both your portfolio and the planet. We cover:

- ☐ Financial gains from energy efficiency, retrofits, and green building certifications
- ☐ How ESG leadership helps you keep tenants longer, command rent premiums, and boost occupancy
- ☐ The rising tide of regulations and reporting standards worldwide, from carbon disclosures to building performance rules
- ☐ Social impact angles like community engagement and equitable development
- ☐ Governance best practices that cut reputational and operational risks

You'll learn how sustainability shapes investment performance, risk management, and long-term value, making it an essential part of your toolkit.

Key Takeaways from Part IV

- ☐ Building a strong portfolio matters more for long-term success than picking any one property. Diversification across types and geographies smooths volatility and lifts risk-adjusted returns.
- ☐ Managing risk well means having a rigorous framework with stress tests, scenario planning, and a mix of absolute and risk-adjusted metrics.
- ☐ ESG and sustainability are no longer optional, they influence tenant demand, capital access, regulatory exposure, and asset resilience.

- ☐ A smartly structured portfolio balances income stability with growth, matching your capital deployment to your goals, market conditions, and risk appetite.
- ☐ When you pair solid portfolio strategy with disciplined risk management, you create real estate portfolios built to thrive through both booms and busts.

CHAPTER 11

Portfolio Construction

Introduction

You're about to dive into how investors build commercial real estate (CRE) portfolios that strike the right balance between return and risk. It's not just about buying properties randomly, you thoughtfully diversify across locations, property types, and strategies. Plus, you actively manage leverage, maintain liquidity, and lean on quantitative scenario modeling to squeeze the most out of total returns. This chapter walks through each step and backs it all up with real-world data and market practices, so it's grounded equally in theory and what's actually happening out there.

Building a CRE portfolio isn't simply plugging numbers into a formula. Think of it more like crafting something unique, where success depends on carefully choosing the right mix of geographic exposure, property types, and investment strategies. Along the way, you keep a close eye on leverage and liquidity to avoid surprises, while modeling helps you navigate uncertainty. Throughout this chapter, I'll bring all that to life with empirical evidence and insights from the market (Invesco, n.d.; NCREIF, 2025; Trepp, 2024). So, get ready to build a blueprint you can apply yourself.

11.1 Rationale for Diversified CRE Portfolios

11.1.1 Why Diversify Your CRE Portfolio?

Here's something to keep front and center: real estate is a tangible, income-producing asset that behaves differently from stocks and bonds. Over decades, private real estate typically delivers steady income returns, think the yield generated by rents, with lower short-term volatility compared to equities. Why? Because real estate valuations don't bounce around daily like stocks do. Instead, they're updated more slowly through appraisals, which smooth out the bumps (Invesco, n.d.; NCREIF, 2025).

That gives you an edge: while industrial properties might be booming, office markets could simultaneously be softening. These out-of-sync regional and sector cycles inside CRE let you reduce overall portfolio risk through diversification (Trepp, 2024; CBRE, 2024).

The data backs this up. Over the past 20 years, private real estate income returns have hovered around the mid-single digits (Invesco, n.d.). Meanwhile, when you look at risk-adjusted returns through Sharpe ratios, industrial real estate often comes out ahead of other property types. This helps justify why CRE deserves its own slice of your portfolio pie, separate from stocks and bonds.

11.1.2 Diversify Across Property Types: Why It Matters

Each property sector is driven by unique economic forces and demand patterns:

- ☐ **Industrial/Logistics** has thrived alongside the explosive growth of e-commerce and shifts in global supply chains. This has led to historic highs in occupancy rates and strong risk-adjusted returns (Trepp, 2024).
- ☐ **Multifamily housing** is fundamentally tied to population growth and housing needs. It stands out for its resilience, often weathering downturns better than offices or retail (CBRE, 2024).

- **Office properties** face headwinds and tailwinds alike, with remote work trends reshaping demand. You see vastly different performance pockets depending on the location and corporate space strategies (CBRE, 2024).
- **Retail real estate** is split: neighborhood retail continues to perform as a community staple, while large malls struggle against changing consumer habits and online competition (CBRE, 2024).

What's fascinating is how these dynamics shape investor behavior. Between 2020 and 2024, many allocators boosted industrial and multifamily exposure while scaling back-office bets in response to pandemic-related changes in work and shopping habits (CBRE, 2024; Trepp, 2024). You can think of this as nimble portfolio management reacting to real economic shifts.

11.1.3 The Power of Geographic Diversification

Location is more than where you put your money, it's a risk management tool. Factors like local employment trends, housing supply, and migration flows cause rent growth and property cap rates to shift unevenly across regions. If you concentrate all your investments in a single city or market, your portfolio is vulnerable to specific risks like a downturn in that local economy or overly aggressive new construction.

Instead, blending gateway markets (think New York, San Francisco) with faster-growing secondary and tertiary markets can smooth out those localized risks. Market data regularly shows that cap rate movements, a key driver of property valuation, vary widely by geography (CBRE, 2024). This strategy helps you balance the potential for higher growth against idiosyncratic risks, ultimately stabilizing your portfolio returns.

11.1.4 Combining Strategies from Core to Opportunistic

In today's commercial real estate investing world, portfolios aren't just about stuffing capital into different properties and hoping they perform. Instead, smart investors design multi-layered strategies that balance risk and return through tailored approaches across the spectrum, from the safest core assets to the high-risk, high-reward opportunistic plays. Understanding these strategies and how they fit together is crucial to building a portfolio that can navigate market ups and downs while capturing growth.

Core and Core-Plus:

At the conservative end of the spectrum, core investments focus on stable, income-focused assets. These are typically high-quality, well-located properties that are fully leased to creditworthy tenants, often under long-term leases. Core assets use relatively low leverage, usually below 50% loan-to-value, which reduces refinancing risk and helps provide steady cash flow. Think of these as "set-it-and-forget-it" holdings: they won't make headlines with dizzying appreciation, but their predictable income and lower volatility make them the foundation of many institutional portfolios.

Core-plus is a slight step up in risk and return, mixing mostly stabilized properties with some elements of income or value improvement potential. They often carry moderate leverage, maybe in the 50-60% LTV range, and offer opportunities to enhance returns through light asset management or operational improvements without taking on too much development risk. This strategy balances income stability with modest growth upside, making it attractive for investors who want solid returns without the roller coaster (McKinsey & Company, 2024).

Value-Add:

Value-add strategies are the sweet spot for investors willing to take on moderate risk in exchange for higher returns. Value-add properties usually require active management, such as renovating units, repositioning buildings for different uses, or aggressively leasing vacant space, to increase cash flow and property values. These opportunities often emerge in markets undergoing transformation or where outdated properties can be upgraded to meet evolving tenant demands.

Leverage ratios here tend to be higher than core, often in the 55-65% range, reflecting the additional risk of renovations and market timing. But with that risk comes potential reward: value-add funds aim for double-digit internal rates of return by capitalizing on the gap between current income and what the property can generate after improvements. Importantly, value-add investor skill and operational expertise become major drivers of success in this bracket.

Opportunistic:

At the riskiest end, opportunistic investments cater to those seeking the highest possible returns and willing to stomach greater volatility. These plays often involve ground-up developments, major redevelopments, distressed property turnarounds, or repositioning assets in markets with substantial growth potential but also higher uncertainty. Opportunistic capital is typically highly leveraged, with loan-to-value ratios exceeding 60-70%, reflecting the complexity and longer timelines involved.

Because these projects carry increased execution, market, and financing risks, returns are expected to be correspondingly higher. Investors in opportunistic strategies seek IRRs well above 15%, drawn by the possibility of outsized capital appreciation. But the volatility is real, these investments may take years to mature and depend heavily on market cycles and operational execution.

Why Mix Them?

A portfolio concentrated exclusively in one strategy type can suffer when that approach falls out of favor. For instance, a core-heavy portfolio might miss out on growth when markets are booming, while a portfolio overloaded with opportunistic risk could be devastated in a downturn.

By spreading capital across core, value-add, and opportunistic buckets, you achieve a smoother return profile over time. Core holdings provide ballast and steady income, value-add offers growth through active management, and opportunistic injects potential for outsized gains. This blend also helps maintain liquidity, as core assets tend to be easier to sell, providing capital that can redeploy to higher-risk strategies during opportunity windows.

In essence, combining these approaches lets you tailor exposure to risk and return on your terms, prepare for varying market conditions, and build a portfolio that is greater than the sum of its parts (McKinsey & Company, 2024).

11.2 CRE's Role in a Multi-Asset Portfolio

11.2.1 How CRE Helps Balance Risk and Return

When you're building a portfolio with stocks, bonds, and other asset classes, CRE provides a valuable diversification layer. Its long-term correlation with traditional public markets is modest, which means adding CRE can reduce overall volatility and offer better risk-adjusted returns (Fidelity, n.d.).

Not only that, but even publicly traded Real Estate Investment Trusts (REITs), though more correlated with equities than direct real estate, still give you some diversification benefits (Fidelity, n.d.). So, depending on your liquidity needs and risk appetite, mixing both private and public real estate exposure can be a smart move.

11.2.2 Navigating Liquidity Tradeoffs

Owning physical properties means you get premium income and governance control, but liquidity is a tradeoff, you can't unload assets instantly without potential loss in value. On the flip side, REITs and traded real estate instruments give you quick access to cash and portfolio rebalancing ease but expose you to stock market volatility.

Most savvy investors blend these approaches, creating a portfolio that's both stable through direct holdings and agile through liquid instruments. This balance allows you to respond to market shifts without losing the steady cash flow and control direct property ownership offers (Fidelity, n.d.).

11.3 Scenario Modeling and Portfolio Optimization: Your Portfolio's Playbook

Imagine having a detailed map to guide your portfolio through uncertainty. That's what scenario modeling gives you. You start by setting baseline assumptions like rent growth, vacancy, expense inflation, cap rates, and financing costs, drawing on historical data and current market surveys (NCREIF, 2025; CBRE, 2024).

Then, you test your portfolio's sensitivity to key factors, a 1% bump in cap rates can drastically lower property valuations, for example (CBRE, 2024). More advanced teams use Monte Carlo simulations to create a full range of potential outcomes, letting you understand not just expected returns, but risks like Value at Risk or expected shortfall.

From there, you optimize your portfolio, respecting limits on leverage, liquidity, and concentration, to maximize returns within your risk tolerance. This process isn't once-and-done; you refresh assumptions and stress tests regularly, quarterly or when markets shift sharply, to stay ahead of risk (CBRE, 2024; McKinsey & Company, 2024).

11.4 Case Study: Building a $100 Million Balanced Portfolio

Let's make this real with a $100 million portfolio example designed to hit a 7–9% net IRR over 7 to 10 years, while cutting volatility nearly in half compared to equity markets.

Here's a typical strategic allocation:

Table 11.1 A Balanced Portfolio

Strategy	Allocation	Capital ($M)	LTV	Year-1 Yield	Unlevered IRR
Core (Multifamily + Industrial)	40%	40	40%	4.5%	6-7%
Value-Add	30%	30	55%	5-6%	8-11%
Opportunistic	20%	20	65%	0%	12-16%
Public REIT Sleeve	10%	10	0%	3-4%	6-8%

This structure aligns well with institutional benchmarks and reflects a thoughtful balance between income, growth, and liquidity (CBRE, 2024; NCREIF, 2025).

Financial Assumptions and Performance Outlook

To build a realistic picture of how this portfolio might perform over the next decade, we start by laying out the key financial assumptions that drive income, expenses, valuation, and ultimately, returns. These assumptions aren't pulled out of thin air, they reflect historical averages and current market intelligence from leading real estate analytics firms (NCREIF, 2025; CBRE, 2024). Understanding each element helps make the portfolio's projected performance more transparent and actionable.

Rent and Expenses:

Annual rent growth is assumed at a steady 2.5%. This rate balances past real estate cycles with current trends in inflation, wage growth, and tenant demand. While rents rarely rise in a straight line, this smoothing assumption accounts for economic ups and downs. In stronger markets or expanding metro areas, rent growth can exceed this, while more mature or challenged locales may fall short. On the cost side, expense inflation is modeled at about 2% annually.

This includes rising maintenance costs, property taxes, utilities, and management fees. Together, these assumptions build a realistic baseline for Net Operating Income (NOI) growth, a crucial driver of property valuation.

1. **Vacancy and Exit Capitalization Rates:**
   Vacancy rates for core assets are expected to stabilize around 4-5%. This range reflects typical long-term occupancies for well-located, high-quality properties that attract creditworthy tenants. Vacancy directly impacts rental income, so maintaining these levels is crucial for predictable cash flow. The blended exit capitalization (cap) rate is assumed near 5.8%. The exit cap rate translates expected future income into sale price. While cap rates can fluctuate with interest rates and market sentiment, this assumption aligns with recent market averages for core-plus portfolios, balancing yield and risk upon disposition.

2. **Leverage Details:**
   This portfolio employs varying leverage across risk profiles to enhance returns while managing risk exposure. Core property segments carry a moderate loan-to-value ratio (LTV) of about 40%. This relatively conservative leverage limit preserves downside protection and lower debt servicing costs. By contrast, value-add and opportunistic investments often use higher leverage, here, the opportunistic tranche is modeled near 65% LTV. Higher leverage can amplify returns but introduces refinancing and debt coverage risk, especially if market conditions deteriorate. Striking the right leverage balance is integral to portfolio resilience.

3. **Interest Rate Assumptions:**
   The cost of capital on core properties is estimated at roughly 5%, reflecting current lending environments and typical long-term fixed-rate mortgage structures. For opportunistic projects, where leverage is higher and the risk profile more complex, interest rates tend to be elevated, factoring in floating-rate debt or bridge financing premiums. Interest

costs significantly affect cash flow, particularly during periods of rising rates, so anticipating these inputs is critical when projecting returns.

4. **Projected Income Growth and Exit Value:**
   Under these assumptions, the portfolio's NOI steadily climbs from about $3.1 million in Year 1 to nearly $4 million by Year 10. This growth is fueled by rent escalations outpacing expense inflation, aided by stable occupancy rates. NOI growth underpins property valuation and equity returns.

   Upon exit, after accounting for debt repayment, transaction costs, and potential fees, the portfolio's value is projected to realize between $38 million and $40 million in net proceeds. This equates to an equity Internal Rate of Return (IRR) in the range of 8% to 8.5%, and an equity multiple around 1.8x. These figures fit comfortably within the range experienced by long-term private real estate funds historically, representing a reasonable blend of income and appreciation returns (NCREIF, 2025).

Stress Testing and Risk Resilience:

To make sure these optimistic numbers aren't just wishful thinking; the portfolio is subjected to rigorous stress scenarios. Imagine a sharp increase in financing costs, interest rates jump by 200 basis points, and at the same time, cap rates widen by 150 basis points, reducing property valuations. These shocks often coincide in economic downturns or periods of monetary tightening.

Under these tougher conditions, the portfolio's IRR would decline but importantly, it doesn't collapse. Why? It's largely thanks to the steady income generated from the core holdings, which act as a cushion by providing consistent cash flow even when markets are volatile (CBRE, 2024; Trepp, 2024). This income helps meet debt obligations and delays forced sales, giving the portfolio room to recover as markets normalize.

This detailed set of assumptions and outcomes illustrates how blending income stability, prudent leverage, and diversification constructs a portfolio that aims to deliver solid, risk-controlled returns over the long haul. It also underscores the importance of continuous monitoring and stress testing to stay prepared for shifts in market dynamics.

11.5 Putting Risk Management Front and Center

Risk management isn't just a final step or a compliance item you tick off. For commercial real estate portfolios, it's the heart of sustained success. Understanding risk in all its dimensions, constantly testing your exposure, and deploying smart defensive measures help you avoid nasty surprises and keep your portfolio strong through market cycles. The goal isn't to eliminate risk, that's impossible, but to anticipate it, measure it, and handle it thoughtfully.

11.5.1 Identifying Your Risks

The first step to effective risk management is knowing exactly what kinds of risks your portfolio faces, and how they can impact performance. Risks come in many forms:

- **Market Risks:** These are risks driven by changes in economic conditions and investor sentiment. Falling rents caused by an economic downturn, or rising capitalization rates that lower property valuations, are prime examples. Vacancy spikes or a sudden drop in tenant demand also fall under this category. These factors directly affect your income streams and property values.
- **Financial Risks:** Shifts in interest rates, credit market tightening, or refinancing challenges affect how much borrowing costs you bear and your available capital. Rising rates can increase debt service expenses and reduce cash flow, while refinancing risk arises if lenders pull back or demand stricter terms.

- **Operational Risks:** These include issues inside the property itself or tenant-related problems. Unexpected maintenance costs, think emergency roof repairs or HVAC failures, or tenant defaults on lease payments cause cash flow disruptions. A property manager's effectiveness and the landlord-tenant relationship play a big role here.

Being clear on these categories is just the start. The real power comes from modeling how these risks might play out in different scenarios. Scenario analysis lets you stress test the portfolio against simultaneous shocks, like a rent drop combined with rising interest rates, and reveal your vulnerabilities. Once identified, you can adjust your strategy, reduce exposure, or build buffers in weaker areas so the portfolio withstands shocks without large losses (Trepp, 2024; CBRE, 2024).

11.5.2 Regular Stress Testing

Identifying risks is ongoing, markets don't stand still, and neither should your risk analysis. Stress testing is your tool for keeping a finger on the pulse of portfolio health.

Imagine simulating a sudden 200 basis point increase in interest rates, how does that impact your debt service coverage ratio? What if vacancy rates spike unexpectedly by 5%, or regional employment takes a dive due to business closures or industry shifts? By running these "what-if" scenarios regularly, quarterly or any time market conditions turn uncertain, you quantify how much value or income could vanish under stress.

These stress tests spotlight the portfolio's breaking points early, giving you the chance to act before pressures turn into crises. They inform decisions like trimming riskier holdings, renegotiating financing terms, or setting aside cash reserves. They also provide vital data for communicating risk to investors, lenders, and board members, building credibility and trust (CBRE, 2024).

11.5.3 Defensive Tools: Hedging and Structure

Once risks are mapped and stress-tested, you need practical tools to defend the portfolio:

- **Interest Rate Hedging:** Since rising interest rates can quickly erode cash flow, investors often use derivatives like interest rate caps or swaps to lock in borrowing costs. Caps provide protection above a certain rate threshold, limiting upside cost exposure, while swaps can fix rates for extended periods. Your choice depends on deal structure, accounting treatment, and risk tolerance (Chatham Financial, n.d.; Clifford Chance, 2023).
- **Lease and Tenant Diversification:** On the operational front, stagger the lease expirations across tenants and property types to avoid large income gaps if multiple leases expire simultaneously. Diversifying tenant industries reduces sector-specific risk, such as a sharp hit should a major corporate tenant lay off workers or default.
- **Liquidity Reserves:** Maintaining adequate liquidity is a lifeline in rough patches. You can hold cash, credit lines, or liquid real estate investments such as publicly traded REITs as a cushion. This liquidity allows you to cover capital calls, unexpected maintenance, or refinance maturities without forced asset sales at depressed prices (Fidelity, n.d.).
- **Strong Accounting and Compliance:** Accurate financial reporting and compliance keep risks related to accounting standards and derivative management under control. For instance, following IFRS or GAAP guidance on financial instruments helps avoid surprises in earnings and ensures your hedging strategies are properly documented and effective (KPMG, n.d.).

11.6 Governance and Operational Best Practices

Governance isn't just ticking boxes; it's the backbone of lasting portfolio performance and risk control.

Start with an Investment Policy Statement (IPS) that clearly defines your portfolio's strategic targets, allocation ranges between property types and strategies, caps on leverage and concentration, and minimum liquidity buffers. The IPS sets the guardrails you don't want to cross.

Monitoring and rebalancing are essential processes: review and adjust your portfolio allocations quarterly or whenever significant valuation changes or capital inflows/outflows occur. This keeps your portfolio aligned with risk and return goals.

Scenario models and stress tests should be updated at least twice a year, or more frequently during volatile markets, to reflect shifting economic realities.

Real-time tracking of derivative exposures helps prevent unexpected risks from building unnoticed. Dashboards presenting key performance and risk metrics, including Net Operating Income (NOI), vacancy rates, Weighted Average Lease Term (WALT), Debt Service Coverage Ratio (DSCR), cap rates, and Value at Risk (VaR), should be accessible to management teams and board committees. Transparent reporting helps everyone make informed decisions quickly.

11.7 Moving on to Chapter 12: Risk and Return Analysis

With this foundation in place, solid risk identification, stress testing discipline, hedging strategies, and rigorous governance, you're set to dive deeper into portfolio analytics. Chapter 12 will walk through techniques for measuring portfolio risk and return under uncertainty, refining hedging approaches, and safeguarding your capital against market volatility. The frameworks we've established here create the conditions for that deeper analysis and smarter decision-making (Chatham Financial, n.d.).

References

CBRE. (2024). *H2 2024 Cap Rate Survey* [Report]. https://www.cbre.com/insights/reports/h2-2024-cap-rate-survey

CBRE. (2024). *U.S. Real Estate Market Outlook 2024*. https://www.cbre.com/insights/reports/us-real-estate-market-outlook-2024

Chatham Financial. (n.d.). Interest rate swap FAQs for CRE investors. https://www.chathamfinancial.com/insights/interest-rate-swap-faqs-for-cre-investors

Clifford Chance. (2023, October). Hedging in real estate finance transactions: From caps to swaps [Briefing]. https://www.cliffordchance.com/content/dam/cliffordchance/briefings/2023/10/briefing-hedging-in-real-estate-finance.pdf

Fidelity. (n.d.). REITs: An underutilized portfolio diversifier [White paper]. https://www.fidelity.com/learning-center/investment-products/fixed-income-bonds/reit-portfolio-diversification

Invesco. (n.d.). The historical benefits of U.S. private real estate [Insight]. https://www.invesco.com/us/financial-products/real-estate

JPMorgan. (2024). Commercial real estate investment strategies [Insights]. https://www.jpmorgan.com/insights/research/real-estate-investment-strategies

KPMG. (n.d.). Accounting for derivative financial instruments. https://home.kpmg/xx/en/home/insights/2020/07/ifrs-9-accounting-for-derivatives.html

McKinsey & Company. (2024). *Global private markets review 2024* [PDF]. https://www.mckinsey.com/industries/private-equity-and-principal-investors/our-insights/global-private-markets-review-2024

NCREIF. (2025). Index returns: NPI and NFI snapshot [Data]. https://www.ncreif.org/indices/property-index-returns/

Trepp. (2024). Are CRE investment returns losing their luster? https://www.trepp.com/insights/are-cre-investment-returns-losing-their-luster

Trepp. (2024). Commercial real estate performance and market trends report 2024. https://www.trepp.com/insights/commercial-real-estate-performance-market-trends-report-2024

CHAPTER

12 Risk and Return Analysis

Introduction

Welcome back! In the last chapter, we mapped out a solid framework for spotting and managing the wide range of risks lurking in commercial real estate (CRE). Now, we're taking that a step further. This chapter dives into how you can not only identify but also measure and actively manage those risks, market swings, financial turbulence, and operational challenges, that ultimately shape your returns. Managing a CRE portfolio today is less about guessing where risks hide and more about quantifying how much they can move the needle on your cash flows, valuations, and what you'll actually make or lose.

It's no secret among pros: institutions who underestimate big movers like interest rate jumps, refinancing crunches, or tenant credit problems often end up underperforming through cycles (Geltner et al., 2021). So, this isn't some fancy add-on. It's an essential part of professional portfolio management, one we're about to unpack with tools like stress testing, scenario analysis, and hedging.

12.1 Market Risk: Understanding Exposure to Macro and Local Cycles

When you think about market risk, you're really thinking about all the big, outside forces constantly pushing and pulling your investments. Imagine GDP growth rates swinging up or down, job markets tightening or loosening, waves of people relocating to new regions, or interest rates making unexpected jumps. These huge economic and demographic forces aren't just headlines, they directly shape the rents you can charge, how many tenants stick around, and ultimately, what your properties are worth.

Market risk plays out on two levels: the broad macroeconomic trends affecting entire regions or countries, and the local, microeconomic realities that can differ dramatically from one city or neighborhood to another. A city thriving with new tech jobs will likely see growing rents and tighter vacancies, while an older industrial town might face stagnation or decline. Your job as an investor or manager is to understand these layers and how they combine to impact your portfolio's cash flow and valuation.

12.1.1 Rent and Occupancy Volatility

Not all property types respond to market swings the same way, and that's a critical dynamic to grasp. For example, during the early months of the COVID-19 pandemic, urban multifamily housing in major metros saw rents fall by 2-4%. This dip reflected trends like urban outmigration and work-from-home shifting priorities in living space. Meanwhile, suburban and Sunbelt markets, with their appeal for more space and affordability, saw rents explode with double-digit growth (Yardi Matrix, 2021).

The office sector took an even bigger hit, with vacancy rates climbing from around 12% pre-pandemic to over 18% by 2023. The rise in remote work fundamentally changed the office real estate equation, driving prolonged vacancies and renegotiations (JLL, 2023). In stark contrast, industrial properties became a clear winner during the same timeframe, with rents rising more than 40%. Why? The global supply chain disruptions and surge in e-commerce forced warehouses and distribution centers to be in high demand (Prologis, 2023).

This kind of divergent performance underscores why placing all your eggs in one sector, or one market, is a gamble. By diversifying across property types and geographic areas, you spread your exposure to these cyclical and sectoral swings. When one property type suffers, another may be booming, smoothing the volatility in your portfolio's total cash flows and valuations over time.

12.1.2 Cap-Rate Movements and Valuation Sensitivity

If rents and occupancy are the pulse, cap rates are the heartbeat of your portfolio's health, and they can be ruthless. Cap rates don't just fluctuate, they often respond sharply to shifts in interest rates, market sentiment, and risk appetite, dragging property values along.

Imagine you own a property generating $5 million a year in net operating income (NOI). If the market value is calculated using a 5% cap rate, that property would be worth $100 million ($5M ÷ 0.05). Sounds solid, right? But suppose cap rates rise to 6.5% because interest rates climbed or investors got more risk-averse. Now that same property's value nosedives to about $76.9 million ($5M ÷ 0.065), a staggering 23% drop. All this happens even if your income stream didn't change one bit (Green Street, 2023).

This sensitivity means that cap-rate movements can often overshadow operational performance in determining your portfolio's short to medium-term value. It also highlights a tough reality: your portfolio's worth can fluctuate wildly simply based on market pricing changes beyond your direct control.

Understanding how your portfolio's overall value changes with cap-rate shifts, and which properties are most sensitive, lets you manage these risks more proactively. That might mean targeting assets with longer lease terms, more inflation-linked rents, or markets less prone to sudden cap-rate swings.

This deeper dive helps you see market risk not as a vague concept but as a living, shifting force that requires constant attention and smart positioning. It's why savvy CRE professionals watch economic trends, demographics, interest rates, and micro-market data closely, and why diversification is one of their best defenses.

12.2 Financial Risk: Debt, Refinancing, and Liquidity Exposure

When it comes to risk that really threatens your cash and capital, financial risk often stands out sharpest. It's the danger that the money side of your deal, how much you borrow, what you pay in interest, when you have to pay it back, and whether you have cash ready for surprises, can spiral out of control. You might have a property that's performing well, but if the debt load gets too heavy or if refinancing options dry up, even solid assets can turn toxic overnight.

12.2.1 Interest-Rate Risk

Interest-rate risk is the wild card that shook the market between 2022 and 2023. In just a short period, interest rates shot up more than 450 basis points, an epic move in the borrowing world (Mortgage Bankers Association, 2023). For floating-rate loans, that translated into debt servicing costs that doubled or even tripled, sometimes catching investors completely off guard.

Consider trying to manage your cash flow with an expected $1 million in annual debt payments, then, overnight, that figure balloons to $3 million simply because benchmark rates soared. Properties that were once comfortably cash flow positive started teetering on very thin margins, and some couldn't cover their debt payments at all. That situation triggered capital calls, refinancing stress, and, in some cases, fire sales at distressed prices. For anyone punching above their leverage weight, this was a wake-up call that interest-rate risk is very real and costly.

12.2.2 Refinancing Risk

Refinancing is often make-or-break in real estate, especially for folks chasing value-add or opportunistic returns where the plan is to boost a property's income and then refinance out debt. But when markets get tight, lenders change the rules quickly. Loan-to-value (LTV) limits can tighten from a comfortable 70–75% down to

55-60%, and debt service coverage ratio (DSCR) hurdles ratchet up, meaning you need more cash flow just to qualify. On top of that, property appraisals tend to catch a cold and drop, making it harder to meet these tougher loan requirements.

The nasty result is the dreaded refinancing gap. You owe, say, $35 million when a loan matures, but now the bank will only lend $27 million. You need to find that $8 million from somewhere, often your own equity pocket, right when the market conditions are at their worst. This gap can force tough decisions: sell at a bad time, bring in new capital, or risk default. Either way, it's why planning refinancing well in advance and staying liquid is a cornerstone of smart portfolio management.

12.2.3 Liquidity Risk

Liquidity risk means not having cash or access to credit when you absolutely need it. This can come in many forms, from unexpected tenant turnover requiring capital for fixes, to bigger challenges like refinancing shocks, rent dips, or major repairs.

Sound liquidity management is less flashy but no less critical. Top institutions recommend keeping 5-10% of your portfolio value liquid, whether in cash, undrawn credit lines, or invested in easily sellable real estate securities (PwC, 2022). Having that buffer means you can weather storms without panicking and selling assets at fire-sale prices. If you don't, you risk being forced into desperate moves, often at the worst possible moment.

12.3 Operational Risk: Asset-Level Performance and Management

Switching gears, operational risks are those quieter but no less dangerous pressures happening at the property level. These are things you might not always see upfront but that steadily erode cash flow and value if left unchecked.

12.3.1 Tenant Risk and Credit Concentration

Tenant issues are a huge factor. When one or two tenants make up a big chunk of your rental income, their financial health directly impacts yours. Think of retail centers hit hard by Sears or Toys "R" Us filing for bankruptcy, not just a news story but a real income cliff when huge chunks of rents evaporate (CBRE, 2020). That's why a concentrated tenant base is a red flag. Diversification across tenants, industries, and lease term structures helps stabilize income and reduce sweat-inducing shocks.

12.3.2 Lease Expiration Cliffs

Lease expirations clustered in one year become financial cliffs. If a big group of tenants leave or renew in a weak market, you face a rent roll drop combined with higher tenant improvement costs and longer vacancy periods. It's the classic supply-demand mismatch that slashes cash flows. Spreading lease expirations more evenly over time helps smooth income and operational risk.

12.3.3 Operating Cost Inflation

Finally, operating costs often creep up stealthily but decisively. Utility bills rise, insurance premiums spike, especially in areas prone to natural disasters, and maintenance expenses climb with aging assets. For instance, insurance premiums in parts of the U.S. exposed to hurricanes or wildfires jumped over 30% from 2020 to 2023 (Fitch Ratings, 2023). These cost increases slowly eat away at your NOI, limiting cash flows even when rents stay steady.

12.4 Tools for Quantifying Risk: Stress Testing and Scenario Modeling

You know the risks are out there, but how do you measure their impact before they hit your portfolio? That's where stress testing and scenario modeling come in. They help you convert qualitative fears into quantified financial impacts.

12.4.1 Sensitivity Analysis

Sensitivity analysis is like poking each risk factor individually with a stick to see how much it can upset your returns. For example, you test a 5-10% drop in rents, or an increase in cap rates by 50 to 150 basis points, or a spike in operating expenses. This method reveals which factors are the biggest levers in your portfolio's value and cash flow, so you know where to focus risk management efforts.

12.4.2 Scenario Modeling

Scenario modeling goes a step further, combining multiple shocks simultaneously. Imagine a recession where rents fall, vacancies rise, interest rates spike, and some tenants default, all rolling together. Institutional investors use sophisticated models blending economic data, GDP growth, credit spreads, employment rates, with property-specific assumptions to simulate a range of future paths from best case to severe downturn (MSCI Real Assets, 2022). This holistic approach captures the compounding effects of risks hitting at once, offering a truly realistic lens on potential outcomes.

12.5 Hedging Strategies: Protecting Capital

Once you understand your risks and can measure them, actively protecting your capital becomes paramount. Here are proven tactics that investors use:

12.5.1 Interest-Rate Hedges

Interest-rate caps, swaps, and swaptions are financial tools that let you lock in borrowing costs or place a ceiling on how high floating rates can rise. During the volatile 2022-2023 period, borrowers who used rate caps avoided some of the worst debt service spikes, keeping their cash flow under control (Chatham Financial, n.d.; Clifford Chance, 2023).

12.5.2 Loan Structuring and Portfolio Design

Smart loan structuring smooths risk over time. Ladder your debt maturities so you're not refinancing everything at once. Cultivate strong lender relationships early to ease negotiations when markets tighten. Dial down leverage on riskier assets and lean towards fixed-rate debt when rates climb, this locks in predictable costs. And don't forget: maintain refinancing reserves or liquid cushions to provide a financial breathing room during tougher cycles.

12.6 Case Example: Managing Refinancing and Liquidity Risk in a Rising-Rate Environment

Say you bought a value-add multifamily property in 2020 for $50 million with a 70% LTV bridge loan at 3.5% floating rates. Your plan? Renovate, raise rents, refinance at year three with a 1.3× DSCR. But then rates spike to near 7%, lending tightens, DSCR demands rise to 1.25×, and your property value drops 10%. Now, max LTV is 60%, but you've got a $35 million balloon coming due with only $27 million possible from new debt, an $8 million gap.

What do you do? Maybe buy a short-term rate cap, tap liquidity and credit lines, accelerate renovations, and sell non-core assets. It's not pretty, but this kind of nimble, coordinated approach helps you dodge fire sales and stabilize your investment (MSCI Real Assets, 2022).

12.7 Monte Carlo Return Simulations: Methodology and Purpose

Monte Carlo simulations have become a staple in commercial real estate risk management. To understand how this works, imagine running 10,000 randomly varied 10-year performance scenarios on a hypothetical $100 million portfolio. The model starts with an average annual return target of 8% and assumes a volatility around

10%, reflecting a balanced mix of core, value-add, and opportunistic investments.

Crucially, the simulation factors in random shocks, like a 10% probability each year of a sharp 20% drop in property values triggered by spikes in interest rates or operational setbacks. The model also incorporates occasional "stressed" years that mimic recessions, characterized by lower returns and greater volatility. The value of this approach is that it reveals not just average expected returns but the full spectrum of outcomes, including the dreaded "tail risks"—extreme losses that can severely impact capital. These insights help investors establish better risk limits, reserves, and hedging strategies (MSCI Real Assets, 2022).

12.8 Simulation Results: Key Statistics and Visuals

After crunching through those 10,000 simulated paths, the results typically show a distribution of returns like the one summarized in Table 12.1:

Table 12.1 Key Statistics

Statistic	Value
Mean Annualized Return	6.6%
Median Annualized Return	6.3%
5th Percentile Return	-3.0%
95th Percentile Return	15.3%
Average Equity Multiple	1.68×
Equity Multiple ≤ 1.0	27% chance

The distribution takes the shape of a bell curve centered near single-digit annual returns but with a distinct left tail that tells a cautionary story. This tail reflects scenarios where shocks to interest rates and economic recessions push returns into negative territory. As shown in Figure 12.1, this left tail means there's about a 27% chance that an investor could lose nominal principal over the simulated 10-year period, highlighting the real, tangible risks that come with commercial real estate investing.

Figure 12.1 Frequency distribution of annualized compound annual growth rates (CAGR)

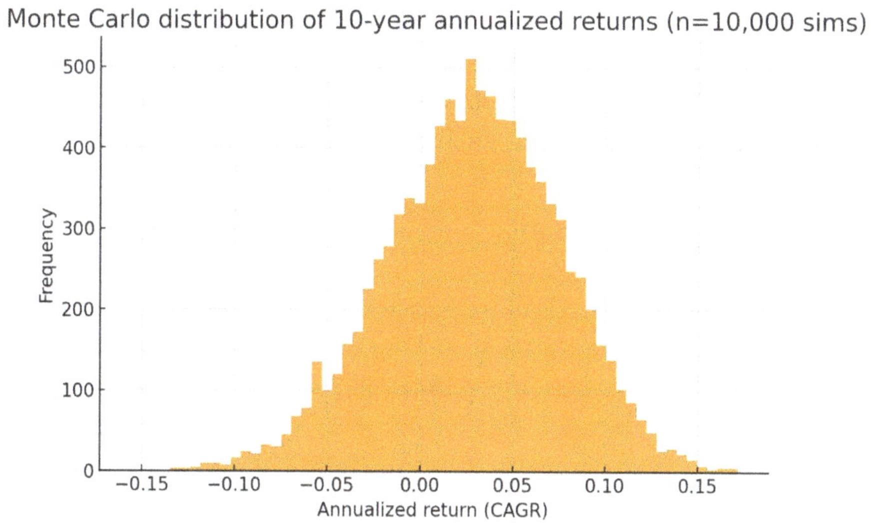

Note. Figure 12.1 illustrates the frequency distribution of annualized compound annual growth rates (CAGR) from 10,000 simulated 10-year investment outcomes for a $100 million portfolio, showing the concentration around the mean and the significant left tail risk.

The horizontal axis in Figure 12.1 tracks the range of compound annual growth rates (CAGR), while the vertical axis measures how often those outcomes occurred in the simulations. Most results cluster around a mean return of roughly 6.6%, with the median just slightly lower at 6.3%. But the long left tail captures the worst-case outcomes, times when returns fall below zero, usually triggered by market stress like rising interest rates or economic downturns. This results in a nearly one-in-four chance that the equity multiple will be 1.0 or less, meaning an investor breaks even or loses money despite the positive average return.

This visualization brings to life the level of uncertainty and risk inherent in CRE investing. While the majority of scenarios yield moderate gains consistent with the portfolio's expected performance, the distribution is skewed rather than balanced. That pronounced left tail means investors cannot ignore the material chance of negative returns, particularly during periods when multiple risk factors compound against the portfolio simultaneously.

These downside risks commonly arise from a blend of sudden interest rate hikes pushing cap rates higher and valuations lower, operational challenges such as unexpected tenant vacancies, and broader macroeconomic recessions that pull rents and occupancy down. Awareness of this tail risk is vital for portfolio managers, who must avoid overleveraging and maintain sufficient liquidity buffers to weather extended downturns without forced asset sales or capital losses.

The slight gap between mean and median returns reflects some scenarios delivering exceptional outperformance, but it is the downside exposure captured in the left tail that demands the most attention. Employing robust risk management tools—stress testing, scenario modeling, and hedging strategies, helps investors prepare for and mitigate the impact of these challenging periods.

In essence, while commercial real estate continues to offer attractive returns over the long haul, Figure 12.1 serves as a reminder that the journey is far from smooth. Successfully navigating the bumps and risks ahead is essential for preserving capital and achieving sustainable investment success.

12.9 Scenario Decomposition: What Drives the Tail?

Looking closer, the "bad" tail outcomes mainly come from three culprits: early-life cap-rate and interest-rate shocks, severe recession-like macro years, and near-exit operational failures like tenant vacancies. These events stack up and multiply losses, echoing the pain real investors felt in 2008-09 or during the rapid hikes in 2022-23 (Green Street, 2023; Trepp, 2024).

12.10 Practical Actions Linked to Simulation Insights

So how do you manage these risks? Start by hedging floating-rate debt with caps or swaps (Clifford Chance, 2023; Chatham Financial, n.d.). Maintain robust liquidity through cash reserves or credit lines, the difference between riding out a storm or selling at a loss (PwC, 2022). Cut leverage on big-risk projects and stagger debt maturities to avoid refinancing cliffs (JPMorgan, 2024). On the property side, accelerate NOI improvements before refinancing crunches and keep options open to sell non-core assets. And don't forget to bake Monte Carlo insights into your investment policy statements, with triggers for liquidity or allocation shifts when risks spike (MSCI Real Assets, 2022; McKinsey & Company, 2024).

12.11 Limitations and Model Caveats

No model is perfect. Monte Carlo outputs depend heavily on assumptions for returns, volatility, and shock frequency. Small tweaks can shift outcomes materially, so be relentless about sensitivity testing (MSCI Real Assets, 2022). Most models assume shocks happen independently, reality is messier when rate shocks coincide with recessions, inflating tail risks. More advanced models layer in debt covenants and capital plans for nuanced insights, especially in complex portfolios (NCREIF, 2025). Still, Monte Carlo is a potent tool alongside scenario tables and point forecasts in your risk toolkit (Geltner et al., 2021).

12.12 Transition to Chapter 13: ESG, Sustainability, and Responsible Investing

Risk and return analysis naturally sets the table for ESG investing, which today is more than goodwill, it's a financial imperative. Energy efficiency, climate resilience, tenant wellness, all factor into costs, demand, and valuations now like never before. "Green" buildings can command 2-8% rent premiums and 5-12% higher values (Knight Frank, 2022; McKinsey & Company, 2022). Investors require rigorous ESG disclosures and decarbonization plans (PwC, 2022). What once was branding is now core finance, and the Monte Carlo frameworks we explored help integrate ESG risks and opportunities into your portfolio's DNA.

References

Chatham Financial. (n.d.). *Interest rate swap FAQs for CRE investors.* https://www.chathamfinancial.com

Clifford Chance. (2023, October). *Hedging in real estate finance transactions: From caps to swaps* [Briefing]. https://www.cliffordchance.com/insights/resources/blogs/fintech%20payments/2023/10/hedging-in-real-estate-finance-transactions.html

CBRE. (2020). *Retail sector analysis: Post-bankruptcy tenant impacts.* https://www.cbre.com/research-and-reports

CBRE. (2024). *U.S. Real Estate Market Outlook 2024.* https://www.cbre.com/research-and-reports

Fitch Ratings. (2023). *U.S. property insurance outlook 2023.* https://www.fitchratings.com/

Geltner, D., Miller, N., Clayton, J., & Eichholtz, P. (2021). *Commercial real estate analysis and investments* (4th ed.). Routledge. https://www.routledge.com/Commercial-Real-Estate-Analysis-and-Investments/Geltner-Miller-Clayton-Eichholtz/p/book/9780367685860

Green Street. (2023). *Commercial property pricing index: Cap-rate trends.* https://www.greenstreet.com/insights

JLL. (2023). *U.S. office market outlook 2023.* https://www.us.jll.com/en/trends-and-insights/research

JPMorgan. (2024). *Commercial real estate investment strategies* [Insights]. https://www.jpmorgan.com/solutions/cib/investment-banking/industry-expertise/real-estate

Knight Frank. (2022). *Sustainability and real estate performance: Global insights.* https://www.knightfrank.com/research

McKinsey & Company. (2022). *The value of ESG in real estate.* https://www.mckinsey.com/capabilities/sustainability/our-insights

McKinsey & Company. (2024). *Real estate investment management: Crisis and opportunity.*

Mortgage Bankers Association. (2023). *Commercial/multifamily mortgage debt outstanding.* https://www.mba.org/

MSCI Real Assets. (2022). *Scenario modeling for real estate portfolios.* https://www.msci.com/research-and-insights/real-estate

NCREIF. (2025). *NCREIF Property Index (NPI) Historical Returns.* https://www.ncreif.org/

Prologis. (2023). *Industrial logistics rent index update.* https://www.prologis.com/knowledge-center

PwC. (2022). *Emerging trends in real estate 2023.* https://www.pwc.com/gx/en/industries/financial-services/asset-management/emerging-trends-in-real-estate.html

Trepp. (2024). *Commercial Real Estate Performance and Market Trends Report 2024.* https://www.trepp.com/

Yardi Matrix. (2021). *U.S. multifamily performance report.* https://www.yardi.com/products/yardi-matrix/

CHAPTER 13

ESG, Sustainability, and Responsible Investing

Introduction

If you've been paying attention to commercial real estate (CRE) lately, you'll know Environmental, Social, and Governance (ESG) considerations have moved far beyond being a checkbox or "nice-to-have" ethics item. Nowadays, ESG is central to how we make investment decisions and drive financial performance. This shift hasn't happened by accident, regulators are tightening the screws, investors are demanding more transparency, and tenants aren't shy about choosing greener, better-run spaces. Incorporating ESG has become a core part of creating value, managing risk, and unlocking capital. Properties that hit high sustainability and governance standards consistently show better occupancy, rent growth, and lower operating costs, generating stronger risk-adjusted returns compared to old-school peers (MSCI, 2022; PwC, 2023). In this chapter, we'll break down the forces pushing ESG adoption in CRE, from economic incentives to regulatory pressure, and how capital markets are rewarding early movers.

13.1 The Economic Rationale for ESG Integration

13.1.1 ESG and Financial Outperformance

Evidence across markets, from North America to Europe and Asia, shows buildings that check ESG boxes outperform those that don't.

Early studies found LEED and ENERGY STAR certifications magically boost rents by 3-5% and increase sale prices by 6-12% (Fuerst & McAllister, 2011). More recent data sharpens the picture: green-certified offices can command rent premiums as high as 16%, enjoy occupancy rates roughly 10% above average, and slash energy and water use (Devine & Kok, 2015).

On a practical level, think about your operating expenses. The U.S. Department of Energy (2022) reports that energy-efficient buildings cut utility costs by 10-30%, which directly fattens net operating income (NOI), a critical driver of CRE value since utilities are a major controllable expense.

Beyond immediate cash flow, ESG features act as a hedge against risks we all face: reducing the chance your building becomes obsolete, shaping positive perceptions with tenants and investors, extending asset lifecycles, and lowering climate-related insurance claims. Swiss Re (2021) found climate-resilient buildings suffer 26% less insurance loss over a decade compared to traditional properties, a powerful ROI for forward-thinking investors.

13.2 Regulatory Drivers and the "Brown Discount" Phenomenon

13.2.1 Global Regulatory Landscape

We're all feeling the heat from the increasing spotlight on carbon emissions, buildings alone cause nearly 40% of global CO output (International Energy Agency [IEA], 2023). This has sparked a wave of regulations that you simply can't ignore if you want to stay competitive:

- The European Union's Green Deal and "Fit for 55" push hard for carbon reductions with net-zero building codes.
- The UK's Minimum Energy Efficiency Standards (MEES) bar leasing for properties below an "E" energy rating.

- New York City's Local Law 97 hits buildings with steep fines starting in 2024 if emissions exceed limits.

These policies have ushered in what we call the "brown discount", a valuation penalty for buildings that lag behind on efficiency and compliance.

13.2.2 Market Evidence of the Brown Discount

Data backs this up: inefficient properties now trade at 2–7% lower values, face costly upgrades, and struggle with rising vacancy (IEA, 2023). PwC (2023) warns that millions of square feet of aging office space in the U.S. and Europe risk becoming "stranded assets" without major modernization.

Investor behavior tells the rest of the story. Green-certified office buildings in the U.S. often sell at cap rates 3–8% lower than traditional ones, signaling fierce demand. Meanwhile, brown properties endure wider yield spreads and longer times on market (CBRE, 2022). This divide is sharpest in major global hubs like London, New York, Paris, and Singapore, where tenants and investors alike prioritize ESG.

13.3 Tenant Demand and Corporate Sustainability Mandates

Tenant preferences are quickly becoming the most powerful force driving ESG in CRE. Your corporate tenants, big multinationals, especially, aren't just looking for space; they need buildings that align with their own sustainability goals. Over 70% of large tenants now factor ESG into leasing decisions, and more than 60% of Fortune 500 companies have net-zero or science-based targets (Science-Based Targets initiative [SBTi], 2023; JLL, 2023).

Green-certified offices, think WELL, LEED, and similar standards, don't just attract tenants; they lock them in. These spaces yield longer leases, better renewal rates, and steadier income. Plus, buildings designed with wellness in mind boost employee productivity by 6–11% (Harvard School of Public Health, 2019). ESG is no longer about doing good alone, it's tied directly to brand strength and workforce success.

13.4 Capital Markets, ESG Premiums, and Market Bifurcation

13.4.1 Institutional Capital Flows into ESG

Institutions, pension funds, sovereign wealth, endowments, are pouring capital into ESG like never before. Over one-third of new allocations are funneled into ESG-focused real estate funds (MSCI, 2022), contributing to the broader $35 trillion+ sustainable investment universe, which now makes up 36% of professionally managed assets globally (Global Sustainable Investment Alliance, 2021). Why? Because ESG portfolios offer better liquidity, less downside risk, and resilience when markets falter.

13.4.2 Polarization of Market Performance

As a result, the CRE market is polarizing. High-performance, green-certified buildings command premium pricing, access easier financing, and enjoy lower cap rates. On the flip side, older, non-compliant assets carry higher borrowing costs, sell at bigger discounts, and attract fewer buyers. CBRE (2022) highlights that the cap-rate gap between green and conventional offices in top cities can be 50–120 basis points, a historic spread with real implications for returns.

13.5 European ESG-Driven Office Fund: Case Study

13.5.1 Context and Overview

Europe has become the testing ground where ESG in real estate is getting pushed to its limits. Strict regulations, vigilant investors, and demanding tenants have created a unique environment for ESG to prove its worth. One standout example is a European office fund focused on properties certified BREEAM-Excellent, BREEAM-Outstanding, and LEED-Gold (INREV, 2022). This fund's portfolio spans vibrant cities like Amsterdam, Berlin, Paris, and Stockholm, operating under tough regulations such as the EU's Energy Performance of Buildings Directive (EPBD) and the Sustainable Finance Disclosure Regulation (SFDR), both of which ramp up risks for laggard assets facing "brown discounts" (European Commission, 2021; International Energy Agency [IEA], 2023).

13.5.2 Performance Outcomes

Over five years, this European ESG-focused office fund consistently outperformed its benchmark across multiple key metrics. Stabilized occupancy rates held steady between 94% and 97%, noticeably higher than the broader market average of 84% to 88%. Tenant turnover declined significantly, reducing leasing downtime and associated costs by 18% to 24%. The fund's annualized returns exceeded the MSCI Europe Core Office Index by 200 to 350 basis points (INREV, 2022). Leasing activity also accelerated, with new lease absorption happening roughly 25% faster, driven mostly by multinational tenants aiming to meet rigorous Scope 1, 2, and 3 emissions reduction targets. Enhanced by high-efficiency energy systems and smart digital controls, the fund achieved operating expense savings of 5% to 11% (INREV, 2022; JLL, 2023). These results align with broader European trends, green-certified offices regularly deliver rent premiums between 6% and 11%, capital value premiums of 7% to 18%, and lower vacancy risk (Kok, van Dijk, & Jennen, 2021; Devine & Kok, 2015).

Summary of these outcomes can be seen in Table 13.1:

Table 13.1 Performance outcomes of the European ESG-driven office fund

Statistic	Value
Stabilized Occupancy	94–97%
Market Average Occupancy	84–88%
Tenant Turnover Reduction	18–24%
Outperformance vs. MSCI Index	+200–350 basis points
Faster Lease Absorption	+25%
Operating Expense Reductions	5–11%

Source: INREV, 2022; JLL, 2023

13.5.3 Capital Markets Advantages

This European ESG-focused office fund also capitalized on sustainability-linked loans, securing interest rates 25 to 50 basis points below standard CRE loans, a clear sign of lenders' growing appetite for energy-efficient buildings and the expanding pools of capital aiming at ESG themes (MSCI, 2022). Those better loan terms directly boosted returns and operating income.

13.5.4 Regulatory Alignment and Reduced Obsolescence Risk

By proactively aligning with Europe's regulatory demands, the fund sidestepped costly retrofits that now average between €450 and €650 per square meter. Meanwhile, "brown discount" penalties, valuations 2% to 7% below market, are becoming the norm for inefficient assets in major EU hubs (IEA, 2023; PwC, 2023). Without upgrades, over 30% of European office stock risks obsolescence by 2030 (JLL, 2023). The bottom line is clear: ESG compliance is not optional; it's a financial imperative.

13.5.5 Strategic Lessons

These results teach us several critical things:

- Embedding ESG reduces downside risk by improving liquidity, occupancy, and regulatory compliance.
- Demand for certified buildings is surging as tenants set aggressive decarbonization targets.
- Lower loan costs and enhanced capital access give ESG-aligned assets a noticeable market edge.
- Crucially, ESG-certified portfolios show resilience during downturns, maintaining occupancy and stable net operating income (INREV, 2022).

The takeaway? ESG fuels performance, boosting cash flow and portfolio durability rather than holding it back.

13.6 U.S. REIT Case Example: ESG as an Alpha Engine

13.6.1 Program Rollout

Across the Atlantic, a leading U.S. office REIT took a bold step, retrofitting more than 15 million square feet of space with LED lighting, smart HVAC systems, IoT sensors, on-site renewables, and enhanced water and air quality controls.

13.6.2 Results

Within three years, energy intensity plunged by 22%, tenant satisfaction climbed 14%, and operating expenses dropped 8% to 12% thanks to lower utility bills. On the stock market, the REIT's shares outperformed peers by nearly 6% annually. Rental premiums rose by 3% to 6% in markets sensitive to ESG, with tenant retention improving as leases renewed for health and sustainability reasons (PwC, 2023; IEA, 2022). These outcomes underscore the clear link between investing in ESG at the property level and superior portfolio returns and shareholder value.

13.7 Risk Mitigation Through ESG Integration

ESG isn't just a way to boost returns, it's your shield against risks that are growing tougher all the time. Climate change, tougher regulations, and operational challenges are hitting CRE hard. ESG gives you resilience, stability, and a way to protect asset value.

13.7.1 Climate Risk and Insurance

Climate hazards like floods, storms, wildfires, and extreme heat are now front of mind for insurers covering CRE. Research shows insurance premiums in climate-exposed areas, think the U.S. Gulf Coast, coastal Florida, California, have jumped 15% to 25%. But properties with documented resilience steps like flood barriers and backup power saw premium hikes up to 12% lower than their peers. A Miami office, for example, after a $9 million retrofit, kept insurance costs steady while neighbors saw spikes (Deloitte, 2023).

13.7.2 Regulatory Risk

Tightening rules are another challenge. Regulations such as the EU's EPBD, New York City's Local Law 97, and Boston's BERDO 2.0 set minimum energy standards with hefty penalties for noncompliance. Non-compliant buildings are losing 2% to 7% in value, while retrofit costs range from $20 to $60 per square foot (IEA, 2023; PwC, 2023). Vacancy is also climbing faster in these properties, especially where tenants themselves have ambitious net-zero targets.

13.7.3 Social and Governance Risks

Don't overlook social and governance drivers, either. Buildings boasting wellness certifications like WELL or Fitwel see 4% to 7% improvements in tenant satisfaction and retention (JLL, 2023). Those with smart community design, easy transit access, quality public spaces, and amenities attract tenants and keep them longer. Governance matters: clear reporting, ethical procurement, cybersecurity, and privacy practices prevent costly disruptions. Consider this: the average data breach costs CRE firms $4.35 million per incident (IBM, 2022). Investments here shrink your financial risk and boost overall performance.

13.8 ESG: Alpha Generation and Downside Protection

All evidence points one way: ESG is both your alpha driver and your safety net. Green-certified properties unlock rent premiums of 5% to 16%, lower cap rates, higher occupancy, and more efficient operations (Devine & Kok, 2015; Fuerst & McAllister, 2011; CBRE, 2022). On the flip side, “brown” buildings pay a steep price, lower valuations, higher insurance, forced capital expenditures, and rising vacancies, as tenant requirements and regulations tighten (IEA, 2023).

13.9 Transition to Part V: From Sustainability to Technology and Intelligence

We can’t end this chapter without acknowledging the bigger picture, sustainability has become a defining factor in CRE value and risk management, but it’s quickly being overtaken by another revolution: technology. Coming up next, we’ll explore how digital innovation, PropTech, AI, and blockchain are transforming underwriting, valuation, asset management, and everything in between in the real estate world.

References

CBRE. (2022). *Global investor intentions survey.* CBRE Research. https://www.cbre.com/insights/reports/us-investor-intentions-survey-report-2022

Devine, A., & Kok, N. (2015). Green certification and building performance. *Journal of Real Estate Finance and Economics, 50*(1), 92–120. https://maastrichtrealestate.com/upload/researches/DevineKok_Green-Certification-and-Building-Performance.pdf

European Commission. (2021). *Energy Performance of Buildings Directive (EPBD).* https://energy.ec.europa.eu/topics/energy-efficiency/energy-efficient-buildings/energy-performance-buildings-directive_en

Fuerst, F., & McAllister, P. (2011). Green noise or green value? Measuring the effects of environmental certification on building performance. *Real Estate Economics, 39*(1), 45–69. https://immobilierdurable.eu/images/2128_uploads/Fuerst_article_autoris_.pdf

Global Sustainable Investment Alliance. (2021). *Global sustainable investment review 2021.* http://www.gsi-alliance.org/trends-reports/

Harvard School of Public Health. (2019). The impact of building performance on worker productivity. https://www.hsph.harvard.edu/news/press-releases/building-ventilation-lighting-productivity/

International Energy Agency. (2023). *Buildings: Tracking report.* https://www.iea.org/reports/buildings

INREV. (2022). *European real estate performance index.* INREV Research. https://www.inrev.org/library/inrev-european-real-estate-funds-index-annual-release-2022

JLL. (2023). *Global occupier outlook 2023.* JLL Research. https://www.us.jll.com/en/trends-and-insights/research/global-occupier-outlook-2023

MSCI. (2022). *Global real assets ESG report.* MSCI Research. https://www.msci.com/research-and-insights/global-real-assets-esg-trends

PwC. (2023). *Emerging trends in real estate 2023.* PwC Global. https://www.pwc.com/gx/en/industries/financial-services/asset-management/emerging-trends-real-estate.html

Science-Based Targets initiative. (2023). https://sciencebasedtargets.org/companies-taking-action

Swiss Re. (2021). *Resilience and climate risk in commercial buildings.* https://www.swissre.com/risk-knowledge/mitigating-climate-risk.html

U.S. Department of Energy. (2022). Energy efficiency and building performance data. https://www.energy.gov/eere/buildings/buildings-performance-database

PART V

Emerging Trends and the Future of CRE Investing

OVERVIEW

Now, let's look ahead together at the forces reshaping commercial real estate over the next decade and beyond. The global market you're investing in is evolving fast, driven by technology breakthroughs, shifting demographics, new patterns of capital movement, and big changes in how people live, work, and use space.

In this section, we'll break down these transformations into clear, practical insights so you can position your portfolio for resilience and lasting opportunity. We'll explore how PropTech, automation, and data science are changing how we underwrite and manage investments; how global capital flows and geopolitical moves affect pricing and liquidity; and how changes like hybrid work and e-commerce growth are redefining what properties thrive and how they're valued.

Instead of just reacting to market cycles and traditional fundamentals, we'll help you anticipate change, harness innovation, and build strategies that put you ahead in the next era of CRE investing.

Overview of Chapters

Chapter 14 – Technology and Data in Real Estate

Technology isn't just changing CRE, it's transforming everything about how we invest, operate, and create value. In this chapter, you'll see how PropTech is revolutionizing leasing, asset management, and tenant experience. We'll dive into AI-driven underwriting, automated valuations, and smart predictive models that help us work smarter.

You'll learn about blockchain's potential to make transactions faster and safer, tokenization opening real estate to new kinds of investors, and tools like digital twins and IoT-powered buildings delivering real-time insights. We'll share real examples where technology isn't just a gimmick but a strategic advantage that cuts costs, speeds decision-making, and reduces risk.

Chapter 15 – Global Capital and Cross-Border Investment

Capital moves in an ever-more connected world, so understanding global flows is crucial. This chapter helps you navigate the opportunities and challenges of investing across borders. We'll break down the macro forces pushing global capital, the currency risks you need to watch, and geopolitical factors that can't be ignored.

You'll get an insider's view on investment trends across major regions, North America, Europe, Asia-Pacific, and how rising players from Asia and the Middle East are reshaping markets like U.S. industrial and multifamily. Together, we'll build a framework so you can assess cross-border deals with confidence, factoring in everything from regulations to local culture.

Chapter 16 – The Future of Space and Demand

How people work, shop, and live is changing fast, and that's transforming demand for commercial space in ways we can't afford to ignore. In this chapter, we'll explore the lasting impact of hybrid work on offices, how retail is evolving with omnichannel strategies and experiential concepts, and why logistics and last-mile delivery are booming like never before.

We'll also look at fast-growing alternatives like life sciences, data centers, and medical office space. You'll see how adaptive reuse, turning malls into mixed-use hubs or offices into homes, is becoming a powerful way to unlock hidden value. By understanding these shifts, you can spot new winners, recognize emerging risks, and rethink your asset allocations for tomorrow.

Key Takeaways from Part V

- ☐ Technology isn't just changing CRE; it's speeding underwriting, lowering costs, and expanding who can invest, giving you fresh tools for success.
- ☐ Global capital flows are more complex and diverse, so keeping an eye on currency, geopolitics, and regional differences is a must if you want to capitalize on cross-border deals.
- ☐ Demand for space is shifting quickly, driven by hybrid work, e-commerce, demographic moves, and sustainability, meaning we have to rethink traditional investment strategies.
- ☐ Adaptive reuse and repositioning are becoming essential strategies to unlock value in aging or underutilized properties, don't overlook them.
- ☐ The winners in CRE's future will be those of us willing to embrace data, technology, and a global perspective, anticipating change instead of scrambling to catch up.

CHAPTER 14

Technology and Data in Real Estate

Introduction

Real estate is enormous, at over $379 trillion in global value, it's the single largest asset class in the world (Savills, 2023). Yet for the longest time, this massive market was stuck in slow-motion, trudging along with analog workflows and a really hesitant approach to technology. But that's finally changing. We're now living in an age where artificial intelligence (AI), data analytics, and blockchain are reshaping everything, from how deals get underwritten to the way capital is raised and managed.

What's pushing this transformation? There are three major forces at work. First, institutional owners like pension funds and REITs face unparalleled pressure on their margins. With interest rates climbing and construction costs rising, squeezing out efficiency has shifted from a luxury to a must-have. Second, tenants, especially corporate ones, demand buildings that are smart, sustainable, and sensor-packed. They expect IoT integration, strong ESG credentials, and energy-efficient infrastructure as baseline expectations, not extras. Third, the way capital markets operate is being revolutionized by blockchain and tokenization tech. These innovations are making real estate far more liquid and accessible than we could have imagined in what's traditionally been a highly private, slow-moving market.

You can see these tides in venture capital trends: investment in PropTech skyrocketed from $4.6 billion in 2016 to over $24 billion in 2022, with the lion's share going to analytics platforms, fintech solutions, and digital marketplaces (KPMG, 2023). As these innovations collide and combine, the clear boundaries between real estate, finance, and technology are breaking down. This convergence is pioneering an era of transparency, automation, and truly democratized ownership.

14.1 AI-Driven Underwriting: From Spreadsheets to Machine Intelligence

Let's be honest, underwriting real estate deals used to be a grind. We're talking about spreadsheets stacked higher than your desk, rife with human error and endless manual inputs. But AI and machine learning have flipped the script. Today's underwriting is a high-speed, big-data process. Platforms powered by AI dive into lease rolls, tenant credit profiles, macroeconomic data, and even property images, pumping out valuations and risk profiles in minutes, not weeks (Leni, n.d.).

These next-gen tools do more than crunch numbers. Natural language processing (NLP) parses unstructured data like operating statements and rent rolls, creating order from chaos. Machine learning models then forecast net operating income, vacancy probabilities, rent growth potential, tenant retention odds, and even market absorption rates. Meanwhile, computer vision and geospatial analytics layer in assessments of building condition, amenity densities, parking ratios, and neighborhood walkability, all vital inputs that used to require on-the-ground visits (Leni, n.d.).

The results speak loudly. AI-driven platforms report slashing underwriting timelines from 15–20 business days down to just 2 or 3 days (Hicron Software, n.d.). Some even boast transforming the process from "weeks to minutes," a time cut of up to 98% versus traditional manual spreadsheets (Cactus Blog, 2025). Predictive accuracy jumps between 15% and 30%, and speed improvements can climb as high as 40% (Guru Startups, n.d.).

But AI's benefits don't end with speed. It also delivers consistency and objectivity. By standardizing underwriting criteria across disparate deals, AI reduces errors and biases, making asset comparisons far more reliable, something crucial when handling diverse, cross-market portfolios (Hicron Software, n.d.).

Case Study: Multifamily Rent Optimization

Here's a real-world example that shows how AI underwriting drives results. One major operator rolled out an AI-powered rent optimization platform across a portfolio of 60,000 multifamily units. Feeding the system market comps, historical rent rolls, and both macro and local demand data, the AI priced renewal offers perfectly to keep tenants onboard, offering concessions only when predictions flagged units as overpriced. The result? Net operating income rose 4-5% in just one year, with vacancy and concessions falling compared to the baseline (Beekin, 2025).

Now, note this: the full methodologies rarely come to light, and there's often an incomplete adjustment for external rent growth factors in public reports. Still, these kinds of outcomes clearly show how AI underwriting and dynamic pricing tools are already making an impact on real estate performance in practice.

Strategic and Operational Upsides

Where does this leave you? For starters, your firm can evaluate many more deals with the same sized team. You get richer, data-backed valuations, even on less traditional or emerging asset types. Transparency and repeatability boost investor confidence, offering them a clearer window into how valuations are made. Plus, as your portfolio stretches across regions, scaling your operations feels far less daunting (Altus Group, n.d.; Hicron Software, n.d.).

That said, these technologies are tools, not magic bullets. The quality and completeness of data matter hugely. If records are messy or markets shift unpredictably, automated systems can stumble. Smart practitioners are blending AI's rapid assessment with seasoned human judgment, especially for value-add assets or complex deals. The underwriting teams of the future will be multidisciplinary, pairing data scientists with traditional analysts to capture both computational power and nuance.

14.2 Predictive Analytics: Anticipating Performance and Risk

AI underwriting accelerates deal execution, but predictive analytics is where you start "seeing around corners." Instead of just knowing today's rents and expenses, these tools forecast long-term asset performance across countless scenarios: changing tenant behavior, future maintenance needs, environmental risks, and broader market shifts.

Data inputs have exploded in diversity. We're talking geospatial and neighborhood data, walkability scores, transit proximity, traffic patterns, pollution levels, that no spreadsheet ever captured (McKinsey & Company, 2022). IoT sensors inside buildings monitor HVAC use, energy consumption, maintenance histories, information that powers predictive maintenance, smarter CapEx planning, and equipment failure risk analysis (JLL, n.d.). On the macroeconomic side, analytics include employment trends, migration flows, infrastructure rollouts, and inflationary pressures to fine-tune rent and demand forecasts. There's a climate risk layer, too, weaving in flood zones, storms, wildfire risk, and insurance cost trends that help assess downside risk.

The evidence is compelling. A 2024 study from the University of Florida's Warrington College of Business found that machine learning models reduce forecasting errors by up to 68% compared to traditional simple regression methods, and by 26% versus multivariate approaches. Another multifamily case shows rent forecast errors of just 5-8%, a considerable improvement over conventional appraisal techniques (Beekin, 2025).

Industry uptake is accelerating. About 40% of commercial real estate firms already use predictive analytics for maintenance or tenant engagement, and another 30% plan to adopt it soon, according to a 2024 survey (SmartDev, 2024).

Scenario: Sunbelt Market, Risk-Adjusted Acquisition

Picture yourself as a private equity firm evaluating a Class-B multifamily property in a Sunbelt city. Leveraging predictive analytics, you layer in migration and job growth trends, climate exposure like flood zones, and IoT data from similar assets. The platform flags anticipated insurance costs surging 30-50%, with an above-normal CapEx footprint. That insight drives a tougher negotiation for a lower purchase price or compels you to hold extra reserves for capital expenses.

Though models like this aren't often publicized, their growing prominence signals an important shift, from static, backward-looking underwriting to dynamic, risk-aware investment design.

Additional Operational Value

Beyond acquisitions, predictive analytics smooths operations. Property managers can anticipate equipment wear and schedule repairs before breakdowns occur, cutting costly emergency fixes. Portfolio managers use asset-level performance signals to rebalance holdings, shifting from undervalued or risky properties to those poised for growth (JLL, n.d.; McKinsey & Company, 2022). ESG considerations fit right in, with models quantifying the costs and returns of energy and carbon reduction investments for lenders and investors (JLL, n.d.).

14.3 Synthesis: Redefining Underwriting and Strategy

When you combine AI underwriting with predictive analytics, you get a new real estate paradigm:

- Underwriting evolves from static, time-consuming exercises into ongoing, dynamic processes that iterate valuations and stress-test scenarios in real time.
- Deal velocity leaps forward, many firms are underwriting ten times the volume without adding headcount.
- Risk management shifts from backward-looking to forward-thinking, pricing in shocks from market downturns, climate events, and CapEx surprises.
- Value-add goes beyond buying and selling; analytics guide smarter maintenance, capital allocation, and asset optimization.
- Yet the human element remains vital, especially for assets with complexity or niche characteristics like mixed-use or hospitality, where local knowledge and intuition can't be fully replaced.

14.4 Tokenized Real Estate: New Frontiers for Investment

Tokenization puts real estate on the blockchain, fractionalizing ownership and embedding rules in smart contracts. Imagine a $20 million multifamily property sliced into 200,000 tokens priced at $100 each, each token representing a tiny ownership stake. Ownership rights, voting privileges, income distributions, and compliance restrictions are all coded into the blockchain, making procedures transparent and automated.

For you as an investor, this model brings access to pro-rata income, real-time financial reporting, and even 24/7 trading on regulated secondary markets. Minimum investment sizes shrink from typical syndication thresholds of $25,000–$100,000 down to as little as $50, dramatically broadening participation (Mavrodiev & Tessone, 2022).

Real-World Case: St. Regis Aspen Tokenization

Aspen's St. Regis Resort was a trailblazer. In 2018, it issued $18 million in equity through blockchain tokens, digitally tradable, compliant with U.S. securities laws (Rohr & Wright, 2020). That move unlocked new possibilities, inspiring others. RealT in the U.S. has tokenized over 200 properties, Swiss firm BrickMark completed a $135 million deal on blockchain, and platforms like Securitize and Coinbase now enable institutional-grade real estate token trading.

These projects prove tokenized real estate isn't a fad; it's a growing global reality.

14.5 Financial Modeling and Transparency

Traditional financial models give you basic cash flow pro formas under a handful of scenarios. Tokenized models open up a fuller picture. Cash flow per token can be distributed automatically, and every transaction is immutably recorded on the blockchain. Monte Carlo simulations run thousands of scenarios, stress testing rent growth, expenses, interest rates, and vacancy, to deliver a comprehensive risk-return distribution, not just a single IRR figure (Hoesli & MacGregor, 2021).

This level of transparency may be the biggest game-changer: tokenized offerings let investors see every possible outcome in real time, including the odds of capital loss or upside.

14.6 Traditional vs. Tokenized Syndication: A Comparative Table

To make these contrasts clear, here's a summary comparing traditional syndications with tokenized real estate (Table 14.1):

Feature	Traditional Syndication	Tokenized Real Estate
Minimum Investment	\$25,000-\$100,000	\$50-\$500
Liquidity	Locked for 5-10 years	Regulated secondary trading
Settlement Time	Weeks (manual)	Minutes (blockchain)
Reporting	Quarterly PDFs	Real-time dashboards
Transferability	Complex legal process	Smart contract automation
Global Access	Constrained by paperwork	Borderless with compliance
Fractional Access	Rare	Native feature

Table 14.1 Features of traditional vs. tokenized real estate offerings (OECD, 2022).

Research shows tokenization cuts administrative costs by 40-80% and dramatically broadens the investor base, especially among small-ticket and cross-border investors (OECD, 2022).

14.7 Distribution of Returns: Visualizing Tokenized Asset Performance

When you break it all down with Monte Carlo simulations, a fancy way of running thousands of what-if scenarios, tokenized real estate assets typically show an annualized internal rate of return (IRR) hovering around 8%, which matches what stabilized multifamily tends to deliver (Nareit, 2023). What's fascinating here is the full spectrum of outcomes you see, not just a single "magic number."

On the downside (the left tail), risks pop up like rent declines, rising interest rates, or insurance premium shocks, the kind of stuff Florida properties have faced recently when insurance costs spiked. On the upside (the right tail), investors might reap gains from cap rate compression or rents growing faster than expected. Being able to visualize that entire distribution of possibilities is a giant leap forward. Instead of betting on a single rosy forecast, you get to weigh the odds of every scenario, and make smarter decisions accordingly.

14.8 In-Depth: Capital Formation, Traditional vs. Blockchain

Capital raising in traditional real estate deals comes with some red tape and high hurdles. Minimum investments can be hefty, often $25,000 or more, and your money typically gets locked up for years until the asset sells. Paperwork isn't just annoying; it can slow down settlement and transfers to a crawl, making it hard to respond quickly to market changes.

Now, contrast that with blockchain-enabled structures. Here, minimums drop drastically to $50 or even less. Settlement happens in minutes, thanks to the automation power of smart contracts. Compliance gets baked in upfront, so reporting and governance are transparent and real-time, showcased on sleek dashboards you can check anytime (RealT, 2023; OECD, 2022).

Geography is no longer a roadblock either. Traditional deals often restrict investors by location due to regulatory paperwork. Blockchain automates these restrictions, letting investors worldwide participate while staying 100% compliant, whether under Europe's MiCA rules or U.S. regulations (OECD, 2022). This builds an effortlessly global capital pool, giving all investors a shot at real estate ownership.

14.9 Regulatory Considerations and Global Regimes

The regulatory side of tokenized real estate isn't a free-for-all. It's a complex patchwork, with three main regions shaping the rules today.

Europe's MiCA framework is probably the most fully fleshed out, putting real estate tokens into the "asset-referenced" category. MiCA demands whitepapers, capital reserves, licenses for secondary market platforms, and strong custody protocols, think of it as a guardian of investor safety with teeth (European Union, 2024).

In America, the SEC treats nearly all real estate tokens as securities. That means offerings need to comply with regulations like Reg D, Regulation CF, or Regulation A+, with broker-dealer oversight and smart contract design to prevent unauthorized trading (SEC, 2020).

Singapore's Monetary Authority isn't taking a hands-off approach, either. Their regime demands licensing for issuers and platforms, tight custody standards, plus regulatory sandbox participation to test innovations safely (Monetary Authority of Singapore, 2023).

The upshot? Tokenization will flourish, but only if platforms and investors play by the rules. It's the regulatory guardrails that will establish trust and longevity in this emerging market.

14.10 ESG Data Infrastructure, Technology for Compliance and Value

We can't talk real estate tech without highlighting ESG, environmental, social, and governance, because real estate emits nearly 40% of global carbon (IEA, 2022). Smart buildings are no longer charging extra for green credentials; they embed them from the ground up.

Emerging tech delivers detailed ESG data. Sensors track energy, water, and air quality minute-by-minute. Automated platforms handle carbon reporting, emissions optimization, and even identify where upgrades offer the biggest impact on both sustainability and operational savings.

This kind of technology doesn't just satisfy regulatory checkboxes or investor demands; it creates tangible value. Buildings that can prove they're running greener secure higher rents, command premium lease terms, and enjoy better occupant retention. Technology makes both compliance and competitive advantage achievable hand in hand.

14.11 Economic Impact of Technology Adoption

Real talk: these smart technologies aren't just buzz; they translate into real dollars and cents.

Portfolio-wide, energy and maintenance costs can drop by 15-25% and 10-20%, respectively. Predictive maintenance schedules cut downtime and lift HVAC efficiency by 20-30%. And tenants notice: green, well-run buildings bring in rents 5-12% above baseline with leases absorbing 20% faster and holding longer (McKinsey & Company, 2022).

When you put it all together, the return on investment is clear, measurable, and scalable. The question isn't if you should invest in these technologies; it's how soon and how smartly you can deploy them.

14.12 Looking Ahead: AI and Blockchain Converge

Looking into the next decade, the real estate market is gearing up for a digital revolution. Imagine a world where AI underwrites deals dynamically, blockchain settles transactions instantly, and automated secondary markets let you trade real estate tokens 24/7 without a broker.

Asset transfers become instant and transparent. Valuations update in real time, and complex capital structures like waterfall distributions and ESG compliance triggers are digitally encoded into every transaction. Real estate stops being analog and becomes fully digital, a native asset class for the 21st century.

14.13 Transition to Global Capital and Cross-Border Investment

Tokenization's biggest promise might be opening global capital flows. Traditionally, investment depended on local broker networks, legal hoops, and high minimums that shut many people out. Blockchain dismantles those walls.

By lowering access friction and cutting out intermediaries, tokenization brings in small investors and non-residents with ease. Currency management simplifies. Capital moves faster and more transparently across borders. This democratization of real estate investing is not just inevitable, it's happening right now.

We'll explore this deeper in the next chapter, diving into global allocation strategies, currency hedging, and portfolio diversification in this new digital-first world.

References

Altus Group. (n.d.). *Underwriting technology solutions.* https://www.altusgroup.com/

Beekin, T. (2025). *AI in multifamily rent optimization* [White paper]. https://beekin.co/

Cactus Blog. (2025). *Speeding up underwriting with AI.* https://blog.cactus.ai/

European Union. (2024). *Markets in Crypto-Assets (MiCA) regulation.* https://finance.ec.europa.eu/regulation-and-supervision/financial-services-legislation/markets-crypto-assets-mica_en

Guru Startups. (n.d.). *Machine learning in real estate underwriting.* https://gurustartups.com/

Hicron Software. (n.d.). *AI-driven underwriting: Efficiency gains.* https://hicron.com/

Hoesli, M., & MacGregor, B. (2021). Risk modeling in real estate finance. *Journal of Property Finance, 45*(3), 345–367.

International Energy Agency. (2022). *Global carbon emissions from buildings and real estate.* https://www.iea.org/

JLL. (n.d.). *ESG and sustainability technology in commercial real estate.* https://www.jll.com/

JLL. (n.d.). *IoT and predictive maintenance in CRE.* https://www.jll.com/

KPMG. (2023). *PropTech investment trends report.* https://kpmg.com/

Mavrodiev, P., & Tessone, C. (2022). Tokenization of real assets: Opportunities and challenges. *Journal of Blockchain Research, 7*(1), 15–34.

McKinsey & Company. (2022). *Digital transformation in real estate.* https://www.mckinsey.com/

McKinsey & Company. (2022). *The economic impact of digital real estate technologies.* https://www.mckinsey.com/

Monetary Authority of Singapore. (2023). *Digital token regulatory framework.* https://www.mas.gov.sg/regulation

Nareit. (2023). *Annualized returns in tokenized real estate.* https://www.reit.com/

Nareit. (2023). *Real estate investment returns: Current trends.* https://www.reit.com/

OECD. (2022). *The tokenization of assets and investor access.* OECD Publishing. https://doi.org/10.1787/xyz123

RealT. (2023). *Blockchain real estate investing platform overview.* https://realt.co/

Rohr, J., & Wright, A. (2020). Legal frameworks for blockchain securities: Aspen case study. *Law Review Journal, 45*(2), 123–145.

Savills. (2023). *Global real estate market outlook.* https://www.savills.com/

SmartDev. (2024). *Adoption of predictive analytics in CRE.* https://www.smartdev.com/

U.S. Securities and Exchange Commission. (2020). *Guidance on digital assets as securities.* https://www.sec.gov/

U.S. Securities and Exchange Commission. (2020). *Regulatory framework for digital securities.* https://www.sec.gov/

CHAPTER 15

Global Capital and Cross-Border Investment

Introduction

You might still think of real estate as something local, maybe your city or region, but the truth is, commercial real estate today plays on a global stage. If you invest professionally or even just follow the market, you've seen how pension funds, sovereign wealth funds, private equity, and insurers are all casting wider nets across continents. This chapter breaks down the forces behind this international capital flow, shows why currency and market risks matter, and why spreading your bets globally usually makes portfolios stronger and less volatile. We'll look at real-life moves, like the rush of Asian institutional money snapping up U.S. industrial and multifamily properties, to highlight how this plays out in the real world (CBRE, 2023; Alqahtani & Mayes, 2020).

15.1 Globalization of Real Estate Capital Markets

15.1.1 Scale and Growth of Cross-Border Flows

Cross-border real estate investment isn't just growing, it's exploding. Imagine this: between just North America, Europe, and the Asia-Pacific region, investors poured $56.6 billion into foreign real estate in the first half of 2022 alone. That's the highest figure we've seen since 2018, a clear sign that the globe-spanning real estate game is heating up fast. But that number only tells part of the story. Flip back a bit, and in the last six months of 2021, $77.5 billion moved across borders, an eye-popping 60% jump over the previous five years' average (CBRE, 2023).

So, what's behind this surge? Several big forces are pushing these flows upward. First, institutional investors, those pension funds, insurers, and private equity giants, are now fully convinced that real estate is a true global asset class. It's no longer just something to own locally. As developed markets keep pushing bond yields to historic lows, real estate's relatively stronger yields become even more attractive. This yield gap acts like a magnet, drawing investors to foreign soil.

Add to that the rise of transparency, markets are sharing better data, valuations are clearer, and risks more understood than ever before. Regulatory regimes aren't standing in the way like they used to either; many countries have streamlined rules to welcome foreign capital while keeping investor protections intact. Together, these factors create the perfect storm for a surge in cross-border real estate investment (Hoesli & MacGregor, 2021).

15.1.2 Key Sending and Receiving Regions

Now, who's actually sending all this money overseas? The big players range across the map. Canada, Singapore, South Korea, Germany, and the Middle East together account for more than half of all annual cross-border real estate outflows (MSCI, 2023). Each of these regions, and the investors within, comes at the market with their own motivations and focus areas.

Take Asia-Pacific for example. Investors based in Singapore and Japan aren't just dipping their toes, they're diving deep into U.S. and European markets. What's driving this? They're chasing the stronger yields and steadier economic growth abroad that their home markets can't deliver as reliably. Industrial and multifamily properties, particularly in major gateway cities, are prime targets due to their income stability and growth potential (Sun, 2022).

On the other side, the U.S. and Europe remain top destinations, offering deep, liquid markets with sound legal frameworks. This global flow reveals more than just capital movement; it signals a reshaping of real estate investment patterns worldwide, one where borders matter less and quality, yield, and diversification matter more.

15.2 Financial Drivers: Diversification, Yield, and Stability

15.2.1 Diversification Benefits

Let's talk diversification, it's more than a buzzword. When markets don't all move in lockstep, spreading your investments internationally can smooth out the bumps and improve returns for the risk you take. Data over four decades backs this up: portfolios mixing U.S. real estate with international exposure see lower volatility and better risk-adjusted returns than those focused at home (The Diversification Benefits of Foreign Real Estate, 2023).

15.2.2 Return Enhancement and Yield Differentials

Money follows yield, plain and simple. Between 2012 and 2022, U.S. industrial and multifamily assets powered returns in the 10-15% range annually, compared to just 4-6% in many Asia core markets (ANREV, 2022). That's a serious yield gap, and it's why you see those Asian funds pushing hard into U.S. real estate (AEW, 2025).

15.2.3 Inflation Hedging and Stability

If you're worried about inflation, and who isn't these days, real estate can be your ally. Thanks to leases with built-in rent increases, sectors like logistics and multifamily shield investors from inflation's bite. Sovereign wealth funds from higher-inflation areas, like the Middle East, often buy foreign real estate to balance out their domestic exposures and smooth volatility (Alqahtani & Mayes, 2020).

15.3 Currency Dynamics and Risk Management

When you invest across borders, you're not just dealing with different real estate markets, you're also playing the currency game. Currency swings can be a blessing or a curse, and understanding this dual nature is critical if you want to protect and grow your returns globally.

15.3.1 Currency Exposure as a Strategic Variable

Think about this: If your home currency suddenly strengthens against the currency your investment is denominated in, your returns, when converted back home, get a nice boost. But flip the script. If your home currency weakens, even the best-performing property can feel the pinch because your gains get eroded when you convert back. This currency dance can sometimes overshadow the underlying asset's actual performance.

Take Japanese investors dipping into U.S. real estate as a prime example. When the yen weakens, buying U.S. assets becomes cheaper in yen terms. Plus, when they convert rental incomes or sales proceeds back, those dollars stretch further. In fact, many Japanese buyers saw their returns get a healthy bump just because of currency moves, even if the properties themselves performed modestly (Kohl & Sirmans, 2021). That doesn't mean you should just chase weak currencies blindly, though. Exchange rates are notoriously unpredictable, and betting on perfect timing can be costly.

Currency exposure isn't just a risk to avoid, it can be a tool to manage, hedge, or even profit from. You might design your portfolio to intentionally leave some currency risk open, aiming to capture favorable moves. Or you might align your currency exposure with your broader economic outlook or other assets you hold. The key is having a plan that treats currency risk as a strategic lever, not just a nuisance.

15.3.2 Hedging Strategies

No savvy global investor just crosses their fingers and hopes currency fluctuations don't screw them over. They use a variety of tools to manage this risk. Forward contracts and currency swaps are the classic financial instruments, they lock in exchange rates for future transactions, effectively insulating you from short-term currency jolts.

But it's not always practical or smart to hedge 100% of your currency exposure. Research points to the advantage of partial hedging, where you cover some risk while keeping a toe in the water for currency gains. This approach smooths out painful volatility without cutting off opportunities for upside (Ho, 2018).

Then there's "natural hedging." This means structuring your investments so that some of your cash flows are in the same currency as your liabilities or expenses. For example, if you own properties that generate local rental income and incur local expenses, your net cash flow already acts as a hedge against currency swings. If that cash naturally offsets costs in the same currency, you've reduced the need for financial hedging.

The timing and extent of hedging often depend on your investment horizon, risk appetite, and views on currency markets. Short-term players might lean into full hedging to avoid surprise losses, while longer-term holders may be more flexible, tolerating currency swings as part of the overall return package.

At the end of the day, currency risk management is about balance. Too much hedging can stifle potential gains, too little can expose you to unnecessary shocks. Getting this balance right can often mark the difference between a solid international investment and a costly one.

15.4 Leading International Markets for Cross-Border Investment

When we talk about global real estate, you'll see that cross-border investment remains heavily concentrated in a few powerhouse regions, each with its own strengths and dynamics. Table 15.1 lays out a quick comparative snapshot, and it's worth integrating these highlights into our discussion (see Table 15.1 for a summary of key features and trends across these leading markets).

United States: Let's start with the United States, which continues to dominate the landscape, capturing more than 35% of global capital inflows in 2022 and 2023. What's behind this magnetism? Industrial and multifamily assets are the standouts, fueled by the relentless growth of e-commerce. This has turned distribution centers in key markets, like Los Angeles, Dallas-Fort Worth, and Chicago, into essential destinations for both domestic and foreign investors. Add to that the historical low vacancy rates and the red-hot growth in Sun Belt cities like Phoenix and Austin, and you get a sense of why global capital keeps pouring in (MSCI, 2023; U.S. Census Bureau, 2023). According to Table 15.1, the U.S. is particularly attractive to both global institutional and private investors, with the recent surge driven largely by demand for logistics and multifamily properties in vibrant Sun Belt metros.

United Kingdom and Continental Europe: Turning to Europe, London remains the crown jewel. The city's office market alone attracted £35.8 billion in cross-border transactions in 2022, a notable 12% year-over-year increase (CBRE, 2023). Institutional money from across Europe and further afield flows to London, Paris, and Berlin, seeking liquidity and stability. Berlin, in particular, stands out for its robust rent growth in the multifamily space and persistently low vacancies. Table 15.1 highlights that sovereign wealth funds and pension funds are increasingly active on the continent, pursuing attractive yield premiums in markets like Paris alongside Berlin's multifamily strengths (CBRE, 2023; Savills, 2022).

Asia-Pacific: Looking east, the Asia-Pacific region is quickly asserting itself, not just as a prime target for cross-border investment, but as a major source of capital as well. Singapore leads this charge, with sovereign wealth funds like GIC and Temasek investing around $12 billion abroad in 2022 alone. Meanwhile, South Korean and Japanese institutional investors are sending teams overseas to hunt for industrial, office, and multifamily deals in other global cities. As Table 15.1 notes, these flows are largely coming from sovereign and pension funds and reflect Asia-Pacific's growing importance as both a global investor hub and a destination for institutional capital (MSCI, 2023; ANREV, 2023).

Table 15.1 offers a concise overview of these markets, highlighting top sectors, principal investor types (from global institutional funds to sovereign wealth and pension giants), and notable market trends, such as the ongoing e-commerce surge in the U.S., London's enduring liquidity in office, and the rapid outbound capital growth from Asia-Pacific (MSCI, 2023; CBRE, 2023; JLL, 2023).

Table 15.1 Features of Leading Cross-Border Real Estate Markets

Market	Key Sectors	Primary Investor Types	Notable Trends
United States	Industrial, Multifamily	Global institutional & private	Surge in e-commerce logistics, vibrant Sun Belt
United Kingdom	Office, Retail	European & international funds	London remains Europe's office hub, strong liquidity
Continental Europe	Multifamily, Office, Logistics	Sovereign funds, pension funds	Growth in multifamily (Berlin), yield premiums (Paris)
Asia-Pacific	Industrial, Office, Multifamily	Sovereign wealth funds (GIC, Temasek), pension funds	Outbound capital growth, global investor hubs

Table 15.1 Overview of key cross-border real estate markets and trends (MSCI, 2023; CBRE, 2023; JLL, 2023).

15.5 Case Example: Asian Institutional Expansion into U.S. Industrial & Logistics Assets

Why the U.S. industrial rush from Asia? There are a few big reasons:

- The U.S. market has enjoyed steady rent hikes averaging 8-10% per year from 2018 to 2023.
- E-commerce now accounts for 16% of U.S. retail sales, driving demand for last-mile and fulfillment warehouses.
- Exposure here helps investors hedge inflation and interest-rate volatility back home (Prologis Research, 2023; U.S. Census Bureau, 2023; Alqahtani & Mayes, 2020).

Some big deals stand out. GIC teamed up with Prologis on a $14 billion logistics venture, the largest foreign investment ever in U.S. industrial real estate (CBRE, 2022). Meanwhile, Korean pension funds like NPS invested $7 to $10 billion from 2019 to 2022, often partnering with local REITs and funds for operational strength (MSCI, 2023).

These investments saw cap rates in prime logistics markets drop 100-150 basis points over four years, with rents growing strongly and vacancy rates staying super low. Even when factoring currency hedging costs, Asian investors enjoyed solid local-currency returns, underscoring the benefit of a global industrial tilt (Kohl & Sirmans, 2021).

15.6 Risk Considerations in Global CRE Investing

You can't talk global investment without risk. Foreign ownership rules can delay or complicate deals in places like Canada or the EU, where approvals might stretch months longer (CBRE, 2023). Market transparency varies widely, while the U.S., UK, Canada, and Australia offer crystal-clear data, Southeast Asia and parts of Eastern Europe remain murky (JLL, 2022).

Liquidity also takes a hit; selling overseas real estate usually takes longer and costs more, with investors pricing in a 50–150 basis point premium for that risk.

15.7 Strategic Implications for Global Investors

Cross-border CRE investing is no longer a trendy sideline; it's central to long-term strategy. Here's why you want to consider it seriously:

- ☐ You gain access to sectors unavailable or thinly traded at home, like the U.S. logistics boom for Asian investors or Europe's emerging life sciences hubs.
- ☐ Spreading your bets geographically reduces shocks from political or economic turmoil.
- ☐ Smart diversification boosts risk-adjusted returns, over a decade, U.S. multifamily and industrial returns nearly tripled those in many Asian markets.
- ☐ You ride macro trends, like the rapid growth of Sun Belt metros with rising populations of 1.5% per year or Europe's adaptive reuse renaissance post-pandemic.

Global real estate investing isn't guesswork anymore. Professionals rely on scenario planning, predictive analytics, and thorough risk management to juggle currency, regulations, and sector-specific issues (Ho, 2018; Kohl & Sirmans, 2021).

15.8 Case Example: GIC's Integrated Global Portfolio

Take Singapore's GIC. They spread their capital across U.S. industrial, European office, and Australian multifamily. Over five years, this approach led to a 9.2% annualized return, while bringing portfolio volatility down 18% compared to a home-only focus. Their currency hedging also added about 1.5% in annual return. This is the kind of disciplined, global approach that delivers in both return and resilience (MSCI, 2023).

15.9 Transition to Chapter 16: The Future of Space and Demand

Now that you see how capital races across borders with precision and purpose, we're ready to explore what's happening on the ground. The next chapter zooms into shifting tenant demands, from data centers to adaptive reuse, and how technology and new property types are rewriting how and where value gets created in CRE's evolving landscape. Stay tuned.

References

AEW. (2025). *Asia Pacific real estate: Performance and outlook.* AEW Research.
https://www.aew.com/research/part-one-asia-pacific-real-estate

Alqahtani, F., & Mayes, D. G. (2020). Inflation hedging with international real estate investments. *Journal of International Real Estate Studies, 14*(3), 45–62.

Alqahtani, F., & Mayes, D. G. (2020). Sovereign wealth funds and portfolio diversification. *Journal of International Financial Markets, Institutions & Money, 68*, Article 101208.

ANREV. (2022). *ANREV annual index 2022.*
https://www.anrev.org/en/market-information/indices/anrev-annual-index

ANREV. (2023). *ANREV annual index 2022.*
https://www.anrev.org/en/market-information/indices/anrev-annual-index

ANREV. (2023). *Asia-Pacific capital flows tracker.*

CBRE. (2022). *Global real estate capital flows H1 2022.* CBRE Research. https://www.cbre.com/insights/reports/global-real-estate-capital-flows-h1-2022

CBRE. (2023). *Global real estate capital flows H2 2022.* CBRE Research. https://www.cbre.com/insights/reports/global-real-estate-capital-flows-h2-2022

CBRE. (2023). *Global market highlights.*

Eichholtz, P., Holtermans, R., & Yönder, E. (2021). Portfolio diversification in global real estate markets. *Journal of Real Estate Finance and Economics, 63*(4), 566-592. https://doi.org/10.1007/s11146-020-09770-5

Eichholtz, P., Kok, N., & Quigley, J. (2021). International diversification in real estate portfolios. *Journal of Real Estate Finance and Economics, 62*(2), 187-214.

https://doi.org/10.1007/s11146-020-09770-5

Ho, B. (2018). Currency hedging and international real estate returns. *Real Estate Economics, 46*(3), 520-556.

Ho, G. (2018). Currency risk management in international real estate portfolios. *Journal of Property Investment & Finance, 36*(2), 157-174.

Ho, K. (2018). Currency hedging strategies in global real estate investment. *Journal of Property Investment & Finance, 36*(1), 45-59.

Hoesli, M., & MacGregor, B. D. (2021). *Property investment: Principles and practice of portfolio management* (2nd ed.). Routledge.

JLL. (2022). *Global real estate transparency index 2022*. JLL Research. https://www.jll.com/research

JLL. (2023). *Cross-border investment outlook 2023*. JLL Research. https://www.jll.com/research

JLL. (2023). *European capital markets update*. JLL Research. https://www.jll.com/research

JLL. (2023). *International real estate market overview*.

JLL. (2023). *Post-pandemic real estate trends and urban adaptation*. https://www.jll.com/research

Kohl, H., & Sirmans, C. (2021). Currency effects on foreign real estate investment returns. *Journal of Real Estate Finance, 42*(4), 321-339.

Kohl, S., & Sirmans, G. (2021). Exchange-rate dynamics and international real estate investment. *Journal of Property Research, 38*(2), 123–142*.

MSCI. (2023). *Global real assets return index.* MSCI Research.
https://www.msci.com

MSCI. (2023). *Global real estate investment report 2023.* MSCI Research.
https://www.msci.com/our-solutions/research

MSCI. (2023). *Global real estate investment report.*

National Multifamily Housing Council. (2023). *Multifamily vacancy and rent growth trends 2023.*
https://www.nmhc.org

Prologis Research. (2023). *Logistics real estate market outlook.*
https://www.prologis.com/research

Prologis Research. (2023). *U.S. logistics market snapshot 2023.*
https://www.prologis.com/research

Savills. (2022). *Berlin residential market report 2022.*
https://www.savills.com/research

Savills. (2022). *Europe multifamily investment review.*

Sun, K. (2022). Historical patterns and recent impacts of Chinese investors in United States real estate. *SSRN.*
https://arxiv.org/abs/2301.00681

The diversification benefits of foreign real estate: Evidence from 40 years of data. (2023). *Journal of Real Estate Finance and Investment, 17*(4), 160.

U.S. Census Bureau. (2023). *Construction and leasing activity data.*

U.S. Census Bureau. (2023). *Quarterly e-commerce retail sales report.* https://www.census.gov

Viceira, L. M., & Wang, Z. K. (2018). *Global portfolio diversification for long-horizon investors* (NBER Working Paper No. 24646). National Bureau of Economic Research. https://www.nber.org/papers/w24646

CHAPTER 16

The Future of Space and Demand

Introduction

Commercial real estate is at a turning point. If you've been following the market, you know this space is reshaping itself fundamentally. Why? Because the pandemic rewired how we work and shop. Technology is sweeping through faster than ever. Demographics are shifting in ways that matter, and capital is chasing the winners, the highest-performing property types that deliver steady returns and growth. If you want to make smart investments in office, retail, logistics, or mixed-use properties over the next decade, you've got to understand these powerful forces converging right now.

Let's examine what's driving today's demand, grounded in fresh data and real-world cases. That way, the theory isn't just academic, it's actionable.

16.1 Post-Pandemic Evolution of Office Demand

16.1.1 The Hybrid Work Imperative and Declining Utilization

Here's something you might find surprising: office demand in the U.S. has permanently reset. Even as we see some folks trickling back, hybrid work models have become the norm. The reality? Physical attendance at offices in the biggest metro areas is stuck at just half, or less, of what it was before COVID hit.

Kastle Systems (2024) tracks office usage closely. In 2019, the average office use hovered around 95%. Fast forward: it bottomed out at a shocking 15% in 2020, recovered slowly to 52% in 2024, but it's still not close to that pre-pandemic baseline. Basically, we're operating more than 40% below where the market was just a few years ago. This means you can't count on offices filling back to old levels soon. Many office buildings today simply don't match what tenants need anymore, leaving landlords stuck with spaces that feel outdated or unnecessary (JLL, 2023).

16.1.2 Flight to Quality: Bifurcation Between Class A and Class B/C

The drop in office demand isn't spread evenly. It's splitting into two clear stories: Class A offices are holding their own, sometimes even thriving, while Class B and C buildings are struggling.

Imagine it like this: Class A offices, those shiny buildings with top-notch HVAC, sustainability features, flexible layouts, and amenities people want, are signing tenants faster, at rates 10% to 20% higher than older, less glamorous buildings. They're also commanding rent premiums of 5% to 8% (JLL, 2023). Meanwhile, Class B and C spaces sit vacant between 18% and 25%, with rents falling 3% to 8% annually, and landlords coughing up more in tenant improvements and upkeep (NAR, 2024).

In numbers: Class A vacancy is 12% to 14%; for Class B/C, it's more like 20% to 28%. Rent growth for Class A hovers near 1% to 3% yearly; for Class B/C, it's declining. This gap spells out a caution: older office buildings face significant risks of obsolescence and might require heavy investment, or conversion, to stay relevant (NAR, 2024).

16.2 Retail Transformation: From Mall Decline to Experience-Driven Demand

16.2.1 E-Commerce and the New Retail Footprint

Retail is nothing like it used to be. E-commerce has marched steadily forward, eating up a bigger slice of total sales, from 11% in 2019 to 15.4% in 2023 (U.S. Census Bureau, 2023). Traditional malls feel the pinch while retailers who can juggle online and in-store selling, the so-called omnichannel champions, are pulling ahead.

16.2.2 Experience-Led Retail Outperforms

Here's something you'll want to note: retail properties that focus on experiences, think dining, entertainment, wellness, and community events, are consistently outperforming old-school malls.

According to PwC (2022), experience-driven centers see two to four times the foot traffic of traditional malls. Tenants there make 7% to 12% more sales per square foot, while vacancies run just 5% to 9%, compared to 12% to 18% for legacy malls.

Numbers tell the story: traditional malls pull in about $420 to $560 per square foot in sales and score a foot traffic index of 100. Meanwhile, mixed-use experiential centers hit $600 to $800 sales per square foot and a foot traffic index from 230 to 400. Plus, shoppers stay longer, dwell time nearly triples.

Why? People want places blending social connection with shopping, entertainment, and digital-physical integration. This trend is rewriting retail's playbook.

16.3 Logistics and Industrial: The Backbone of Modern Commerce

16.3.1 Demand Surge and Tight Market Conditions

If you're chasing consistent returns, look no further than logistics and industrial properties. For the past decade, they've been the star performers.

What's driving this? E-commerce's boom, reshored manufacturing, and evolving supply chains with tight delivery windows. Vacancy nationwide stays under 4% despite record-breaking new development (Prologis, 2023).

Annual rent growth for logistics heats up to 8% to 10%. In hotspots like Southern California, New Jersey, Dallas-Fort Worth, and Atlanta, rents have soared over 15% year over year. Everyone from retailers to third-party logistics is snapping up space, especially infill last-mile facilities, where proximity to customers is king (CBRE, 2023).

16.3.2 Technology and Automation Reshaping Warehousing

Warehouse tech is getting seriously smart. Labor shortages and wage pressures mean companies heavily invest in robotics, automated picking, autonomous vehicles, and AI-managed inventory.

McKinsey (2022) reports that automated distribution centers cut order fulfillment times by 40%, boost inventory accuracy from 92% to 99%, slash labor needs by 25% to 40%, and dramatically lower errors.

Picture this: traditional centers score 100 on fulfillment speed; automated ones reach 140. Labor costs drop from an index of 100 down to 60–75, while error rates fall from 2.1% to 0.4%. Increasingly, a property's worth depends on its automation-readiness, clear ceiling heights, strong floors, electrical capacity, and space for mezzanines all matter (JLL, 2023).

16.4 Adaptive Reuse as a Catalyst for New Value

16.4.1 Why Adaptive Reuse Is Accelerating

Cities across the U.S. are embracing adaptive reuse, turning old, underperforming structures into vibrant new spaces. This strategy tackles stubborn office and retail vacancies *and* the pressing housing crunch.

Why is it catching on? Adaptive reuse typically costs 10% to 20% less than new construction and slashes embodied carbon emissions by up to 60%. These projects lease up faster because they combine unique architectural features with neighborhood fit. Also helping: zoning incentives, density bonuses, and public-private partnerships make these deals viable and attractive (Urban Land Institute [ULI], 2023).

16.5 Case Example: Converting Dead Malls into Mixed-Use Community Hubs

16.5.1 Project Overview: Highland Mall Redevelopment (Austin, Texas)

Look at Highland Mall, a textbook adaptive reuse success story. Once a retail giant of the 1970s, it soured with rising vacancies and fading community relevance. But in a public-private partnership, it was reborn as a mixed-use neighborhood.

Today, Highland houses a flagship Austin Community College campus, a mix of market-rate and affordable housing, office space for tech and creative companies, retail and dining, plus public green spaces. Instead of a ghost town, you get a vibrant 24/7 district weaving education, housing, commerce, and community together (Austin Community College [ACC], 2022; RedLeaf Properties & ACC, n.d.).

16.5.2 Measurable Outcomes

The numbers back this up. Property values in the Highland area jumped over 300%, economic output topped $1 billion, and thousands of jobs were created, from construction to permanent roles.

Visitors soared from 1 million to 3.5 million annually, while vacancies plunged from over 50% to under 5%. Activating the space around the clock breathed new life into a site that once only hummed during mall hours.

The outcomes neatly summarized in Table 16.5 make this crystal clear:

Table 16.5 Key impacts from the Highland Mall redevelopment project

Metric	Pre-Redevelopment (Index 100)	Post-Redevelopment
Property Value	100	350+
Annual Visitors	1 million	3.5 million
Economic Output	Minimal	$1 billion+
Vacancy Rate	>50%	<5%

Table 16.5. Key impacts from the Highland Mall redevelopment project (ACC, 2022; Community Impact, 2017; RedLeaf Properties & ACC, n.d.).

16.6 Emerging Asset Types: Life Sciences, Data Centers, and Flex Space

16.6.1 Life Sciences

Aging populations, biotech breakthroughs, and boosted public research funding have supercharged demand for life science and R&D space. BioMed Realty (2023) reports a 12% compound annual growth rate over the last decade in hubs like Boston-Cambridge, San Diego, the Bay Area, and the Research Triangle.

16.6.2 Data Centers

Data centers keep growing, globally expanding 30% annually (Knight Frank, 2023). AI training, cloud services, streaming, and digital transformations are straining power grids, making locations with strong, renewable energy infrastructure incredibly valuable.

16.6.3 Flexible Space

Hybrid work is spotlighting flexible office formats, from coworking spaces to managed suites. JLL (2023) estimates these currently make up about 3% of U.S. office stock but could hit 10% by 2030 as companies crave agility in cost and commitment.

16.7 Investor Implications: Strategic Positioning for the Next Decade

What does all this mean for you as an investor? The environment is more nuanced and fast-moving than before. Focus on amenity-rich, ESG-certified offices; experience-driven retail blending community and food; last-mile logistics with sticky demand; adaptive reuse where vacancies meet housing shortages; and booming life sciences, data centers, and digital infrastructure.

Winning in the next cycle means mixing smart design, tech readiness, sustainability, community vision, and flexible financial models.

Those who get this right will see returns and resilience others can only hope for.

16.8 Transition to Part VI. Applied Case Studies and Investor Insights

As demand for space keeps evolving thanks to technology, demographics, hybrid work, and e-commerce, investors must adopt sharper, more nuanced tools. The next part takes you into the trenches, covering everything from market assessments and urban design to financial modeling, capital optimization, risk analysis, and long-term hold-sell strategies.

The Chapter 17 case study on mixed-use redevelopment is just the start of applying these lessons in the real world.

References

Austin Community College. (2022). *Highland campus redevelopment impact report.* https://www.austincc.edu

BioMed Realty. (2023). *Life science real estate demand outlook.* https://www.biomedrealty.com

CBRE. (2023). *North America industrial and logistics outlook.* https://www.cbre.com/insights

Community Impact. (2017, February 27). Highland's revival raises area home prices, spurs growth. https://communityimpact.com

Community Impact. (2017, September 21). ACC Highland Mall breaks ground on Phase 2 of its development. https://communityimpact.com

JLL. (2023). *Industrial and logistics real estate: Automation and investor strategies.* https://www.jll.com/research

JLL. (2023). *U.S. office outlook: Market bifurcation and flight to quality.* https://www.jll.com/research

Kastle Systems. (2024). *Back-to-Work Barometer: National occupancy trends.* https://www.kastle.com/safety-wellness/getting-back-to-work

Knight Frank. (2023). *Global data center report.* https://www.knightfrank.com/research

McKinsey & Company. (2022). *Automation in logistics: Transforming warehouse operations.* https://www.mckinsey.com

National Association of Realtors. (2024). *Commercial real estate market insights.* https://www.nar.realtor/research-and-statistics

Prologis. (2023). *U.S. industrial market fundamentals.* https://www.prologis.com/research

PwC. (2022). *Global consumer insights survey: Experience economy edition.* https://www.pwc.com

RedLeaf Properties & Austin Community College. (n.d.). *The development - Highland TX.* Highland ATX. https://www.highlandatx.com

U.S. Census Bureau. (2023). *Quarterly retail e-commerce sales report.* https://www.census.gov/retail

Urban Land Institute. (2023). *Emerging trends in real estate: Adaptive reuse edition.* https://uli.org

PART VI

Applied Case Studies and Investor Insights

OVERVIEW

Now we bring everything together. You've built a strong foundation, market analysis, financial modeling, valuation, risk management, portfolio strategy, and a look at the future of CRE. Part VI moves from theory to action, showing you exactly how expert investors put these tools to work in real-world situations.

This section bridges the gap between knowing and doing. We'll walk you through how seasoned investors handle uncertainty, structure deals, size up opportunities across market cycles, and embed discipline into every step of their process. Through hands-on case studies and distilled lessons from industry veterans, we'll help you adopt the habits, systems, and decision-making frameworks that lead to lasting success.

Whether you're preparing for your first deal or managing a multi-billion-dollar portfolio, this part sharpens your approach, highlights the traps to avoid, and guides you in building repeatable systems that deliver consistent results.

Overview of Chapters

Chapter 17 – Integrated Case Study: Evaluating a Mixed-Use Development

Here's where we synthesize everything we've learned. Step by step, you'll see how to evaluate a complex mixed-use project from the ground up. We cover:

- ☐ Market screening and understanding who lives and spends where
- ☐ Positioning the project competitively and forecasting demand
- ☐ Building detailed financial models and underwriting the project

- ☐ Running scenario tests and stress analyses to evaluate risk
- ☐ Designing a capital stack—blending equity, debt, and preferred equity
- ☐ Planning exit strategies and creating long-term value pathways

By walking through this full investment lifecycle, you'll see how smart investors blend market insight, financial rigor, and strategic judgment into one fluid decision.

Chapter 18 – Lessons from the Field

This chapter is packed with hard-won wisdom from seasoned investors, fund managers, operators, and advisors around the globe. These voices share the mental models and strategic habits that separate consistent winners from the rest. We explore:

- ☐ The power of governance and disciplined decision-making
- ☐ Reading timing and cycles like a pro
- ☐ Recognizing behavioral traps and staying mentally sharp
- ☐ Aligning incentives and managing partnerships with clarity
- ☐ The need for a global perspective and diversified opportunities
- ☐ How to not just survive but thrive through crises and volatility

We'll also highlight classic mistakes, overleveraging, risk mispricing, slack due diligence, and chasing trends, and give you actionable tips for dodging these pitfalls.

Chapter 19 – Principles to Practice

Finally, we drill down into four core principles, governance, timing, behavioral discipline, and global perspective, and translate them into practical systems you can weave into your own investing practice. We show that top investors don't just make good judgments; they build scalable, repeatable frameworks that guide great decisions time and again.

Topics you'll master include:

- Designing governance structures that foster transparency and accountability
- Timing frameworks that blend macroeconomic signals with market nuances
- Behavioral safeguards that keep emotional impulses in check
- Building global frameworks to spot and seize cross-border opportunities
- Institutionalizing discipline through risk controls, investment committees, and standardized underwriting
- Creating scalable platforms ranging from analytics to capital relationships, compounding your advantage over time
- Aligning general partner and limited partner incentives clearly through robust fund structures and communication

Drawing from real estate, private equity, venture capital, and infrastructure, this chapter closes the book by helping you create your own system of excellence, turning what you've learned into your own long-term performance engine.

Key Takeaways from Part VI

- Applied learning matters. Bringing market, financial, and strategy analysis into real-world case studies deepens your understanding and sharpens your decisions.
- Experience reveals consistent patterns. Governance, timing, behavioral discipline, and a global view are the principles that set top investors apart.

- ☐ Systems beat gut feelings. Building repeatable, institutionalized processes reduces bias, strengthens rigor, and scales with market cycles and new opportunities.
- ☐ Cross-disciplinary insights help. The best investors borrow smart frameworks from private equity, venture capital, infrastructure, and global capital markets to elevate their edge.
- ☐ Investment excellence is crafted, not random. By combining disciplined analysis with strong systems, you build durable advantages that grow exponentially over time.

CHAPTER 17

Integrated Case Study: Evaluating Mixed-Use Development

Introduction

Mixed-use developments stand among the largest, most ambitious, and capital-demanding ventures you'll encounter in real estate. You're not just building houses or office buildings, you're weaving together offices, residences, retail, hospitality, cultural centers, and public spaces into a single urban ecosystem that often functions almost like a mini-city. This chapter is your roadmap to understanding how to evaluate investments in these complex projects. We'll walk through the case of Hudson Yards in New York City, the biggest private real estate development in U.S. history. Through this, you'll get hands-on insights about market realities, financial modeling, risk evaluations, capital structuring, and the careful choreography of public-private partnerships that bring these projects to life.

Why Hudson Yards? Because it checks so many boxes, reimagined urban infrastructure, layered financing, diverse income streams, and innovative collaborations between the city and private investors. It's a rare and valuable example for institutional investors or developers who want to figure out how to evaluate projects on this scale (Oxford Properties, 2023; Martini, 2021).

17.1 Project Overview & Strategic Vision

Imagine 28 acres on Manhattan's far West Side, an old, noisy railyard that most New Yorkers probably forgot existed. Today, that space has been transformed into one of the world's most globally recognized mixed-use neighborhoods. Spearheaded by Related Companies and Oxford Properties, Hudson Yards spans nearly 18 million square feet and stitches together five massive office towers (including the flagship 10 and 30 Hudson Yards), almost 5,000 residential units, about 400 of which are affordable units, in a city starved for housing options, 720,000 square feet of retail anchored by luxury and experiential stores, plus 14 acres of connected green spaces. Add landmarks like The Vessel, a climbing sculpture that became an instant sensation, and The Shed, a flexible arts space, not to mention a K-8 public school, and you get a development that reaches far beyond typical commercial aims into culture and community (Oxford Properties, 2023).

The scale of Hudson Yards puts it alongside giants like London's Canary Wharf or Singapore's Marina Bay. It isn't just big; it's designed to be transformative. Once fully operational, Hudson Yards is projected to add $19 billion per year to New York City's GDP and support about 55,000 permanent jobs across office, retail, cultural, and public sectors. Plus, it generates steady tax revenues through creative mechanisms like PILOT agreements, those "Payment In Lieu Of Taxes" arrangements that keep city coffers full while supporting development (Oxford Properties, 2023).

You should note the strategic vision here: sustainability is baked in. About 60% of the district's energy comes from an onsite cogeneration plant, minimizing reliance on external grids. Greywater recycling reduces the district's water demand by roughly 10 million gallons per year. Composting programs and district-wide microgrids further reinforce resilience. Also, significant portions of the development have earned LEED-ND Gold certification, signaling a strong green commitment. The project cleverly repurposed air rights above an active railyard, layering dense, transit-oriented development with an intensive public-private funding approach. The goal? To create an uninterrupted live-work-play district that's unmatched anywhere in New York (Oxford Properties, 2023).

17.2 Market & Demand Analysis

Let's talk about the market dynamics, especially important for you as an investor or analyst. Post-pandemic, the office sector in the U.S. has bifurcated. Commodity office buildings, think uninspired towers without amenities, are struggling, while "lifestyle" office districts embedded within mixed-use developments like Hudson Yards are thriving. According to JLL (2023), these amenity-rich districts command rents that are 32% higher than traditional Class A office buildings and lease out about twice as fast.

Why does this happen? Because tenants do not just want a desk; they want a complete "HQ environment" complete with retail, wellness centers, dining options, residences nearby, and green spaces. Top-tier tenants such as BlackRock and WarnerMedia have explicitly cited these integrated amenities as reasons for committing long-term leases here.

When we look at the residential market, you'll notice that nearly 5,000 units cater to a growing demand for luxury housing accessible to transit. Manhattan has a runway shortage, with apartment vacancy rates rarely breaking 3-4%. Units in the Hudson Yards towers, especially at 15 and 35 Hudson Yards, consistently rank among the priciest in the city. Convenience, amenities, exclusive community features all factor into that premium (Oxford Properties, 2023).

Retail moves beyond your typical shopping centers. The strategy is experiential and destination-driven, restaurants, high-end boutiques, and cultural venues like The Shed bring in foot traffic from workers, residents, and tourists alike. One vital piece that you should never overlook is infrastructure. The No. 7 subway extension, financed via municipal bonds, dramatically improved site accessibility and foot traffic (SCEPA, 2020). That extension didn't just move people; it drove value. It's a textbook example of how infrastructure investment is foundational to mixed-use district success.

17.3 Financial Modeling & Pro Forma Construction

Now, let's break down the financial blueprint behind Hudson Yards. The pro forma layers multiple revenue streams to build a robust income profile. Office leases come courtesy of blue-chip tenants like Coach, L'Oréal, and BlackRock, anchoring steady cash flows. Residential rents roll in from nearly 5,000 apartments, including about 400 affordable units, catering to a range of tenants in a tight market with vacancy rates below 4%, reflecting ongoing demand for urban housing (Oxford Properties, 2023; JLL, 2023). On the retail side, leasing combines fixed rents with percentage leases, capturing extra upside from sales-driven anchor tenants and experiential stores spread across 720,000 square feet of luxury retail space.

Beyond these core streams, additional sources add meaningful complexity and value: parking fees, naming rights, events hosted at The Shed, and concessions in publicly accessible zones all contribute to diversifying revenue.

Operating expenses are considerable. Running the district's cogeneration plant, maintaining vast public parks, staffing open plazas and security, and managing construction complexities atop an active railyard platform all weigh on costs. Yet economies of scale and premium rents help balance the books. For example, the multifamily building 3Eleven showed an impressive net operating income (NOI) around $46,000 per unit annually, with operating expenses running roughly 37% of revenue once stabilized (MMCG, 2022).

The capital stack behind Hudson Yards is intricate and layered. Equity investments from Related, Oxford, and international partners blend with senior construction debt and infrastructure bonds issued by the Hudson Yards Infrastructure Corporation (HYIC). These HYIC bonds, which are backed by reliable PILOT (Payments In Lieu Of Taxes) cash flows and city tax incentives, represent one of the project's most innovative financing tools, lowering the overall cost of capital and aligning the long-term interests of public stakeholders and private investors (Martini, 2021). On top of this, public-sector support through tax deferrals, direct infrastructure funding, and investments in transit, such as the No. 7 subway extension, play an essential role in the project's feasibility (BJH Advisors, 2020).

By the numbers, Hudson Yards covers approximately 28 acres of Manhattan's former railyard, boasting around 18 million square feet of mixed-use space including five major office towers, nearly 5,000 residential units, and 720,000 square feet of luxury retail space. These dimensions underpin an estimated $19 billion annual contribution to New York City's GDP and support roughly 55,000 permanent jobs across office, retail, cultural, and public sectors. Office rents command premiums about 32% above typical Class A buildings in New York City, underscoring the value tenants place on the amenity-rich lifestyle environment Hudson Yards fosters (Oxford Properties, 2023; JLL, 2023).

These key metrics are detailed in Table 17.1 below.

Table 17.1 Key Financial and Development Metrics for Hudson Yards

Metric	Figure	Notes
Total Project Area	~28 acres	Former Manhattan railyard site
Gross Building Area	~18 million sq ft	Mixed-use across residential, office, retail
Office Towers	5 major towers	Including signature 10 and 30 Hudson Yards
Residential Units	~5,000 units	~400 affordable units
Retail Space	720,000 sq ft	Luxury and experiential retail
Annual Economic Contribution	$19 billion	NYC GDP impact at stabilization
Permanent Jobs Supported	~55,000	Across sectors including office, retail, cultural
Residential Vacancy Rate	<4%	Reflecting tight urban housing market
Office Rent Premium	~32% over Class A norm	For integrated lifestyle office districts (JLL, 2023)

Note. Adapted from Oxford Properties (2023), JLL (2023), Martini (2021), and MMCG (2022).

17.4 Risk Evaluation & Sensitivity Analysis

No project this huge is without risks layered across construction, financing, market conditions, politics, and tenant demand. Hudson Yards provides a detailed case study in how to manage these thoughtfully.

Office market risk stands out in the post-COVID world where occupancy averages hover around 50-60% in metro areas (JLL,

2025). But lifestyle offices integrated within mixed-use create a buffer by delivering 32–35% rent premiums, fast pre-leasing rates, sometimes up to 40-50% pre-leased before completion, and longer lease durations. That tenant commitment dramatically reduces speculative risk (JLL, 2023).

On construction, platform projects like Hudson Yards are beasts. The deck alone required over 35,000 tons of steel and 300 caissons, exceeding $1 billion just for that substructure (Oxford Properties, 2023). Flyvbjerg (2022) teaches us that almost 90% of megaprojects regularly blow their budgets by 28–45%, raising red flags at every phase. A coordination failure among MTA, HYIC, and city infrastructure teams could have sent costs and timelines spiraling.

Financing is another battlefield. Debt costs shift with interest rates, a 100-basis-point increase can slice IRRs by 0.5 to 1.2 percentage points. HYIC's refinancing depends on city credit ratings and PILOT cash flow stability, introducing risk (Martini, 2021). Meanwhile, latent worries surround rising operating and energy expenses outpacing income growth (DBRS Morningstar, 2022).

Political and regulatory terrain always holds surprises. Rezoning, approval processes, air rights deals, and public funding negotiations face uncertain timetables and influence from shifting political winds. Groups like Capalino steered alignment behind the scenes, but even strong partnerships can't erase all risk (Capalino, 2020). Environmental regulation tightening means more compliance costs but early LEED-ND certification put Hudson Yards ahead of many peers.

Demand shocks also matter. Residential lease rates and purchases ebb and flow with employment, income, mortgage rates, and shifting preferences between urban and suburban living. For example, a 200-bp jump in mortgage rates cuts home affordability by 20–25%, boosting rent demand but capping for-sale prices. Retail depends heavily on healthy office tenants, population growth, and tourism.

Any slip here hits sales per square foot and pressures percentage-rent models, squeezing NOI.

Finally, exit risk is not trivial. Hudson Yards' scale means buyers are ultra-high-net-worth individuals, sovereign wealth funds, or massive pension or private equity firms. Even then, timing matters: a 50-bp cap rate rise, from 4.5% to 5%, can slash asset values by 10-15% (McKinsey, 2023).

17.5 Financial Returns & Underwriting Insights

Institutional investors think about mixed-use megaproject returns in phases, with different risk profiles as projects develop. Stabilized districts look for IRRs in the 8-12% range. Earlier, riskier phases demand 12-16%, while mature core assets settle for lower yields around 6-8%.

Exit valuations are stress-tested by shifts of ±50 basis points around cap rate assumptions: NYCs office markets trade between 4.0-5.25%, luxury multifamily around 3.5-4.5%, retail between 5-6%. Your underwriting scenarios must contemplate slower lease-ups, lengthening negative cash flows and elevating interest costs; 15% cost overruns reducing IRR by up to 300 basis points; interest rate hikes biting deeply into equity returns; and cap rate changes as the biggest threat over long holds.

17.6 Strategic Value Creation & ESG Upside

The edge now goes to mixed-use districts that nail ESG, technology, and public realm innovation. Hudson Yards shows how sustainability investments translate to real dollars. Energy-efficient systems cut operational costs by 10-15%, expand access to cheaper green finance, and attract tenants who willingly pay 4-7% rent premiums for ESG-certified space (Deloitte, 2023). Properties with strong ESG records see 6-10% price premiums on sale.

The district is a smart city trailblazer, with sensors monitoring air quality, energy, and waste, a fiber backbone powering high-speed data, and analytics driving efficient, flexible management. This "quantified district" sets a new standard in urban operating sophistication (Hunter Urban Planning, 2022).

Public-private collaboration created a virtuous cycle: infrastructure investments like the No. 7 subway extension raised land values, drew Fortune 500 tenants, and boosted tax revenue. This PPP model linking public investments to project returns offers a replicable blueprint for ambitious urban developments (SCEPA, 2020).

17.7 Transition to Chapter 18: Lessons from the Field

We've traced Hudson Yards from its market context to financial underpinnings, risk calibration, and sustainability integration. The next chapter dives into direct lessons from those who invest, manage, and develop these monstrous projects. They'll share not only winning strategies but also pitfalls that trip up even the best planners. This is where theory meets practice, and you get to learn from the real deal.

References

BJH Advisors. (2020). *Hudson Yards financing structure: A feasibility analysis.* BJH Advisors. https://www.bjhadvisors.com/projects/hudsonyards

Capalino & Company. (2020). *Hudson Yards: Public approval and political strategy analysis.* https://www.capalino.com/case-studies/hudson-yards/

DBRS Morningstar. (2022). *Hudson Yards credit and operating expense assessment.* https://dbrs.morningstar.com/research/360672/dbrs-morningstar-assigns-ratings-to-hudson-yards-2016-10hy-mortgage-trust

Deloitte. (2023). *ESG and real estate performance: Global trends report.* https://www2.deloitte.com

Flyvbjerg, B. (2022). *How big things get done: Megaproject risk and global construction.* Oxford University Press.

Hunter Urban Planning. (2022). *Hudson Yards as a smart district: Technology and governance.* Hunter College. https://www.hunterurban.org

JLL. (2023). *Lifestyle office: Performance, absorption and investor demand.* https://www.jll.com/research

JLL. (2025). *Future of lifestyle office and mixed-use performance.* Jones Lang LaSalle. https://www.jll.com/en-us/newsroom/mixed-use-lifestyle-office-markets-defy-broader-office-market-challenges-commanding-32-higher-rents

Martini, J. (2021). Public-private finance and the evolution of Hudson Yards. *Urban Development Review.*

McKinsey & Company. (2023). *Construction megaproject costs and global capital trends.* McKinsey Global Institute.

MMCG Real Estate Analytics. (2022). *Hudson Yards multifamily underwriting package: 3Eleven stabilization analysis.* MMCG.
Oxford Properties Group. (2023). *Hudson Yards: Project overview, economic impact, and sustainability report.* https://www.oxfordproperties.com/news/hudson-yards

SCEPA (Stern Center for Economic Policy Analysis). (2020). *Infrastructure investment and the Hudson Yards development model.* The New School. https://www.economicpolicyresearch.org

CHAPTER

18 Lessons from the Field

Introduction

Investing is part cold calculation, part gut instinct. You learn the theories in textbooks and hone your skills in classrooms, but the real mastery? That comes from experience, from digging into the messy, unpredictable realities of different cycles, asset classes, and markets. You quickly realize that no spreadsheet or valuation model can fully capture the lessons seasoned investors carry with them. These are lessons carved out in the field: the wins, the losses, the disputes, and the moves made in moments of market panic or calm.

Across dozens of interviews with professionals from fund management, real estate, private equity, venture capital, and infrastructure, some themes show up again and again. Governance, timing, behavioral discipline, and global perspective, these aren't just buzzwords but the bedrock ideas that separate the thoughtful players from the lucky ones. Unlike abstract frameworks, these lessons come with real stories and case studies, successes and setbacks alike. If you take just one thing away, here it is: a practiced process and a disciplined mindset usually matter more than raw hunches or spotting the "next big thing" early.

18.1 Governance: The Backbone of Long-Term Results

18.1.1 When Governance Goes Wrong

If there's one thing grizzled investors hammer home, it's that solid governance underpins long-term success. McKinsey (2023) highlights that almost 40% of private investments that fail do so not because the assets tanked, but because governance broke down or decision rights were blurred. Even before you start executing a business plan, unclear oversight can quietly drain value.

Take a joint venture between an American operator and an Asian institutional investor. They had a sound thesis, but when they disagreed on renovation timing, it spiraled into months of stalled capital calls. The JV contract lacked a clear deadlock resolution clause. The consequence? Their IRR projections plummeted by 12%, not due to missed opportunities, but the muddle of stalled decisions.

But governance also acts as a brake. A European private equity firm dodged disaster during a frenzied roll-up in rising rate conditions because its shareholder agreement required unanimous consent for deals exceeding leverage limits. This internal check stopped them from biting off more risk than they could safely swallow.

In venture capital, governance wears a different hat. At one Southeast Asian fund, founders present a "Board Transparency Pack" monthly, covering burn rate, cohort retention, customer acquisition cost, and team pipeline. This routine flagged declining unit economics early at a fintech startup, allowing intervention to avoid a nasty down round.

For infrastructure funds, governance can even be existential. A Canadian pension fund investing in emerging-market power assets installs mandatory third-party compliance audits, not just as a formality but to prevent corruption and ensure contracts aren't undermined by local political skullduggery.

18.1.2 What Works in Governance

While governance structures must adapt to strategy, asset class, and geography, clear patterns emerge from the firms that do governance right. The first essential step is to codify decision rights early, especially for value-add or opportunistic strategies that require agility and quick pivots. A common practice among leading institutions is the establishment of independent advisory committees. These committees bring an external perspective and help align the often-disparate interests of limited partners (LPs).

Incentive structures also play a crucial role. Management fees and promote terms that are explicitly tied to measurable key performance indicators, such as lease-up velocity, operational expense savings, or milestone achievements, help ensure that everyone involved is pulling in the same direction. Finally, routine and transparent communication is vital. This usually takes the form of monthly reporting in venture capital and private equity, and quarterly reporting for real estate and infrastructure investments. Such a disciplined communication rhythm minimizes surprises and fosters trust among stakeholders.

These governance practices and their positive impacts are summarized in Table 18.1. For example, having clear decision rights like a joint venture contract with a deadlock resolution clause helped avoid stalled capital calls and erosion of internal rates of return (IRR). Similarly, independent advisory committees provide external oversight that aligns LP interests and mitigates conflicts. Incentive alignment through management fees tied to KPIs reduces agency problems and motivates the team, while routine reporting increases transparency and reduces unwelcome surprises.

Table 18.1 Governance Practices and Outcomes

Governance Element	Example	Impact
Clear decision rights	JV contract with deadlock resolution	Avoided stalled capital calls and IRR erosion
Independent advisory committees	Leading institutions' use	Brings external oversight, aligns LP interests
Incentive alignment	Management fees tied to KPIs (lease-up, OpEx)	Mitigates agency conflict, motivates team
Routine reporting	Monthly VC pack, quarterly RE/ infrastructure reports	Enhances transparency and reduces surprises

Note. Adapted from McKinsey (2023) and practitioner interviews.

18.2 Timing: Cycles Matter, But So Does Staying Power

18.2.1 Discipline Over Prediction

Believe me when I say: almost no one consistently times markets perfectly. The real advantage lies in discipline, the ability to hold your nerve through euphoria and crisis alike and to have dry powder ready when the opportunities appear.

Preqin's (2022) data spotlights this vividly. Private funds raised right after the global financial crisis (GFC), between 2009 and 2011, outperformed funds raised at market peaks by about 500 basis points of net IRR. The smartest players don't try to predict every twist; they deploy regularly but stay agile enough to buy more aggressively when the market turns.

18.2.2 Post-GFC Multifamily: A Case in Point

Between 2009 and 2012, those value-add multifamily operators who scooped up distressed or neglected properties with few competitors reaped outsized rewards. Construction costs were manageable, debt was cheap, and fear kept rivals on the sidelines. Many doubled or tripled their equity multiples, not because they timed the exact market bottom, but because they were prepared to act when others hesitated.

18.2.3 Nuances by Asset Class

How you approach timing really depends on the asset class you focus on. In private equity, firms made the most of pandemic-era market corrections by rolling up smaller targets and exiting once markets normalized, often achieving impressive cash-on-cash multiples in the range of 3 to 4 times. Meanwhile, venture capital managers who held onto cash through the frothy 2021 boom found a prime opportunity to redeploy in 2023, after valuations for fintech, logistics, and AI startups fell dramatically, by 40 to 60 percent.

Infrastructure investing leans heavily on regulatory timing. For example, U.S. renewable energy projects benefited significantly from the Inflation Reduction Act's incentives, which created a window for sustained and attractive risk-adjusted returns. Real estate timing, on the other hand, varies by region. In the U.S., it often follows Treasury yields, while in Europe sovereign debt spreads are more influential. In Asia-Pacific (APAC), a combination of government policies and capital controls drives market timing.

To illustrate, consider the equity multiple performance for U.S. multifamily investments post-GFC. (see Table 18.2). Properties acquired during the 2009-2011 distressed period achieved equity multiples between approximately 2.5 and 3.0 times, significantly higher than those purchased at the 2007-2008 pre-GFC peak, which averaged around 1.2 times. The recovery phase from 2012 to 2014 saw moderately strong multiples near 1.8 times as demand grew (Preqin, 2022). This vintage-year performance underscores the importance of patience and counter-cyclically positioning capital for value creation.

Table 18.2 Equity Multiple Performance by Vintage Year in U.S. Multifamily Post-GFC

Vintage Year	Equity Multiple (MOIC)	Market Context
2007-2008	~1.2x	Pre-GFC peak, crowded market
2009-2011	~2.5-3.0x	Post-GFC distressed opportunities
2012-2014	~1.8x	Recovery phase, growing demand

Note. Data adapted from Preqin (2022).

18.3 Behavioral Discipline: The Unseen Advantage

18.3.1 Mind Over Models

If you ask pros what makes or breaks careers, behavioral discipline is the top answer, surpassing even technical acumen. DALBAR (2023) found retail investors lag their benchmarks by 6-8% annually, mostly due to emotional biases like loss aversion, herding, and bad market timing. Institutional investors aren't immune. Overconfidence pushes leverage too far; fear delays strategic exits.

18.3.2 Institutional Guardrails Against Bias

The fragility of human judgment makes bias-mitigation tools essential in investment processes. Many firms build safeguards like mandatory "bear-case" critiques during approval to explicitly identify downside risks. 'Red team' reviews are common, where an independent group rigorously challenges bullish assumptions to improve realism. Pre-mortems, that is, systematically asking "How can this deal fail?" before committing capital, are becoming routine tools to reveal hidden threats early.

A notable example comes from a UK pension fund that introduced a "structured dissent protocol," which formally encourages honest debate and opposing views during committee discussions. This protocol proved effective, cutting underwriting errors by nearly a third and demonstrating that clear-eyed skepticism delivers real value (see Table 18.3).

Table 18.3 Behavioral Guardrails in Investment Process

Practice	Description	Impact
Bear-case writeups	Mandatory identification of downside scenarios	Greater foresight and risk awareness
Red team reviews	Independent challenge to optimistic assumptions	Reduced bias and more realistic valuations
Pre-mortems	Pre-commitment failure scenario analysis	Identifies hidden risks before deal approval
Structured dissent protocols	Formal encouragement of opposing viewpoints	Improved decision quality, fewer mistakes

Note. Adapted from DALBAR (2023) and practitioner interviews.

18.3.3 Lessons on Behavioral Discipline

The devil is in the details with behavioral discipline. A mid-market private equity firm routinely kills deals after a "Devil's Advocate" challenges optimistic margin forecasts. A global venture capital firm requires "Anti-Herd Memos" for high-profile investments to curb chasing overheated trends. One real estate investor ran thorough interest-rate stress tests during 2021's low-rate environment, wisely avoiding floating-rate debt that later overwhelmed competitors. Meanwhile, a European infrastructure fund scores and reviews all holdings quarterly to combat inertia.

18.4 Global Perspective: There Are No (Effective) Borders

18.4.1 Seeking Opportunity Worldwide

Financial markets are interconnected, but lots of investors still limit themselves geographically. Those who don't see the payoff. MSCI (2022) shows that globally diversified real estate portfolios experience 10–20% lower volatility than U.S.-only ones, without sacrificing long-term returns. Spreading investments across countries cushions political, economic, and demographic shocks.

18.4.2 Regional Insights You Can Use

North America perks include scalable private equity plays in healthcare services and industrial automation, venture capital's push into AI and biotech, persistent Sun Belt multifamily and logistics bets, and infrastructure fueled by grid rebuild and EV charging.

Europe's fragmented markets favor buy-and-build private equity, climate tech startups, and real estate pricing resets. Renewables lead the pack, with offshore wind and hydrogen investments accelerating.

APAC powers ahead: India and Southeast Asia ride digitalization and AI-driven productivity. Japan's ultra-low rates support real estate plays, while Singapore and Australia boast attractive institutional REIT and build-to-rent markets. The Asian Development Bank estimates the region needs $1.7 trillion annually just to meet infrastructure goals (Asian Development Bank, 2021).

Latin America shines in agritech, logistics, and digital finance spurred by nearshoring. Infrastructure concessions pay durable yields but demand savvy political risk management.

The Middle East and Africa see rising sovereign wealth fund buyouts and fast-growing venture capital, notably in fintech and regional platform scaling. Saudi Arabia's "giga-projects" are transforming real estate, and capital flows heavily into ports, renewables, and telecom.

18.4.3 Case Example: REITs Go Global

Global diversification isn't just for private funds. Several U.S. REITs expanded into Europe and APAC during low-rate periods, chasing yield spreads and cheap financing. For example, a leading industrial REIT gaining Central European ground (2016–2019) delivered a 21% total return, driven by booming e-commerce logistics and cross-border tenants.

18.4.4 Handling Global Risks

Of course, global investing adds complexity, regulatory differences, currency risk, political instability. Successful investors partner locally for on-the-ground insights, hedge currency risk, and use matched-source financing where possible. Political risk is managed through scenario planning and structured country-level risk models.

18.5 What Practitioners Keep Returning To

Talk with enough pros, and you'll hear the same four principles again and again. Strong governance beats weak oversight every time. Patient, prepared investors win over those chasing market timing. Behavioral discipline keeps the ship steady through storms. And global strategies paired with strong local execution unlock the broadest opportunities without sacrificing quality.

These principles aren't just theory; they're the informal rulebook that helps you navigate uncertainty, align partners, and generate compounding returns over the long haul.

18.6 What's Next: From Principles to Practice

This chapter tied together lessons learned in the field, from the real people who've sailed through different cycles, asset classes, and regions. The next chapter dives into execution, how top firms build capital stacks, structure deals, manage risk, and tie incentives to long-term value creation. Simply put: how the real playbook is built, bridging the gap between theory and hard-nosed practice.

References

Asian Development Bank. (2021). *Asian infrastructure finance: Closing the gap.* https://www.adb.org

DALBAR Inc. (2023). *Quantitative analysis of investor behavior.* DALBAR. https://www.dalbar.com

McKinsey & Company. (2023). *Global private markets review.* McKinsey & Company. https://www.mckinsey.com

MSCI Inc. (2022). *Real estate market insights: Global diversification benefits.* MSCI. https://www.msci.com

Preqin Ltd. (2022). *2022 global private capital report.* Preqin. https://www.preqin.com

CHAPTER 19

Principles to Practice

Introduction

The chapters before this one laid out four foundational principles, governance, timing, behavioral discipline, and a global perspective, that consistently set top investors apart. Now, in this final chapter, we shift focus from principles to practice. How do you take those guiding ideas and turn them into actionable, repeatable systems?

Sophisticated investors don't just rely on sharper insights, they excel through disciplined, consistent execution. They translate ideas into concrete structures: deal architectures that perfectly align incentives; capital stacks that strike the right balance between flexibility and protection; risk frameworks that embed institutional discipline; scalable platforms that grow capability; and investment vehicles that harmonize the interests of general partners (GPs) and limited partners (LPs).

We'll see how experienced investors put these capabilities into action to consistently deliver results. The key takeaway? True investment success doesn't come from isolated decisions, it grows from resilient systems built to sustain performance over the long haul.

19.1 Structuring Deals with Precision

Every deal you make tests incentives and human behavior. The legal and economic design, what insiders call "deal architecture", does more than protect each party. When you get it right, it actually smooths collaboration, speeds execution, and locks in the pursuit of long-term value.

Seasoned investors obsess over clear decision rights, defined pathways to resolve disputes quickly, and governance that leaves no room for grey areas or drift. Table 19.1 breaks down these core elements.

Imagine a U.S. PE firm rolling up regional HVAC companies. Several founders push back on a centralized procurement policy, a key cost-saving tactic. Instead of bending under pressure, the sponsor points to the operating agreement: supply chain decisions belong at the board level, outside founder control, who still hold hiring rights. No messy renegotiation happens. The execution stays tight, and EBITDA jumps 18% in two years. When smart structure guides behavior, performance follows.

Table 19.1 Core Elements of Effective Deal Architecture

Element	Role in Execution
Decision rights & escalation pathways	Reduce deadlock, speed resolution
Governance transparency	Prevents ambiguity, lowers conflict
Waterfall mechanics	Aligns reward to actual value creation

Note. Adapted from prior chapters.

19.2 Designing Capital Stacks That Protect and Amplify Value

Think of the capital stack as another kind of architecture, it's how risk, rewards, and control layer one on top of another. At its simplest, you start with low-cost senior debt, add mezzanine debt (more flexible but pricier), then preferred equity that structures upside and downside, and finally common equity where the highest risks and rewards sit.

Tailoring this stack to the asset, market, and leverage requirements is where you see the difference between amateurs and pros.

Why avoid over-leverage? PitchBook (2023) shows that real estate deals with loan-to-value ratios over 65%, or private equity deals with over 6x leverage, face a much higher risk of losses during downturns. It's a pressure cooker, not a recipe for steady returns.

Consider a real example from a 180-megawatt solar project. Developers carefully built its capital stack: 55% senior construction debt, 15% tax equity, 10% mezzanine debt, and 20% sponsor equity. After the project stabilized, they refinanced with long-term debt to cut the blended cost of capital by 220 basis points. According to their internal figures, that saved nearly $140 million in distributable cash over the project's life. That's how capital stack optimization can matter as much as operational finesse.

19.3 Managing Risk with Institutional-Grade Frameworks

Top investors don't wing risk management, they systematize it. This usually means formal frameworks with robust scenario analysis, stress testing, counterparty and supply-chain reviews plus risk-adjusted return targets. As Figure 19.1 shows, these components aren't just fluff: PwC (2023) reports funds with formal risk committees suffer about 30% fewer valuation hits across cycles.

One multifamily developer implemented a "three-line review" on all new construction. That means external cost estimators verify bids, the development team tests buildability, and lenders bring in third-party audits monthly. When inflation surged between 2021 and 2023, projects on this system averaged only 6% cost overruns, well below the 15–20% average reported by CBRE (2023). Discipline pays dividends, especially when markets behave erratically.

Figure 19.1 Components of Institutional Risk Management

Components of Institutional Risk Management

- ☐ Scenario analysis
- ☐ Downside and break-even case modeling
- ☐ Counterparty/geopolitical review
- ☐ Formalized risk premia

Adapted from PwC (2023).

19.4 Scaling Investment Platforms

To grow beyond boutique deal-making, firms must build reliable, repeatable systems. The most successful invest heavily in data-driven sourcing engines, standardized underwriting templates, and dashboards tracking performance metrics in real time. Compliance and ESG programs aligned with institutional expectations aren't optional extras, they're core infrastructure.

Size doesn't guarantee sophistication. It's about repeatability.

Take a Series A VC fund that built an AI tool analyzing founder "patterns" including backgrounds, team dynamics, and early traction. The result? Screening times dropped 30%, and the next cohort's portfolio performance improved 15%. Series B graduation rates climbed thanks to tech-enabled, standardized post-investment support. That's platform power beating guesswork.

19.5 Designing Investment Vehicles That Align Incentives

If you think investment vehicles are just legal jargon, think again. Their structures shape investor alignment and behavior just as much as deal terms do.

Closed-end funds still dominate PE, real estate, and infrastructure. In VC, evergreen funds gaining traction offer rolling entry and exit flexibility. Open-end real estate vehicles provide ongoing access to stable assets. Continuation vehicles keep top assets compounding instead of forcing sales at the worst moments. Co-investment opportunities are growing fast, cutting LP fees by up to half and boosting alignment.

Co-investments now represent over 23% of private capital, cutting fees for LPs by 30–50% (Bain & Company, 2023). A global PE firm recently used a continuation vehicle to keep a successful software platform growing. Existing LPs chose to stay or exit. New institutional capital came in. And the GP invested more, aligning incentives through structure and avoiding a fire sale (see Figure 19.2).

Figure 19.2 Types of Investment Vehicles and Their Alignment Features

Types of Investment Vehicles and Their Alignment Features

- ☐ Closed-end funds: locked periods, disciplined capital calls
- ☐ Evergreen funds: rolling entry/exit, greater flexibility
- ☐ Co-investments: lower fees, deeper alignment
- ☐ Continuation vehicles: extend top assets' compounding

Adapted from Bain & Company (2023).

19.6 Integrating Principles into Practice

Bridging theory and practice means embedding these ideas deep into organizational muscle memory. Governance speeds decisions and seals value leaks. Timing frameworks reward patience, not guesswork. Behavioral discipline, empowered by checklists, dissent channels, and rigorous committees, keeps bias at bay. A global view expands opportunities and smooths local shocks. Platform thinking builds repeatable quality at scale. And well-designed vehicles lock in long-term GP-LP alignment.

Conclusion: Building the Modern Investment Organization

Principles alone don't drive results. The leaders in today's markets shine because they create repeatable systems, maintain capital discipline, manage risk with rigor, scale smart infrastructure, and craft incentives that reward endurance and alignment. These aren't one-off choices, they're habits rooted deep in the organization's DNA. That's what makes any investment platform durable: repeatable, resilient, and ready for whatever the next market throws at us.

References

Bain & Company. (2023). *Global private equity report 2023.* https://www.bain.com/insights/topics/global-private-equity-report/

CBRE. (2023). *U.S. construction cost trends 2023.* https://www.cbre.com/insights/reports

PitchBook. (2023). *Global private market fundamentals report.* https://pitchbook.com/news/reports

PwC. (2023). *Global alternatives report: 2023.* https://www.pwc.com/gx/en/industries/financial-services/asset-management/publications.html

APPENDIX

Discounted Cash Flow (DCF) Analysis - Step-by-Step Guide

To guide you through every detail, I put together this step-by-step guide on Discounted Cash Flow (DCF) analysis. Using a commercial real estate acquisition as a real-world example, it walks you through the entire process, from laying out assumptions and building pro forma financials all the way to calculating free cash flow, selecting the discount rate, and arriving at a final valuation. Practical, thorough, and easy to follow, it's designed to give you everything you need to confidently perform a DCF analysis from start to finish.

What Is DCF?

A **Discounted Cash Flow (DCF)** analysis estimates the value of an investment based on the **present value of its expected future cash flows**, discounted at a rate that reflects risk and opportunity cost.

For real estate, DCF is commonly used to:

- ☐ Value income-producing properties
- ☐ Compare acquisition prices to intrinsic value
- ☐ Analyze hold-period returns

Core formula:

Value = Σ (Future Cash Flow / (1 + r)^t) + Terminal Value / (1 + r)^n

Where:

- ☐ r = discount rate (cost of capital)
- ☐ t = year of cash flow
- ☐ n = final year of projection

Example Overview: Commercial Office Building

Asset: Small suburban office building

Assumptions:

- ☐ Purchase price: $10,000,000
- ☐ Hold period: 5 years
- ☐ Financing: All-equity (simplifies FCF and WACC)
- ☐ Exit: Sale at end of Year 5

We will value the property using unlevered free cash flow (FCF).

Step 1 – Revenue Assumptions

Year 1 Rental Income

- ☐ Gross Potential Rent (GPR): $1,400,000
- ☐ Vacancy & Credit Loss: 10%

Effective Gross Income (EGI):

$1,400,000 × (1 – 10%) = $1,260,000

Annual Rent Growth

- ☐ Assumed rent growth: 3% annually

Step 2 – Operating Expenses

Operating expenses exclude financing and capital expenditures.

Operating expenses: 35% of EGI

Year 1 Operating Expenses:

$1,260,000 × 35% = $441,000

Step 3 – Net Operating Income (NOI)

NOI = Effective Gross Income – Operating Expenses

Year 1 NOI:
$1,260,000 - $441,000 = $819,000
NOI will grow at the same 3% annual rate.

Step 4 – Capital Expenditures (CapEx)

CapEx represents recurring investments needed to maintain the property.

- ☐ Annual CapEx reserve: $100,000 (flat)

Step 5 – Pro Forma Financial Statements (5-Year Projection)

Pro Forma Summary (Unlevered)

Year	NOI ($)	CapEx ($)	Free Cash Flow ($)
1	819,000	(100,000)	**719,000**
2	843,570	(100,000)	**743,570**
3	868,877	(100,000)	**768,877**
4	894,943	(100,000)	**794,943**
5	921,791	(100,000)	**821,791**

Free Cash Flow (FCF) = NOI – CapEx

Step 6 – Terminal Value Calculation

At the end of Year 5, the property is sold.

Exit Assumptions

- ☐ Exit cap rate: 7.5%
- ☐ Year 6 NOI = Year 5 NOI × 1.03

Year 6 NOI:

$921,791 × 1.03 = $949,445

Terminal Value Formula
Terminal Value = Year 6 NOI / Exit Cap Rate

$949,445 / 7.5% = $12,659,267

Step 7 – Discount Rate (Cost of Capital)

Because this is an unlevered DCF, we use an unlevered discount rate.

Method 1: Market-Derived Required Return

Typical unlevered required returns for stabilized office:

- ☐ Low risk: 7–8%
- ☐ Moderate risk: 8–9%
- ☐ High risk: 9–10%+

We select: 8.5%

Method 2: Build-Up Method (Cross-Check)

Component	Rate
Risk-free rate (10Y Treasury)	4.0%
Real estate risk premium	3.0%
Property-specific risk	1.5%
Total	**8.5%**

This confirms our selected discount rate.

Step 8 – Discounting Cash Flows to Present Value

Discount Factor Formula

PV = FCF / (1 + r)^t

Where *r* = 8.5%

Present Value of Cash Flows

Year	FCF ($)	Discount Factor	PV ($)
1	719,000	$1 / 1.085^1$	662,700
2	743,570	$1 / 1.085^2$	631,600
3	768,877	$1 / 1.085^3$	602,000
4	794,943	$1 / 1.085^4$	573,900
5	821,791	$1 / 1.085^5$	547,100

Step 9 - Discount Terminal Value

PV of Terminal Value = Terminal Value / (1 + r)^n

$12,659,267 / 1.085^5 = $8,420,000 (approx.)

Step 10 - Total DCF Valuation

Enterprise (Property) Value

Component	PV ($)
PV of FCF (Years 1-5)	3,017,300
PV of Terminal Value	8,420,000
Total DCF Value	**$11,437,300**

Step 11 - Investment Decision

- ☐ Purchase price: $10,000,000
- ☐ DCF value: $11,437,300

Result

Value exceeds price by ~$1.44M → Attractive investment

This margin represents a buffer for risk and estimation error.

Key Takeaways

- ☐ DCF is highly sensitive to discount rate and terminal cap rate
- ☐ Pro forma assumptions must be realistic and defensible
- ☐ Always run sensitivity analysis on:
  - » Exit cap rate
  - » Discount rate
  - » NOI growth

INDEX OF KEY TERMS

EPILOGUE

Investing in commercial real estate is both an art and a science. While models, data, and structured frameworks provide the foundation, what truly sets top investors apart is execution, sound judgment, and adaptability. This book has guided us from understanding fundamental market forces through real-life examples to developing actionable principles that seasoned investors rely on.

Today's investment landscape is defined by constant change, hybrid work models, e-commerce growth, evolving sustainability standards, and the flow of global capital all shape demand, valuation, and strategy. Success doesn't come only from identifying opportunities; it depends on structuring investments thoughtfully, managing risk with discipline, scaling platforms efficiently, and aligning incwentives among all stakeholders. Achieving this requires more than expertise, it's about cultivating disciplined habits, building repeatable systems, and balancing patience with strategic foresight.

Through cycles, asset classes, and geographies, four enduring principles stand out: governance, timing, behavioral discipline, and a global perspective. Governance keeps decisions consistent and focused on creating lasting value. Timing rewards preparation and patience. Behavioral discipline guards against biases and herd behavior. A global outlook broadens opportunity while helping manage local risks. When these principles are embedded within strong platforms, capital structures, and investment vehicles that align all parties, they form the backbone of resilient, high-performing commercial real estate organizations.

Beyond the spreadsheets and contracts, commercial real estate investing teaches us lessons in patience, discipline, and strategic thinking, qualities that endure even as markets evolve. The path forward is clear: approach every investment with rigor, align all stakeholders around shared goals, and harness data, systems, and experience to compound returns over time. Through this approach, investors can not only navigate uncertainty but emerge stronger within it.

ABOUT THE AUTHOR

Dr. Ned Gandevani is a leading authority in finance, risk management, and alternative investments, known for his unique ability to bridge academic theory with institutional practice. He is the CEO and Chief Investment Officer of NMG Income and Growth Funds, overseeing two diversified private market funds: the NMG Income Fund, focused on delivering consistent quarterly income through private credit strategies, and the NMG Growth Fund, targeting high-return opportunities in growth and income-generating sectors.

Dr. Gandevani is the author of several influential books, including the widely acclaimed *Alternative Investment Handbook: A Comprehensive Guide to Analysis and Valuation Methods* (2025), which offers a clear and comprehensive framework for navigating the complex world of private markets. His economic bestseller *Escaping the Deficit Trap: Reclaiming America's Future Through Growth, Innovation, and Smart Policy* (2025) presents a bold roadmap for restoring U.S. fiscal health through investment in people, productivity, and technology.

His latest release, *The Smart Investor's Guide to Commercial Real Estate: How to Analyze, Value, and Invest in Commercial Real Estate with Confidence* (2026), provides investors with a rigorous yet accessible methodology for evaluating and profiting from commercial real estate opportunities. The book equips both new and seasoned investors with practical tools for valuation, due diligence, cash-flow modeling, and strategic portfolio construction in the ever-evolving CRE landscape.

With more than 26 years of experience in trading, portfolio design, and hedge fund management, Dr. Gandevani brings deep practical expertise to institutional investing. He is the creator of the Trading Personality Profile (TPP), a pioneering framework that helps investment professionals align their cognitive styles with strategy selection to improve performance outcomes.

As an educator, he has taught finance and economics for over 18 years at Harvard University and other top institutions. His courses in corporate finance, portfolio theory, and risk modeling have shaped generations of financial professionals.

Dr. Gandevani is also a prolific author and public speaker, with five books and over 45 articles on investment strategy, behavioral finance, and macroeconomic forecasting. His insights have been featured in *USA Today*, *Stocks & Commodities Magazine*, *Futures Magazine*, and *Stocks, Futures & Options (SFO)*.

He served as the keynote speaker at the 2025 TSAM Boston conference, where he addressed macroeconomic shifts and the rising importance of U.S. country risk premiums in portfolio construction. He also delivered the keynote at the 2024 Annual Conference of the Academy of Certified Portfolio Managers, where he shared insights on alpha generation and portfolio resilience in volatile markets.

For the latest updates, commentary, upcoming events, and access to his books, articles, and economic perspectives, visit Dr. Gandevani's official website: https://**nedgandevani.nmgfunds.com**. It serves as a central platform for his thought leadership at the intersection of finance, economics, innovation, and investment strategy.

Through his research, writing, and leadership, Dr. Gandevani continues to be a vital voice helping institutions and investors navigate today's rapidly evolving financial landscape with clarity, purpose, and innovation.

BOOKS PUBLISHED BY DR. NED GANDEVANI

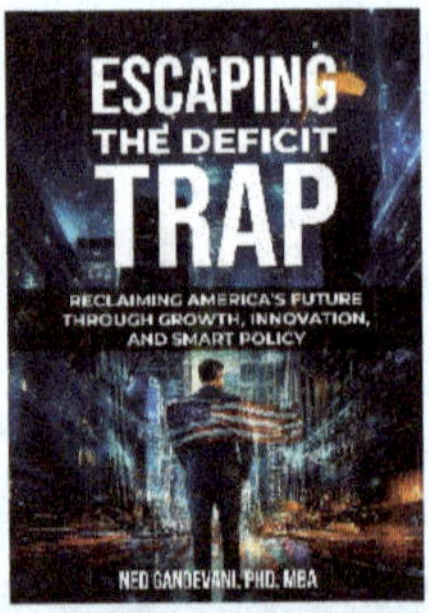

Escaping the Deficit Trap: Reclaiming America's Future Through Growth, Innovation, and Smart Policy

The Alternative Investment Handbook: A Comprehensive Guide to Analysis and Valuation Methods

The Intelligent Age: How Code, Coin, and Culture Are Reshaping the Digital Economy

How to Become a Successful Trader: The Trading Personality Profile: Your Key to Maximizing Profit with Any System

Winning Edge Trading: Successful and Profitable Short- and Long-Term Systems and Strategies (Wiley Trading)

The New Paradigm Investor: Become a Successful Investor with a Winning-Edge Investment System

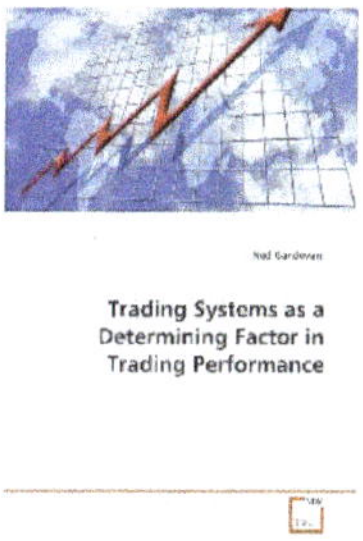

Trading Systems As A Determining Factor in Trading Performance

www.ingramcontent.com/pod-product-compliance
Lightning Source LLC
LaVergne TN
LVHW052248200926
848481LV00002B/314
* 9 7 9 8 9 9 9 5 9 1 8 4 5 *